Epistemic Modality in Standard Spoken Tibetan:

Epistemic Verbal Endings and Copulas

Zuzana Vokurková

KAROLINUM PRESS
PRAGUE, 2017

KAROLINUM PRESS
Karolinum Press is a publishing department of Charles University
Ovocný trh 560/5, 116 36 Prague 1, Czech Republic
www.karolinum.cz

Cover by Jan Šerých
Printed in the Czech Republic by Karolinum Press
First English edition

A catalogue record for this book is available from the National Library of the Czech Republic.

ISBN 978-80-246-3588-0
ISBN 978-80-246-3598-9 (pdf)

The original manuscript was peer-reviewed by Nicolas Tournadre, Associate Professor of
Linguistics at the University of Paris 8, a member of the Centre National de la Recherche
Scientifique (Lacito), and Co-Director of the Tibetan language collection at the Tibetan and
Himalayan Digital Library at the University of Virginia; Françoise Robin, Faculty Member,
Tibetan department of L'Inalco, l'Université Sorbonne Paris Cité; and Professor Bohumil Palek,
Faculty of Arts, Department of Linguistics, Charles University, Prague.

CONTENTS

Acknowledgements

As this monograph is largely based on my Ph.D. dissertation, I would like first of all to express thanks to my Ph.D. supervisors, Nicolas Tournadre from the University of Provence, France, and Bohumil Palek from Charles University, Prague, Czech Republic, for their valuable help with my dissertation, their guidance, encouragement and insight. I am also especially grateful to Professor Nicolas Tournadre for giving me the idea to study this part of the Tibetan grammar. Furthermore, I would like to thank my Tibetan teachers and consultants: Mr Dawa (professor at Tibet University, Lhasa), Mrs Tsheyang (professor at Tibet University, Lhasa), Mr Tenpa Gyaltsen (a former employee of the PICC Insurance Company, Lhasa), Mrs Soyag (professor at Tibet University, Lhasa), Mr Sangda Dorje (professor at Tibet University, Lhasa), Mr Ngawang Dakpa (professor at Inalco, Paris), Mr Tenzin Samphel (professor at Inalco, Paris), Mr Dorje Tsering Jiangbu (a former professor at INALCO, Paris), Mr Tenzin Jigme (a former professor at Charles University, Prague), Mr Thubten Kunga (professor at Warsaw University), Mrs Pema Yonden (teacher, Dharamsala, India), Mr Dondub, Mr Thinle Gyaltsen, Mr Nyima Tashi, Mr Sonam Dorje, Mr Pasang, and Mr Pasang Tsering (Tibetans from central Tibet); and many others. Last but not least, I would like to thank Françoise Robin (professor at Inalco, Paris) for reviewing my work and for her valuable comments.

I am thankful to LACITO/CNRS (PICS 2554) and the French Ministry of Education for financing my research work in central Tibet and India during the years 2003–2005. The latter also granted me a scholarship for my doctoral studies in France. In addition, I would like to express my gratitude to the Sasakawa Young Leaders Fellowship Fund for awarding me a grant making possible my studies at Tibet University in 2004–2005. Last but not least, I am thankful to Charles University of Prague for awarding me a post-doctoral grant to publish this book on epistemic verbal endings in standard spoken Tibetan.

I also owe many thanks to my friends and colleagues for their suggestions and commentaries concerning Tibetan examples of epistemic modality and their English equivalents. Equally important was the help in the final stages with editing and proofreading. I am very much grateful to Rachel Mikos for the proofreading and stylistic improvement.

Last but not least, I want to thank my family for their invaluable support, unceasing patience and tolerance. Without them, I would not have been able to persevere in my research work and to bring my dissertation and this book to completion.

ABBREVIATIONS

ABL :	ablative
ABS :	absolutive
Ag :	agent
ASSOC :	associative
CAUS :	causative/causative particle
COMP:	comparative
CONTR :	controllable
EGO :	egophoric
ENDO :	endopathic
EPI :	epistemic
ERG :	ergative
FACT :	factual
FP :	final particle
GAR :	verbal suffix marking the complement of a verb of motion
GEN :	genitive
GNR :	generic
h :	humilific
H :	honorific
HAB :	habitual
IMM :	suffix marking the immediate
IMP :	imperative
impers :	impersonal
IMPF :	imperfective (past, present, future)
ImpP :	imperative particle
IND :	indicative
INF :	infinitive
INFR :	inferential
M :	masculine
NEG :	negative
NOM :	nominalizer
N-CONTR :	non-controllable
OBL :	oblique
Pa :	patient
PAS :	past
PFV :	perfective past
PERF :	perfect
pl :	plural
POLITE :	particle expressing politeness
PRS :	present

Q :	question particle/interrogative particle
QP :	quotation particle
REC :	receptive
RES :	resultative
RepS :	marker of the reported speech
RES :	resultative
SENS :	sensory
sg :	singular
SST :	standard spoken Tibetan
SUB :	subjunctive
TAM :	tense-aspect-modality
VBZ :	verbalizer

INTRODUCTION

Key terms

In this study, I revisit the notion of epistemic modalities in standard spoken Tibetan, the topic of my dissertation "Epistemic Modalities in Spoken Standard Tibetan" defended at Charles University (Prague, Czech republic) and the University of Saint-Denis (Paris 8, France) in 2008. This monograph deals with *standard spoken Tibetan* (SST, the Tibetan term: *spyi.skad*). This term corresponds more or less to the dialect of Lhasa (*lha.sa.skad*) and the surrounding areas. It is a variety of central Tibetan (*dbus.skad*) and is used as a *lingua franca* by Tibetans living in the Tibetan autonomous region (T.A.R.) and in the Tibetan diaspora in India, Nepal and other countries. Standard spoken Tibetan is spoken by about one and a half million people, 130,000 of whom live in the diaspora.

Another key term employed in this work is *epistemic modality* or *epistemicity* (see Boye 2006; Bybee, Fleischman 1995; de Haan 2005; Nuyts 2001a; Palmer 1986, 1990). This can be defined as the expression of the speaker's evaluation of the probability of a state of affairs (Nuyts 2001). It shows "the status of the speaker's understanding or knowledge" and "the degree of commitment by the speaker to the truth of what he says" (Palmer 1986: 51), or "the extent to which the speaker is committed to the truth of the proposition" (Bybee, Perkins, Pagliuca 1994: 179). In this monograph, epistemic modalities are defined in terms of the degree of the speaker's certainty of the actuality of his utterance.

Epistemic modalities are closely connected with another important linguistic parameter — *evidentiality*. Evidentiality specifies the speaker's commitment to what he says in terms of the kind of evidence he is basing his statement upon (Palmer 1986). It is often defined as a grammatical means of expressing a source of information (Aikhenvald 2004), or more broadly, as the expression of the speaker's access to information, considering as well the subjective strategy or perspective of the speaker in representing a particular state of affairs (see Mélac 2014; Tournadre, LaPolla 2014). Epistemic modality and evidentiality are at times regarded as two separate linguistic categories (see Aikhenvald 2004; de Haan 2005; Nyuts 2001), at times as parts of the same linguistic category, and in other cases the first one is considered as a sub-category of the latter (Papafragou 2000), or vice versa (Willet 1988). Having a large conception of modality, unlike van der Auwera, Plungian (1998), Aikhenvald (2004, 2011)[1] and Gosselin (2005),[2] and in

---

[1] "That evidentials may have semantic extensions related to probability and speaker's evaluation of the trustworthiness of information does not make evidentiality a kind of modality." Aikhenvald (2004: 7–8).

accordance with Palmer (1986), Bhat (1999) and Tournadre (2004), I consider evidentials as a modal type. In this monograph, therefore, 'evidential' and 'epistemic' are treated as two parts of the same linguistic category.

In various languages, epistemic modalities are expressed by different lexical and grammatical means, e.g. modal verbs and affixes. In Tibetan, however, epistemic modalities are not expressed by modal verbs, as is the case with many languages of the world but by other lexical and grammatical means. These lexical means include, in particular, epistemic adverbs. However, the chief means to be found in the spoken language are morpho-syntactic, consisting of a system of epistemic verbal endings and copulas, which will be discussed in detail in this monograph. As it is the case in many languages with a verb-final word order, in Tibetan, grammatical meanings, e.g. modality or tense, are marked at the end of the verbal domain by verbal suffixes, verbal markers or verbal endings depending on the adopted terminology. In this study, the term *verbal endings* is employed.

Verbal endings indicate the end of a sentence. Some verbal endings function primarily as markers of evidential meanings. These are termed *evidential verbal endings*. The use of these verbal endings is obligatory in spoken Tibetan but most of the time optional in the literary language. In addition to evidential verbal endings, there are also verbal endings which primarily express various degrees of the speaker's certainty of the actuality of his utterance. These are called *epistemic verbal endings* in this monograph. They correspond to the epistemic use of English modal verbs, such as 'may' or 'must', and to epistemic adverbs, such as 'surely', 'apparently', 'likely', 'probably'. Both types of verbal endings may be grouped under the term *TAM verbal endings*[3] because they all express, in addition to modality, various tense-aspects. They do not express the grammatical categories of gender, voice and number.

While all the attention of scholars has mainly been concentrated on evidentiality (evidential verbal endings and copulas) — which is particularly rich in Tibetic languages — very little has been written about epistemic modality (epistemic verbal endings and copulas) in Tibetic languages. However, as we will see, epistemic verbal endings constitute a very complex system in SST (and other languages of the family). In consequence, I have decided to focus my interest on this aspect of Tibetan grammar. In this work, my intention is to classify all types of epistemic verbal endings and copulas that are more or less frequently employed in SST and to analyze them from the formal, semantic, pragmatic and syntactic viewpoints.

---

[2] "On se gardera par ailleurs de confondre l'instance de validation, qui fonde la modalité, avec la source de l'information, qui relève de la problématique de « l'évidentialité », quoique ces deux phénomènes entretiennent des liens étroits et qu'il soit parfois difficile de les distinguer…" (Gosselin 2005: 30–40).
[3] TAM stands for tense-aspect-modality.

Fieldwork and corpus

Taking into account the fact that there are few written sources on epistemic modalities in SST (see chiefly Hu 1989, Tournadre, Sangda Dorje 2003, Wang 1994, Zhou, Xie [eds.] 2003), the main part of my research work has been comprised of fieldwork. In the course of my fieldwork, I have had to overcome several difficulties concerning the building of paradigms of the many epistemic verbal endings used in SST. One difficulty was found in the rarity of occurrences of some forms in the actual spoken language necessitating a method of elicitation. Other difficulties were the divergences among Tibetan consultants who, though they all speak standard Tibetan, hail from different locations and have their own idiolects and therefore use different epistemic verbal endings and copulas. And last but not least, I faced the problem of hypercorrection. As a matter of fact, some of my consultants, more or less unconsciously, relied on the written language.

Although I worked with Tibetan consultants in Tibet, India and Europe, focus is placed on the Lhasa variation of SST. My fieldwork began in Central Tibet (Lhasa) in 2002 when I began to collect material on Tibetan secondary verbs[4] and verbal endings for my D.E.A. thesis defended in October 2002 at the University of Paris 8, France. I continued my work in Northern India (Dharamsala) in 2003. At that time, I concentrated on the expression of epistemic modalities in the language spoken by the Tibetans living in the diaspora, *spyi.skad*, comparing it with Lhasa Tibetan, *lha.sa.skad*. Between 2004 and 2006, I spent over a year in Lhasa studying the epistemic modalities in SST and in some Tibetan dialects as well. During this time, I also worked with Tibetan consultants living in Europe (France, Poland, Czech republic). Between 2012 and 2015, I returned to Lhasa several times to verify the results of my previous fieldwork and to check the examples employed in this monograph.

My main Tibetan consultants are Dawa (born in Lhasa, professor at Tibet University), Tsheyang (born in Lhasa, professor at Tibet University), Tenpa Gyaltsen (born in Lhasa, former employee at the PICC insurance company), Soyag (born in Hor, resident in Lhasa for 20 years, professor at Tibet University) and Dondrub (born near Lhasa, studied in India, tourist guide). I also worked with Ngawang Dagpa (born in Lhasa, lived in India, resident since the 1960s in France, professor at Inalco, France), Tenzin Samphel (born in Nepal, resident since the 1990s in France, a former professor at Inalco, France), Pema Yonden (born in Lhasa, living in India from the age of three, teacher of Tibetan), Tashi (born near Lhasa, security guard), Sangda Dorje (born in Lhasa, associate professor at Tibet University), Tenzin Jigme (born in India, a former professor

---

[4] For the term "secondary verbs", see Section 3.1.

at Charles University, Czech Republic), Dorje Tsering Jangbu (born in Amdo, lived in Lhasa, a former professor at Inalco, France), Thupten Kunga (born in Nepal, professor at Warsaw University, Poland), Damchoe Thewo (born in Amdo, lived in India, student), Thinle Gyaltsen (born in Maldo Gongkar, resident in Lhasa for 30 years, restaurant owner), Nyima Tashi (born and lives in Lhasa, driver), Pasang (born near Lhasa, driver), Pasang Tsering (born in Phenpo, lives in Lhasa, electrician); I occasionally consulted other Tibetan consultants as well.

The corpus on which my research is based has been obtained from several sources: the most important one being an inquiry of Tibetan native speakers, followed by spontaneous conversations and recordings of a test on epistemic modality (see below), as well as other sources, including Tibetan television shows, and texts composed in spoken Tibetan.

Since no extensive study of epistemic modality in spoken Tibetan had been completed to the state, my first task was to identify all the different types of epistemic verbal endings and to construct their paradigms. I therefore began by asking Tibetan consultants about the existence of different verbal endings and the influence of various parameters on their use. I collected a corpus of examples illustrating the various paradigms. Since certain verbal endings are very rare in the spoken language, it would be virtually impossible to obtain all existing forms of the various types of epistemic verbal endings by merely hoping for an occurrence in conversation. A certain section of my examples, therefore, are not directly drawn from conversations but are elicited.

My next step was to verify the data acquired during my work with my consultants. For this purpose, I prepared a series of spoken tasks in which my consultants would be prompted to use various epistemic verbal endings. I attempted to find such situations in which native speakers would naturally use epistemic verbal endings. Since the Tibetan language encodes the cognitive process differently according to the type of access to information (whether it is visual, stemming from memory, or through sense perception), the spoken task I proposed to my consultants consisted of three parts. The first part was based on visual experience, the second on memory and the third one on physical sensation, or touch.

In the first part, I asked my consultants to talk about three photographs that I showed them. The photographs represented an unknown man, an unknown woman and a non-specified landscape with a lake. I asked my consultants to guess who the people were and where the lake was. In the second part, the consultants spoke about their or their family's past and future: what they remembered from their past and what they thought their future would be like. And in the third part, I prepared several objects and hid them under a cover. The consultants had to judge what the hidden things were. First, they only could observe the general shape of the things. Then, they could touch them from outside the cover, and finally from inside the cover.

To summarize the results of the test broadly, the first outcome was that in all parts of the test, the consultants tended to use epistemic verbal endings. The following outcome was that in the third part, all the consultants but one used one or another type of epistemic verbal ending when they judged the objects by mere sight. But when they could touch them, they used evidential verbal endings, not epistemic verbal endings. The test also demonstrated a certain degree of idiolect employed by each consultant in the use of epistemic verbal endings. The most interesting case was the total absence of any epistemic verbal ending in the utterances of one consultant (a man from Lhasa, 26 years old) who preferred the use of epistemic adverbs combined with evidential verbal endings instead. The test further demonstrated that epistemic adverbs are a very frequent means of expressing epistemic modalities in spoken Tibetan and that they are often employed with epistemic verbal endings.

Structure of the monograph and of the Tibetan examples

The monograph consists of three chapters. The first chapter introduces the various lexical and grammatical means of expressing epistemic modalities in standard spoken Tibetan. It concentrates on the system of epistemic verbal endings and copulas (1.2), analyzing them from different points of view: formal (1.2.1), functional (1.2.2) and syntactic (1.2.3). The final part of the chapter discusses the co-occurrence of a lexical and grammatical means of expressing epistemic modalities, i.e. epistemic adverbs and epistemic verbal endings (1.3).

The second chapter is a classification and a detailed analysis of the epistemic verbal endings and copulas that are employed in spoken Tibetan. They are classified into eleven types. Each type is described from a morphological, semantic, pragmatic and syntactic point of view, and illustrated by examples.

The last chapter focuses on the compatibility of secondary verbs with epistemic verbal endings. The first part describes secondary verbs (3.1) and the second part deals with the combinations of epistemic verbal endings (or epistemic auxiliaries) with seventeen secondary verbs which are most frequently used in standard spoken Tibetan (3.2).

The examples from spoken Tibetan are given in the Tibetan orthography using Wylie transliteration (Wylie 1959). Although current pronunciation differs a great deal from the written language, it is nonetheless possible to convert transliterated sentences into the actual pronunciation by means of several phonological rules. Each example consists of four lines: the first one is written in Tibetan script, the second one is registered in Wylie transliteration, the third one is the English interlinear gloss,[5] and the fourth one is the English translation and the context of the utterance or a commentary in brackets (see below). Tibetan words with more than one syllable are written with a dot between the syllables.[6] Grammatical morphemes are attached by a dash. Various meanings of one morpheme are joined by the mark "+". The morphemes in the process of grammaticalization are connected by the mark ":".

Tibetan has an archaic system of verbal stems used in different tenses (see Bailey, Walker 2004; Beyer 1992; Wang Zhijing 1994; Zeisler 2004). However, the system of verbal inflection has been considerably reduced in the spoken language and tense and aspect are most of the time conveyed by verbal endings. The verbal stems do not, in general, have an influence on the interpretation of the verbal endings. Unlike literary Tibetan, most of the verbs have lost their inflectional diversity in the spoken language and have one generalized stem for all tenses. As a result, I will use, when appropriate, the invariable stem for all tenses in the examples and will not mark the original tense of the stem as in classical or literary Tibetan. In some cases, two (or exceptionally three) stems are still used in SST: the past and the present-future (and exceptionally the imperative). These will be marked in brackets after the lexical meaning of the verb, i.e. (PAS), (PRS), (IMP).

Line 1:	ཕལ་ཆེར་མི་གཅིག་སླེབས་པ་འདྲ།					
Line 2:	*phal.cher*	*mi*	*cig*	*slebs*	*- pa.'dra*	
Line 3:	probably	person	a	come	- PFV+EPI 2 +SENS	
Line 4:	It looks like someone has come. (The speaker can hear knocking on the door or the dog barking.)					

---

[5] I.e. morpheme by morpheme translation; lexical morphemes are, however, not analyzed.
[6] The negative counterparts of affirmative verbal endings are also written with dots between syllables, e.g. *yod.kyi.red* (affirmative) and *yod.kyi.ma.red* (negative). They are not further analyzed in negative and TAM morphemes. Although such analysis would be possible with most evidential verbal endings, it would be rather complicated and often impossible with the majority of epistemic verbal endings. For more details, refer to Vokurková (2008: 58).

I. THE EXPRESSION OF EPISTEMIC MODALITY IN STANDARD SPOKEN TIBETAN

In various languages, epistemic modalities may be conveyed via different lexical and grammatical means. Regarding lexical expression, aside from modal verbs (e.g. may, could, must), epistemic meanings may be encoded in the lexicon by means of epistemic verbs (verbs of cognition, such as: believe, guess, seem, be sure, doubt, think, say), by epistemic adverbs (e.g. probably, likely, maybe, possibly) (Givón 1984: 318), and by other lexical means (e.g. adjectives, nouns). The world's languages also use various grammatical means for conveying modality, whether morphological and syntactical, such as modal particles, verbal affixes, or word order (see Brown 2006; Bybee 1985, Haspelmath 2005).

In standard spoken Tibetan, possibility and probability are not conveyed by modal verbs[7] but through other lexical and grammatical means. The main means in the spoken language are epistemic adverbs for the lexical expression (1.1), and a system of verbal affixes which I designate as *verbal endings* for the grammatical expression (1.2). In SST, there are two groups of verbal endings that are clearly distinguished in employing the criterion of epistemicity:

1) Evidential verbal endings that principally express an evidential meaning and certain information i.e. the speaker presents his utterance as certain (for evidentiality in Tibetan see: Section 1.2.2.3; Garrett 2001; Mélac 2014; Oisel 2013; Tournadre, Sangda Dorje 2003, Vokurková 2008; for evidentiality see: Aikhenvald 2004, 2011; Aikhenvald, Dixon [eds.] 2003; Barnes 1984; Chafe, Nichols [eds.] 1986; Guentcheva [ed.] 1996; Guentcheva, Landaburu [eds.] 2007; Johanson, Utas 2000; Tournadre, LaPolla 2014, ex. 1).

(1)   མོ་རང་ལྷ་སར་འགྲོ་གི་རེད།

mo.rang	lha.sa	- r	'gro	- gi.red
she	Lhasa	- OBL	go (PRS)	- FUT+FACT

She will go to Lhasa.

2) Epistemic verbal endings that principally convey an epistemic meaning. By using these endings, the speaker expresses different degrees of certainty of the actuality of his utterance (for

---

[7] The verb *srid* „be possible" is an exception because its lexical meaning is epistemic. However, unlike modal verbs in European languages which have both, modal and epistemic, meanings, *srid* only has an epistemic meaning. For more details on *srid*, see Section 3.2.6.

epistemicity in Tibetan see: Tournadre, Sangda Dorje 2003; Tournadre, Shao [to be published], Vokurková 2008, 2009, 2011a, 2011b; Zhou, Xie 2003; for epistemic modality, see: Boye 2006; Choi 1995; Nuyts 2001a, 2001b, ex. 2). This morpho-syntactic system will be discussed in detail in Section 1.2.

(2)   མོ་རང་ལྷ་སར་འགྲོ་གི་ཡོད་ཀྱི་རེད།

    mo.rang   *lha.sa*   *- r*   *'gro*   *- gi.yod.kyi.red*
    she   Lhasa   - OBL   go (PRS)   - IMPF+EPI 2+FACT
    In all likelyhood, she will go to Lhasa.

1.1 THE LEXICAL EXPRESSION OF EPISTEMIC MODALITY

1.1.1 EPISTEMIC ADVERBS

Epistemic adverbs are the most important lexical means of expressing epistemic modalities in SST. They may be employed in the same sentence either with an evidential or an epistemic verbal ending. The co-occurrence of epistemic adverbs with evidential endings as in example (3a) with both the epistemic adverb *phal.cher* and the evidential verbal ending *gi.red* is a common way of expressing epistemic modality in SST. Nonetheless, Tibetans often prefer sentences with an epistemic verbal ending either combined with an epistemic adverb, as in example (3b) with both the epistemic adverb *phal.cher* and the epistemic ending *gi.yod.kyi.red,* or without it as in example (3c) with the epistemic verbal ending *gi.yod.kyi.red.*

(3)   ཁོང་ཕལ་ཆེར་ཡོང་གི་རེད།

   a)   *khong   phal.cher   yong   - gi.red*
        s/he+H   probably   come   - FUT+FACT

        She will probably come. (A reply to the question as to whether she will come. For some reason, the speaker tends to think that she will.)

   ཁོང་ཕལ་ཆེར་ཡོང་གི་ཡོད་ཀྱི་རེད།

   b)   *khong   phal.cher   yong   - gi.yod.kyi.red*
        s/he+H   probably   come   - IMPF+EPI 2+FACT

        She will probably come. (A reply to the question as to whether she will come. She said she would come so the speaker thinks she will.)

   ཁོང་ཡོང་གི་ཡོད་ཀྱི་རེད།

   c)   *khong   yong   - gi.yod.kyi.red*
        s/he+H   come   - IMPF+EPI 2+FACT

        She will probably come. (A reply to the question as to whether she will come. She said she would come so the speaker thinks she will.)

Regarding the degree of probability: in example (3a), my consultants suggest that the degree of the speaker's certainty is higher than in examples (3b) and (3c). This is due to the fact that (3a) contains an evidential ending, which generally conveys the speaker's certainty (100%); the epistemic meaning is only expressed by the epistemic adverb *phal.cher* 'probably'. In contrast, examples (3b) or (3c) contain an epistemic ending which conveys a degree of certainty lower than 100%, and thus the degree of certainty is perceived as slightly lower than in the case of sentences containing an evidential ending, as in example (3a).

Furthermore, it is worth noting that Tibetans when speaking in an epistemic context often prefer uttering a sentence that includes an epistemic adverb in order to stress the uncertainty of the statement they are making, as in examples (3a) and (3b). They tend to use epistemic adverbs, regardless of whether the verbal ending is evidential[8] or epistemic. In sentences containing both an epistemic adverb and an epistemic verbal ending, as in example (3b), it is often the adverb that is stressed in the utterance and that emphasizes the degree of probability. The final epistemic meaning, however, arises from an interaction of both the lexical and the grammatical epistemic means, in addition to being influenced by the pragmatic circumstances of the utterance.

Epistemic adverbs differ in the degree of certainty they convey and they can be divided into at least three groups according to these degrees of certainty: adverbs expressing possibility (close to 50%), adverbs expressing probability (close to 75%) and adverbs expressing near-absolute certainty (close to 100%).

1.1.1.1 Epistemic adverbs expressing possibility

In the epistemic adverb *gcig.byas.na*, the degree of certainty expressed is approximately 50% or more. From a syntactic viewpoint, *gcig.byas.na* is generally employed at the beginning of a sentence. It is usually translated in English by the adverbs 'perhaps', 'maybe' or 'possibly' (bKrashis Tsering, Liu 1991) and 'perhaps', 'maybe' (Goldstein 2001). It is very common in SST. Below is an example of the use of this adverb in a sentence:

---

[8] They are, however, not used with sensory evidentials (direct evidentials in Garett's terminology, see Garett 2001: 87):

ཁྱེད་རང་གི་དེབ་ག་པར་ཡོད་རེད། ∫ འདུག

khyed.rang	*-gi*	*deb*	*ga.par*	*yod.red/'dug*
you+H	-GEN	book	where	*exist* (FACT/SENS)

Where is your book?

གཅིག་བྱས་ན་ཉལ་ཁྲི་སྒང་ལ་ཡོད། ∫ ཡོད་རེད། ∫ * འདུག

gcig.byas.na	*nyal.khri*	*sgang*	*-la*	*yod/yod.red/* 'dug*
maybe	bed	top	-OBL	exist (EGO/FACT/SENS)
gcig.byas.na	*sa*	*sgang*	*-la*	*yod/yod.red/* 'dug*
maybe	floor	top	-OBL	exist (EGO/FACT/SENS)

Maybe it's on the bed, maybe it's on the floor.

(4)　　　གཅིག་བྱས་ན་ཕུར་བུ་ཡོང་གི་རེད།

> gcig.byas.na　　phur.bu　　yong　　- gi.red
> perhaps　　　　Phurbu　　come　　- FUT+FACT

Maybe Phurbu will come. (A reply to the question as to who will come. The speaker doesn't know any details.)

In the epistemic adverb *ha.lam*, the degree of certainty expressed is low, perhaps even lower than that of the previous adverb. It is less frequently used than the previous epistemic adverb. It is translated in English as 'nearly, 'more or less', 'approximately', 'roughly' (Goldstein 2001). In negative sentences, *ha.lam* does not convey an epistemic meaning: it corresponds to 'hardly', 'scarcely' or 'barely'.[9]

(5)　　　ཁོང་ཧ་ལམ་ཡོང་གི་རེད།

a)　*khong*　　*ha.lam*　　*yong*　　- *gi.red*
　　s/he+H　　more or less　　come　　- FUT+FACT

　　She will perhaps come. (The speaker doesn't know any details. It is just his mere supposition.)

ཉི་མ་ལ་དགོངས་པ་ཧ་ལམ་རག་ཡོད་ས་མ་རེད།

b)　*nyi.ma*　- *la*　　*dgongs.pa*　　*ha.lam*　　*rag*　- *yod.sa.ma.red*
　　Nyima　- OBL　　leave of absence　more or less　get　- IMPF+EPI 2+SENS+NEG

　　It seems Nyima didn't get a leave of absence. (Nyima doesn't look happy.)

The adverb *yang.na* is more often employed in its non-epistemic meaning of 'either or' and 'otherwise' in the spoken language. The degree of certainty expressed by this adverb is approximately 50%. From a syntactic viewpoint, *yang.na* generally follows the agent. It can be translated in English by the adverb 'maybe'.

(6)　　　བསྟན་པ་ཡང་ན་སོག་ཡུལ་ལ་འགྲོ་གི་ཡོད་ཀྱི་རེད།

> *bstan.pa*　　*yang.na*　　*sog.yul*　　- *la*　　*'gro*　　- *gi.yod.kyi.red*
> Tenpa　　maybe　　Mongolia　　- OBL　　go (PRS)　- IMPF+EPI 2+FACT

Maybe Tenpa will go to Mongolia. (The speaker knows that Tenpa is interested in Mongolia.)

---

[9] For example:

ཁོང་གིས་ཧ་ལམ་བཟས་མ་སོང་།

> *khong*　　- *gis*　　*ha.lam*　　*bzas*　　- *ma.song*
> s/he+H　　- ERG　　hardly　　eat (PAS)　- PERF+SENS+NEG
> He hardly ate.

19

1.1.1.2 Epistemic adverbs expressing probability

As suggested by my consultants, the degree of certainty expressed by the epistemic adverb *phal.cher* is higher than that of the previous group (more or less 75%). Syntactically, *phal.cher* may precede or follow the agent of an event though the latter is far more common. It is translated in English as 'possibly', 'maybe' or 'perhaps' (bKrashis Tsering, Liu 1991), or 'most probably', 'most likely' (Goldstein 2001). As a result of my research, I suggest using the English adverb 'probably' as the most suitable translation. This adverb is frequently employed in SST.

(7) ཁོང་ཕལ་ཆེར་ཡོང་གི་རེད།

khong	*phal.cher*	*yong*	*- kyi.red*
s/he+H	probably	come	- FUT+FACT

She will probably come. (See example 3a.)

The degree of certainty expressed by the epistemic adverb *spyir.btang* is quite high (about 75%). From a syntactic point of view, *spyir.btang* may precede or follow the agent of an event. It is usually translated in English by the adverbs 'in principle', 'usually' or 'generally' (Goldstein 2001). It is very frequent in the spoken language.

(8) ཁོང་སླེབས་དུས་ང་སྤྱིར་བཏང་ཡི་གི་འབྲི་མཁན་བསྡད་ཡོད།

a)

khong	*slebs*	*- dus*	*nga*	*spyir.btang*	*yi.ge*	*'bri*
s/he+H	arrive	- when	I	generally	letters	write (PRS)

- mkhan	*bsdad*	*- yod*
- NOM	stay	- PERF (EGO)

When she came in, I was in principle writing letters. (A reply to the question as to what the speaker was doing. The speaker is trying to recall.)

ཁོ་རང་སྤྱིར་བཏང་ཕྱིན་པ་ཡོད།

b)

kho.rang	*spyir.btang*	*phyin*	*- pa.yod*
he	generally	go (PAS)	- PFV+EPI 3+EGO

In principle, he went [there]. (The speaker talked to him.)

1.1.1.3 Epistemic adverbs expressing high probability or near-absolute certainty

The adverbs conveying the meaning of near-absolute certainty are most often associated with evidential verbal endings, as seen in examples (9)–(13). Nevertheless, they are sometimes employed with epistemic verbal endings, as in example (14) below.

The epistemic adverb *yin.cig.min.cig* expresses a high degree of certainty (about 100%). It is generally employed with evidential verbal endings. It may only be used in future contexts, not in the past or the present. It is translated in English as 'must', 'in any case', 'without fail' (Goldstein 2001).

(9)　ཁོང་ཡིན་ཅིག་མིན་ཅིག་ཡོང་གི་རེད།

khong	*yin.cig.min.cig*	*yong*	- *gi.red*
s/he+H	in any case	come	- FUT+FACT

In any case, she will come.

Just as the previous adverb, the epistemic adverb *gtan.gtan* (also spelt as *brtan.brtan*) expresses a high degree of certainty (about 100%). It is frequently used in SST. It is translated in English as 'certainly' or 'surely' (Goldstein 2001). It is usually used with evidential verbal endings, and quite rarely with epistemic verbal endings. Its use is illustrated in the example below:

(10)　ཁོང་གཏན་གཏན་ཡོང་གི་རེད།

khong	*gtan.gtan*	*yong*	- *gi.red*
s/he+H	certainly	come	- FUT+FACT

She will certainly come.

There is another epistemic expression with the verb *gtan.'khel* which is semantically similar to the previous adverb. The verb *gtan.'khel* (used with the verbalizer *byed*) conveys the meaning of 'determine', 'decide' or 'fix (a date)'. When used after a nominalized verb it may be translated in English by 'decidedly'. Just as the adverb *gtan.gtan*, it is often employed in the spoken language.

(11)　ཁོང་ཡོང་ཡག་གཏན་འཁེལ་རེད།

khong	*yong*	- *yag*	*gtan.'khel*	*red*
s/he+H	come	- NOM	decide	be (FACT)

Decidedly, she will come.

The adverb *brgya.cha brgya* is another epistemic adverb expressing a high degree of certainty. Its literary translation is 'a hundred percent' (Goldstein 2001) and it can be translated in English as 'definitely'. It is preferably used with evidential verbal endings, not with epistemic verbal endings. This epistemic adverb is very frequent in Lhasa.

(12)   ཁོང་བརྒྱ་ཆ་བརྒྱ་ཡོང་གི་རེད།

khong   brgya.cha brgya   yong   - gi.red
s/he+H   definitely   come   - FUT+FACT

She will definitely come.

1.1.1.4 Differences in the use of epistemic adverbs

As stated above, the two means of expressing epistemic modalities in SST — lexical and grammatical — are often combined. The use of the epistemic adverbs listed above depends on the type of epistemic verbal ending employed and more importantly, on the speaker's degree of certainty. It is true that the epistemic adverb is often the primary means for determining the degree of probability of an utterance, but epistemic meaning as a whole is also influenced by other linguistic and pragmatic indicators (for example, intonation or the speaker's idiolect). Compare the following examples:

(13)   གཅིག་བྱས་ན་ཁོང་ལྷ་སར་ཡོང་གི་ཡོད་ཀྱི་རེད།

a)   *gcig.byas.na   khong   lha.sa   - r   yong   - gi.yod.kyi.red*
       perhaps   s/he+H   Lhasa   - OBL   come   - IMPF+EPI 2+FACT

       She will perhaps come to Lhasa. (The speaker knows that she wants to look for a new job. He is making a guess.)

    ཁོང་ཕལ་ཆེར་ལྷ་སར་ཡོང་གི་ཡོད་ཀྱི་རེད།

b)   *khong   phal.cher   lha.sa   - r   yong   - gi.yod.kyi.red*
       s/he+H   probably   Lhasa   - OBL   come   - IMPF+EPI 2+FACT

       She will probably come to Lhasa. (The speaker knows that she wants to look for a new job. He is slightly more sure of himself.)

    ཁོང་གཏན་གཏན་ལྷ་སར་ཡོང་གི་ཡོད་ཀྱི་རེད།

c)   *khong   gtan.gtan   lha.sa   - r   yong   - gi.yod.kyi.red*
       s/he+H   surely   Lhasa   - OBL   come   - IMPF+EPI 2+FACT

       She will surely come to Lhasa. Or: She must come to Lhasa. (The speaker knows that she wants to look for a new job. He is quite sure of himself.)

The use of various epistemic adverbs expressing different degrees of the speaker's certainty, as seen in the above example, shows that the semantic range of some epistemic verbal endings is quite large. In general, it is possible to combine the majority of epistemic verbal endings with the epistemic adverbs of the first and second degree (1.1.1.1 and 1.1.1.2), for example *gcig.byas.na* 'perhaps' and *phal.cher* 'probably'. The use of the epistemic adverbs of the third degree (1.1.1.3), for example *gtan.gtan* 'certainly' or *yin.cig.min.cig* 'necessarily, absolutely', with epistemic verbal endings is more restricted as they are semantically less compatible with the general meaning of probability which epistemic endings convey. Look at the following sentences: while examples (14) and (15) are grammatical, example (16) sounds strange to many native speakers and should be considered as exceptional or even ungrammatical. Similarly, other examples with the adverb *gtan.gtan* and the epistemic verbal ending *a.yod*, as in (17), or that with the adverb *yin.cig.min.cig* and the epistemic verbal ending *gi.yod.pa.'dra*, as in (18), are problematic or even perceived as unacceptable by native speakers:

(14)   གཅིག་བྱས་ན་ཁོང་གིས་བྱས་པ་འདྲ།

gcig.byas.na	*khong*	*- gis*	*byas*	*- pa.'dra*
perhaps	s/he+H	- ERG	VBZ (PAS)	- PFV+EPI 2+SENS

It seems he might have done it. (It is similar to his way of doing things. The speaker is less certain.)

(15)   ཕལ་ཆེར་ཁོང་གིས་བྱས་པ་འདྲ།

phal.cher	*khong*	*- gis*	*byas*	*- pa.'dra*
probably	s/he+H	- ERG	VBZ (PAS)	- PFV+EPI 2+SENS

It seems he probably did it. (It is similar to his way of doing things. The speaker is more certain.)

(16)   ?   ཁོང་གིས་གཏན་གཏན་བྱས་པ་འདྲ།

?	*khong*	*- gis*	*gtan.gtan*	*byas*	*- pa.'dra*
	s/he+H	- ERG	certainly	VBZ (PAS)	- PFV+EPI 2+SENS

It seems he must have done it. (It is similar to his way of doing things. The speaker is almost certain.)

(17)   ?   ཁོང་ལ་ངའི་ལྡེ་མིག་གཏན་གཏན་བརྙེད་ཨ་ཡོད།

?	*khong*	*- la*	*nga*	*-'i*	*lde.mig*	*gtan.gtan*	*brnyed*
	s/he+H	- OBL	I	- GEN	key	certainly	find

- a.yod
- PERF+EPI 3+EGO+NEG

She can't have found my key. (She was not at the place where the speaker thinks he lost it.)

(18)   *   མོ་ཡིན་ཅིག་མིན་ཅིག་བོད་ལ་འགྲོ་གི་ཡོད་པ་འདྲ།

*	*mo*	*yin.cig.min.cig*	*bod*	*- la*	*'gro*	*- gi.yod.pa.'dra*
	she	necessarily	Tibet	- OBL	go (PRS)	- IMPF+EPI 2+SENS

Intended statement: It seems she will certainly go to Tibet.

Nonetheless, epistemic adverbs of the third degree are sometimes employed with epistemic verbal endings, for example *gtan.gtan* is used with the ending *pa.yod,* as in the example below:

(19)   ཁོང་གཏན་གཏན་ཕྱིན་པ་ཡོད།

khong	*gtan.gtan*	*phyin*	*- pa.yod*
s/he+H	certainly	go (PAS)	- PFV+EPI 3+EGO

He must have left. (A reply to the question as to whether he has gone [somewhere]. The speaker lives with the person in question in the same house.)

1.1.2 OTHER LEXICAL MEANS

In standard spoken Tibetan, there are various other lexical means in addition to epistemic adverbs that convey epistemic meanings. These include verbs of cognition or judgement, nominal constructions with a noun or an adjective, and so forth. For example, the epistemic verbs (e.g. *bsam* 'think') are quite frequently used as epistemic markers. Look at the following examples (20) and (21) with the verb *bsam* 'think':

(20)   རྐུབ་བཀྱག་འདི་ངས་ཁྱེར་ཡོང་པ་ཡིན་བསམ་གྱི་འདུག

rkub.bkyag	*'di*	*nga*	*- s*	*khyer*	*yong*	*- pa.yin*
chair	this	I	- ERG	bring	come	- PFV (EGO)

bsam	*- gyi.'dug*
think	- PRS+SENS

I think it was me who brought this chair. (A reply to the question as to who brought the chair.)

(21)   ངས་སྟོད་ཕད་ལ་བླུགས་ཡོད་བསམས་བྱུང་།

nga	*- s*	*stod.phad*	*- la*	*blugs*	*- yod*	*bsams*
I	- ERG	bag	- OBL	put	- PERF+EGO	think

- byung
- PFV+EGO

I thought I put it in the bag. (A reply to the question as to where the knife is. The speaker believes that the knife is in the bag but is not sure. The knife may be in the bag, but it is equally possible that the knife is not in the bag.)

The above example corresponds in meaning to the following sentence with the epistemic ending *yod.pa.yod*. However, they differ in the degree of certainty: while example (21) is often perceived as less certain (close to 50%),[10] example (22) is perceived as more certain:

(22)　　ངས་སྟོད་ཕད་ལ་བླུགས་ཡོད་པ་ཡོད།

nga	*- s*	*stod.phad*	*- la*	*blugs*	*- yod.pa.yod*
I	- ERG	bag	- OBL	put	- PERF+EPI 2+EGO

As far as I remember I put it in the bag. (A reply to the question as to where the knife is. The speaker does not remember clearly, but he thinks the knife is in the bag.)

It is impossible to employ epistemic verbal endings in a sentence that functions as an object of the verb *bsam* 'think' as shown in the following example with the epistemic verbal ending *pa.'dug* (23a). In such a sentence, the only possible grammatical usage is to employ an evidential verbal ending, as in example (23b):

(23)　　* ངའི་བསམ་པར་ཆར་པ་བཏང་པ་འདུག་བསམ་གྱི་འདུག

a)

* *nga*	*- 'i*	*bsam.pa*	*- r*	*char.pa*	*btang*	*- pa.'dug*
I	- GEN	thought	- OBL	rain	VBZ	- FUT+EPI 3+SENS

bsam	*- gyi.'dug*
think	- PRS+SENS

Intended statement: I think it looks like rain. Or: I think it will definitely rain.

ངའི་བསམ་པར་ཆར་པ་བཏང་གི་རེད་བསམ་གྱི་འདུག

b)

nga	*- 'i*	*bsam.pa*	*- r*	*char.pa*	*btang*	*- gi.red*
I	- GEN	thought	- OBL	rain	VBZ	- FUT+FACT

bsam	*- gyi.'dug*
think	- PRS+SENS

I think it is going to rain.

Furthermore, there are nominal constructions with a noun or an adjective conveying an epistemic meaning that are frequently used in the spoken language, such as the expression containing the adjective *'dra.po* 'similar' and the existential copula *'dug/mi.'dug*, meaning literally 'It seems/doesn't seem like…', as in example (24):[11]

---

[10] The opinions of my Tibetan consultants as to the degree of probability of this sentence differ. Some consultants suggest that it conveys the meaning of possibility, others claim that it conveys the meaning of probability.

[11] This nominal construction should not be mistaken with the construction of a lexical verb combined with the epistemic verbal ending *pa.'dug* (for more details see Section 2.7.1) which is employed in the future tense, and not in the past.

(24) ཉི་མར་ཐལ་ཆེར་དགོངས་པ་རག་པ་འདྲ་པོ་མི་འདུག

    a)

nyi.ma	*- r*	*phal.cher*	*dgongs.pa*	*rag*	*- pa*	*'dra.po*
Nyima	- OBL	perhaps	leave of absence	get	- NOM	similar

mi.'dug
exist (NEG+SENS)

It doesn't seem like Nyima got leave of absence. (The speaker guesses the expression on Nyima's face. Nyima looked annoyed as he left the boss's office.)

གༀ ཁོ་ནག་ཆུ་ནས་རེད་པས། ཁༀ ཨོ། འདྲ་པོ་སེ་ཅིག་འདུག

    b) A:

kho	*nag.chu*	*- nas*	*red*	*- pas*
he	Nagchu	- ABL	be (FACT)	- Q

          B:

o	*'dra.po*	*- se*	*cig*	*'dug*
oh	similar	- sort of	a	exist (SENS)

A: Is he from Nagchu?
B: Oh, he looks like one [a person from Nagchu].

Another example of a nominal epistemic construction is the expression consisting of a verb, the nominalizer *yag,* the noun *re.ba* 'hope' and an existential copula. This construction is employed for future contexts and its meaning is literally 'There is no hope of…':

(25) ཉི་མར་ཐལ་ཆེར་དགོངས་པ་རག་ཡག་གི་རེ་བ་མི་འདུག

nyi.ma	*- r*	*phal.cher*	*dgongs.pa*	*rag*	*- yag*	*- gi*
Nyima	- OBL	perhaps	leave of absence	get	- NOM	- GEN

re.ba   *mi.'dug*
hope   exist (NEG+SENS)

There is probably no hope of Nyima's getting any leave of absence. (The speaker speculates, given the amount of work he knows that Nyima has to do.)

Another way of expressing doubts with lexical means is the expression containing the noun *nyen.kha* meaning 'danger' and an existential copula as shown in the following example:

(26) ཁོང་ཚོ་སྤོ་ལོ་ཐོབ་ཡག་གི་ཉེན་ཁ་ཡོད་རེད།

khong	*- tsho*	*spo.lo*	*thob*	*- yag*	*- gi*	*nyen.kha*	*yod.red*
s/he (H)	- pl	ball	gain	- NOM	- GEN	danger	exist (FACT)

They will probably win the match. Or: They risk winning the match. (Lit.: 'There's a danger of their winning the ball.' A reply to the question as to who is going to win the match. They are a good team. So the speaker thinks that they could win.)

Similarly, the following conditional clause also has an epistemic meaning: *nga - s byas - na* corresponding to the English 'I think' or 'My opinion is' (Lit.: 'If I did'), as shown below:

(27)　　ངས་བྱས་ན་ཁོང་ནང་ལ་ཡོད་མ་རེད།

nga	- s	byas	- na	khong	nang	- la	yod.ma.red
I	- ERG	VBZ (PAS)	- if	s/he+H	home	- OBL	exist (FACT+NEG)

I don't think he is at home. (A reply to the question as to where he is. The speaker is expressing his opinion or belief.)

Another way of conveying epistemic meanings is the expression *'dug.se lta - dus* corresponding to the English 'When seeing [it] like this':

(28)　　འདུག་སེ་ལྟ་དུས་ང་ཁོང་ལ་ཡིད་ཆེས་ཡོད།

'dug.se	lta	- dus	nga	khong	- la	yid.ches	yod
like this	look (PRS)	- when	I	s/he+H	- OBL	belief	exist (EGO)

I think I believe him. Or: Upon thinking it over I (tend to) believe him. (A reply to the question as to whether the speaker believes the statement of another person.)

Lastly, the expression containing the nominalizer *yag*, the genitive particle *gi* and the noun *bzo* 'shape' followed by the verb *bstan* 'show' is another example of the lexical expression of epistemic modality:

(29)　　ནད་པ་འདི་དྲག་ཡག་གི་བཟོ་བསྟན་གྱི་མི་འདུག

nad.pa	'di	drag	yag	- gi	bzo	bstan	- gyi.mi.'dug
patient	this	recover	NOM	- GEN	shape	show	- PRS+SENS+NEG

It looks like this patient is not recovering. (Lit.: The patient does not show [any] shape of recovering.)

1.2 THE GRAMMATICAL EXPRESSION OF EPISTEMIC MODALITY

1.2.1 FORMAL ANALYSIS OF EPISTEMIC VERBAL ENDINGS AND COPULAS

In this section, the system of epistemic verbal endings that appear in the spoken language will be discussed from a formal viewpoint. These verbal endings will be classified according to different parameters and will also be discussed from the point of view of affirmative and negative polarity. The final part deals with epistemic copulas.

1.2.1.1 Classification and synchronic representation of epistemic verbal endings

Diachronically, epistemic verbal endings often consist of the same nominalizers and auxiliaries as evidential verbal endings. Most of the epistemic verbal endings were diachronically formed by a process of 'double suffixation'. They have two basic functions: they express tense-aspect and epistemic modality (Tournadre & Sangda Dorje 2003: 175–176). Tense-aspect is often expressed by the first formant and epistemic modality by the second formant. During the process of double suffixation a new modal meaning (epistemic modality) developed and this meaning is mainly conveyed by the second part of the new suffix (e.g. *gi.yod.pa.'dra, yod.sa.red*).[12] For example, consider the epistemic verbal ending *gi.yod-pa.'dra* where the first formant *gi.yod* corresponds to the imperfective and the second formant *pa.'dra* expresses probability.

Nevertheless, this morphemic analysis does not work for all epistemic verbal endings, e.g. *mi.yong.ngas, pa.yod, yong.nga.yod, yod.'gro, yod.'gro'o* and *med.'gro, med.'gro'o*, which cannot be divided in two formants. The endings with the morpheme *'gro/'gro'o*, for example, cannot be analysed in two suffixes since the polarity, and thus the epistemic meaning of these endings does not depend on the polarity of the auxiliaries *yod* and *med* but on the intonation of the whole ending (see Section 2.3). Consequently, in synchrony *yod.'gro, yod.'gro'o* and *med.'gro, med.'gro'o* cannot be analyzed in formants.

---

[12] The fact that during the process of double suffixation a new modal meaning develops (epistemic modality) and is expressed by the second part of the new suffix (e.g. *yod.pa.'dra, yod.bzo.'dug*), seems to confirm the hypothesis that modality is, in general, in a more distant position from the main verb than other verbal categories. (see François 2003: 30)

In addition, epistemic endings also imply an evidential meaning (see 1.1.2.2), which is usually conveyed by the whole ending. As a result, it is better to consider that in SST epistemic endings are non-analyzable units, even though diachronically they were composed of two suffixes. They are written with dots between syllables, not with a hyphen showing the morphemic structure. The synchronic representation of epistemic endings is, therefore, TA+EPI+EVI (tense-aspect + epistemic modality + evidential modality), and not TA-EPI-EVI.

Out of many Tibetan epistemic endings, some are frequently used in the spoken language, others are rare or literary.[13] There are a dozen of different types of epistemic endings that are employed in SST. These are: *yod.kyi.red,*[14] *yod.pa.'dra, yod.'gro, a.yod, yod.sa.red, yod-mdog.kha.po-red/'dug, yod.pa.yod, yong.nga.yod,* and *yod.bzo.'dug,* which are paradigm-like (i.e. each type consists of several verbal endings differing in the tense-aspect, see 1.2.2.1.1), and the verbal endings *pa.'dug, pa.yod, yong* and *mi.yong.ngas* which are not paradigm-like.

In this work, epistemic endings are mainly characterized according to the tense-aspect they refer to (see 1.1.2.1), the degree of probability (see 1.1.2.2) and the evidential meaning (see 1.1.2.3). This is illustrated by the following examples with the epistemic endings *gyi.med.'gro'o* and *yod.sa.red*. In example (30a), *gyi.med.'gro'o* is interpreted as the imperfective future, epistemic degree 1 and the factual evidential. In example (30b), *yod.sa.red* corresponds to the present perfect, epistemic degree 2 and the sensory evidential:

(30) ཁོ་གྲོགས་པོ་ལ་སྤོ་ལོ་གཡར་གྱི་མེད་འགྲོའོ།

a) *kho grogs.po - la spo.lo g.yar - gyi.med.'gro'o*
   he   friend - OBL ball   lend - <u>IMPF+EPI 1+FACT</u>

   He might lend the ball to his friend. (A reply to the question as to whether the child will lend someone the ball. The speaker infers from the fact that friends, in general, lend things to each other.)

---

[13] In literary Tibetan, there are also different ways of expressing various degrees of certainty. The most common means in SST, epistemic copulas and epistemic verbal endings, occur in literary Tibetan as well. The epistemic copulas used in literary Tibetan are, for example, *yod.las.che, yod.shas.che, yod.thang (yod.na.thang), yod.zhan.'dra, yod.bzo.'dug, yod.tshul.'dug, yod.tshod.'dug, yod.nges.la, yod.shag.la* and the corresponding essential copulas, e.g. *yin.las.che,* or other markers following the lexical verb, e.g. V + *tshod.'dug* (for more details and examples, see *Bod-rgya tshig-mdzod chen-mo* 1993, *Bod-kyi-dus-bab* [Tibet Times], Goldstein 2001, Oisel 2013).

   Some of the above mentioned copulas and verbal endings may appear in the spoken language but the majority of them are only reserved for written Tibetan. Below is an example with the epistemic copula *yin.las.che*:

   གནས་ཚུལ་དེ་བདེན་པ་ཡིན་ལས་ཆེ།

   gnas.tshul de bden.pa yin.las.che
   event   that true   be (EPI)
   This event may be true. (Goldstein 2001: 1001)

[14] I chose the perfect form to represent each type of verbal endings. See also Section 1.2.2.1.

ཕུན་ཚོགས་ཀྱིས་ཁ་ལག་བཟོས་ཡོད་ས་རེད།

b) *phun.tshogs* - *kyis* *kha.lag* *bzos* - *yod.sa.red*
   Phuntshog - ERG meal make (PAS) - <u>PERF+EPI 2+SENS</u>

It seems Phuntshog has cooked. (The speaker can smell it.)

1.2.1.2 Polarity: Affirmative and negative epistemic verbal endings

Epistemic verbal endings may be classified according to the parameter of polarity (for negation see: Bernini, Dryer 1988; de Haan 1997; Haegeman 1995; Miestamo 2005; Ramat 1996; van der Auwera 1998b, 2001) as expressed by affirmative and negative endings. In general, affirmative epistemic endings convey positive polarity and negative epistemic endings negative polarity. As a rule, whenever it is possible to use an affirmative ending, it is also possible to use its negative counterpart. Diachronically, negative endings are formed by adding the negative morphemes *ma* or *mi* to the affirmative ending or by using the negative auxiliaries *med, min* as opposed to their affirmative counterparts.

Negative polarity is often expressed by the second formant of the epistemic ending as illustrated in example (31) below, but less frequently by the first formant as shown in (32b). Example (31a) illustrates an affirmative epistemic ending, whereas example (31b) demonstrates a negative one.

(31)   ཁོ་སློབ་གྲྭར་འགྲོ་གི་ཡོད་ཀྱི་རེད།

   a) *kho* *slob.grwa* - *r* *'gro* - *gi.yod.<u>kyi.red</u>*
      he school OBL go (PRS) - IMPF+EPI 2+FACT

      He probably goes to school. (The speaker bases his assertion on the fact that the person in question is still young.)

   ཁོ་སློབ་གྲྭར་འགྲོ་གི་ཡོད་ཀྱི་མ་རེད།

   b) *kho* *slob.grwa* - *r* *'gro* - *gi.yod.<u>kyi.ma.red</u>*
      he school OBL go (PRS) - IMPF+EPI 2+FACT+NEG

      He probably does not go to school. (The speaker bases his assertion on the fact that the person in question is an adult.)

(32)   ཁོང་མོ་ཊ་མང་པོ་བཏང་གི་ཡོད་པ་འདྲ།

   a) *khong* *mo.Ta* *mang.po* *btang* - *gi.yod.pa.'dra*
      s/he+H car a lot VBZ - IMPF+EPI 2+SENS

      It seems he drives a lot. (The speaker can observe that the person's car is often not parked in front of the house.)

ཁོང་དེང་སང་མོ་ཊ་བཏང་གི་མེད་པ་འདྲ།

b) *khong*   *deng.sang*   *mo.Ta*   *btang*   - *gi.med.pa.'dra*
    s/he+H   these days   car   VBZ   - IMPF+EPI 2+SENS+NEG

It seems he isn't driving his car these days. (The speaker can see that recently, the car has often been parked in front of the house.)

Nevertheless, there are exceptions to the above rule, e.g. the formally negative endings with the auxiliary *'gro'o* (e.g. *med.'gro'o*), which are pronounced with a rising intonation and denote positive polarity. See the example below with the epistemic type *'gro*, in which (33a) is formally negative (*med*) but semantically positive (with rising intonation) and (33b) is formally positive (*yod*) but semantically negative (with falling intonation, for details see 2.3):

(33)   ཁོང་གིས་ཁ་ས་ལས་ཀ་བྱས་མེད་འགྲོའོ།

    a) *khong*   - *gis*   *kha.sa*   *las.ka*   *byas*   - *med.'gro'o*
        s/he+H   - ERG   yesterday   work   VBZ (PAS)   - PERF+EPI 1+FACT

    She probably worked yesterday. (Yesterday was Monday.)

          ཁོང་གིས་ཁ་ས་ལས་ཀ་བྱས་ཡོད་འགྲོའོ།

    b) *khong*   - *gis*   *kha.sa*   *las.ka*   *byas*   - *yod.'gro'o*
        s/he+H   - ERG   yesterday   work   VBZ (PAS)   - PERF+EPI 1+FACT+NEG

    She probably didn't work yesterday. (It was the weekend.)

Similarly, the epistemic endings employing the morpheme *a* (e.g. *a.yod*) which are diachronically interrogative, convey semantically a negative polarity (expressing a high degree of certainty about the non-actuality of the action) although they are formally positive. Epistemic endings with the morpheme *a* have no formally negative equivalents that would imply positive polarity, e.g. *a.med, *gi.a.med, *a.ma.yong. Compare the following examples:[15]

(34)   ཁོང་གིས་ཁ་ས་ལས་ཀ་བྱས་ཨ་ཡོད།

    a) *khong*   - *gis*   *kha.sa*   *las.ka*   *byas*   - *a.yod*
        s/he+H   - ERG   yesterday   work   VBZ (PAS)   - PERF+EPI 3+EGO+NEG

    I doubt he worked yesterday. (The speaker knows that the person was ill.)

    *   ཁོང་གིས་ཁ་ས་ལས་ཀ་བྱས་ཨ་མེད།

    b) * *khong*   - *gis*   *kha.sa*   *las.ka*   *byas*   - *a.med*
          s/he+H   - ERG   yesterday   work   VBZ (PAS)   - PERF+EPI 3+EGO

    Intended statement: I have no doubts that he worked yesterday.

---

[15] For more details, refer to Section 2.4.

Another formally negative but semantically positive verbal ending is *mi.yong.ngas.*[16]

In SST, either preverbal or postverbal negation may occur in sentences containing an epistemic verbal ending. In the former case, the negative particle *ma* precedes the lexical verb followed by an affirmative verbal ending. In the latter case, the verb is followed by a negative verbal ending. Preverbal negation is limited to some epistemic endings, usually the perfective past endings with the nominalizer *pa*. In the same manner, the preverbal position of the negative particle *ma* is also found in sentences with the evidential perfective past endings *pa.red* and *pa.yin,* as in example (35a). However, these sentences are less frequent in the spoken language and generally convey a sense of 'not wanting to do [a given action]'. Instead, the negative perfect endings *yod.ma.red* and *med* are used (35b):

(35)   ཁོ་རང་མ་ཕྱིན་པ་རེད།

a) *kho.rang   ma   - phyin   - pa.red*
     he   NEG   - go (PAS)   - PFV+FACT

He didn't go. (often meaning 'because he didn't want to')

ཁོ་རང་ཕྱིན་ཡོད་མ་རེད།

b) *kho.rang   phyin   - yod.ma.red*
     he   go (PAS)   - PFV+FACT+NEG

He didn't go.

This explains why this tendency is also attested in negative sentences with perfective past epistemic endings. In the following examples (36a) and (36b), the lexical verb is preceded by the negative particle *ma*:[17]

(36)   ཁོང་ལྷ་སར་མ་ཕྱིན་པ་ཡིན་གྱི་རེད།

a) *khong   lha.sa   - r   ma   - phyin   - pa.yin.gyi.red*
     s/he+H   Lhasa   - OBL   NEG   - go (PAS)   - PFV+EPI 2+FACT

She probably did not go to Lhasa. (It was a usual working day, not a day off. So the speaker thinks it's likely that she didn't go to Lhasa.)

རང་མདང་དགོང་གཉིད་ཡག་པོ་མ་ཁུག་པ་འདྲ།

b) *rang   mdang.dgong   gnyid   yag.po   ma   - khug   - pa.'dra*
     you   last night   sleeping   well   NEG   - get (sleep)   - PFV+EPI 2+SENS

You seem not to have slept well last night. (The speaker can see that the person addressed looks tired.)

---

[16] For more details, refer to Section 2.10.1.
[17] See e.g. Tournadre, Sangda Dorje (2003: 129–130, 166). Zhou Jiwen, Xie Houfang [eds.] (2003: 113).

Nonetheless, native speakers often prefer sentences with post-verbal negation. It is therefore more common to use the negative ending *med.pa.'dra* for the above sentence, as shown in example (36c).

རང་མདང་དགོང་གཉིད་ཡག་པོ་ཁུག་མེད་པ་འདྲ།

c)	*rang*	*mdang.dgong*	*gnyid*	*yag.po*	*khug*	*- med.pa.'dra*
	you	last night	sleeping	well	get (sleep)	- PERF+EPI 2+SENS+NEG

You seem to have not slept well last night. (The speaker can see that the person addressed looks tired.)

Preverbal negation is often ungrammatical; see, for example (37a), employing the epistemic construction *yod-mdog.kha.po-red.* Only the postverbal negation is grammatical, as in example (37b). Some, but not all Tibetans also accept sentences with the negative auxiliary *med* instead of *yod* preceeding the suffix *mdog.kha.po*, as seen in (37c); see Section 2.6 for more details:

(37) * ཁོང་མ་ཕྱིན་ཡོད་མདོག་ཁ་པོ་རེད།

a)	* *khong*	*ma*	*- phyin*	*- yod*	*- mdog.kha.po*	*- red*
	s/he+H	NEG	- go (PAS)	- PERF	- EPI 1	- AUX (FACT)

Intended statement: It looks like he has not gone (there).

ཁོང་ད་ལྟ་གཞིས་ཀ་རྩེར་སླེབས་ཡོད་མདོག་ཁ་པོ་མ་རེད།

b)	*khong*	*da.lta*	*gzhis.ka.rtse*	*- r*	*slebs*	*- yod*	*- mdog.kha.po*
	s/he+H	now	Shigatse	- OBL	come	- PERF	- EPI 1
	- ma.red						
	- AUX (FACT+NEG)						

It seems he has not yet arrived in Shigatse. (It usually takes five hours to get to Shigatse. Three and a half hours have gone by since he left.)

? ཁོང་གིས་ཡི་གེ་བྲིས་མེད་མདོག་ཁ་པོ་རེད།

c)	*? khong*	*- gis*	*yi.ge*	*bris*	*- med*	*- mdog.kha.po*	*- red*
	s/he+H	- ERG	letter	write (PAS)	- PERF AUX (NEG)	- EPI 1	- AUX (FACT)

She probably did not write [any] letters.

The negation of the predication (preverbal negation) and the negation of the verbal ending (postverbal negation) usually convey a similar meaning. There may, however at times be a difference in the scope of negation between the two, as illustrated in the examples below: in example (38a) the scope of negation is limited to the verb, while in example (38b) the entire predication is negated:

(38)   ཁོང་གིས་སྐད་ཆ་འདི་མ་བཤད་པ་ཡིན་གྱི་རེད།

a) *khong - gis skad.cha 'di ma - bshad - pa.yin.gyi.red*
    s/he+H - ERG speech this NEG - say - PFV+EPI 2+FACT

He probably didn't say this. (i.e. It is likely that he didn't say this, but that he said something else.)

ཁོང་གིས་སྐད་ཆ་འདི་བཤད་པ་ཡིན་གྱི་མ་རེད།

b) *khong - gis skad.cha 'di bshad - pa.yin.gyi.ma.red*
    s/he+H - ERG speech this say - PFV+EPI 2+FACT+NEG

I don't believe he said [it]. (i.e. It must have been someone else who said it.)

1.2.1.3 Epistemic copulas

In spoken Tibetan, there are copulas which convey an epistemic meaning and may therefore be termed *epistemic copulas*. Just as with evidential copulas, they are divided in two types: essential and existential. The essential copulas contain the element *yin* (expressing essence) and the existential copulas the element *yod* (expressing existence, possession, location and attributive predication).[18] The following is a list of epistemic copulas used in SST (in both the affirmative and negative forms):

Affirmative essential	Affirmative existential	Negative essential	Negative existential
yin.gyi.red	*yod.kyi.red*	*yin.gyi.ma.red*	*yod.kyi.ma.red*
yin.pa.'dra	*yod.pa.'dra*	*min.pa.'dra*	*med.pa.'dra*
yin.'gro, *min.'gro'o*	*yod.'gro,* *med.'gro'o*	*yin.'gro'o,* *min.'gro*	*yod.'gro'o,* *med.'gro*
yin.sa.red	*yod.sa.red*	*yin.sa.ma.red*	*yod.sa.ma.red*
a.yin	*a.yod*	–	–
yin-mdog.kha.po-'dug/red	*yod-mdog.kha.po-'dug/red*	*yin-mdog.kha.po -mi.'dug/ma.red*	*yod-mdog.kha.po- mi.'dug/ma.red*
yin.pa.yod	*yod.pa.yod*	*yin.pa.med,* *min.pa.yod*	*yod.pa.med,* *med.pa.yod*
–	*yong*	–	*mi.yong*
(*yong.nga.yod*)	*yong.nga.yod*	(*yong.nga.med*)	*yong.nga.med*
yin.bzo.'dug	*yod.bzo.'dug*	*yin.bzo.mi.'dug*	*yod.bzo.mi.'dug*

---

[18] Just as with evidential copulas, existential epistemic copulas have an identical form with perfect epistemic endings, e.g. *yod.kyi.red* may function as a copula when used with a noun phrase, or as a verbal ending when used after a verb.

The use of epistemic copulas is illustrated by the following pair of examples, one employing the essential copula *yin.gyi.red*, and the other, the existential copula *a.yod*:

(39) ཁོང་སྒྲོལ་མ་ཡིན་གྱི་རེད།

    a) *khong   sgrol.ma   yin.gyi.red*
       s/he+H   Dolma   be (EPI 2+FACT)

       Probably, she is Dolma. (The speaker doesn't personally know the woman in question, but he knows that someone called Dolma lives in this location.)

    ཁོང་ནང་ལ་ཨ་ཡོད།

    b) *khong   nang.la   a.yod*
       s/he+H   home   exist (EPI 2+EGO)

       I don't think she is at home. (The speaker knows that she usually doesn't spend her evenings at home.)

1.2.2 FUNCTIONAL ANALYSIS OF EPISTEMIC VERBAL ENDINGS

In this section, epistemic verbal endings will be discussed from their semantic and functional characteristics. These endings can be classified primarily according to the tense-aspect they convey, the degree of probability, and the evidential meaning. They also, however, convey other meanings (e.g. deontic). Finally, the relation of epistemic verbal endings to the category of person and the parameter of frequency and geographic variation will be discussed.

1.2.2.1 Epistemic verbal endings as markers of tense-aspect

On Tense and Aspect see: Bache 1985, 1995; Bybee, Dahl 1989; Bybee, Perkins, Pagliuca 1994; Chung, Timberlake 1985; Cohen 1989; Comrie 1976, 1985; Confais 1995; Dahl 1985, 2000; Hopper 1982; Kunert 1984; Moeschler 1998; Saussure 1998; Tedeschi, Zaenen (eds.) 1981.

1.2.2.1.1 The tense-aspect paradigm of epistemic verbal endings

As stated above, in spoken Tibetan, there are several types of epistemic endings that are used fairly frequently. The majority of these types are paradigmatic, i.e. they are comprised of three different endings, each of them referring to a different tense-aspect. Diachronically, most of these endings are made up of two formants (see 1.2.1.1). The first formant is always identical to those endings that express the same tense-aspect (e.g. *gi.yod* for all imperfective endings, *yod* for all perfect endings), whereas the second one differs (e.g. *pa.'dra, sa.red, bzo.'dug*). The epistemic paradigm is as follows:

1. The perfective ending with the first formant *pa.yin* is used with the past perfective.		

2. The perfect ending with the first formant *yod* is used with the past, past events having relevance to the present, and at times the immediate present.

3. The imperfective ending with the first formant *gi.yod* (or *kyi.yod, gyi.yod*)[19] is used with the imperfective past, the long-term present and the future.

Below is a table and examples with the type *yod.kyi.red* illustrating the epistemic paradigm:

1	Perfective past	*pa.yin.gyi.red*[20]
2	Perfect and the immediate present	*yod.kyi.red*
3	Imperfective (past, long-term present and future)	*gi.yod.kyi.red*

(40) ཁོང་རྒྱ་གར་ལ་ཕྱིན་པ་ཡིན་གྱི་རེད།

a) *khong   rgya.gar - la   phyin   - pa.yin.gyi.red*
   s/he+H   India   - OBL   go (PAS)   - PFV+EPI 2+FACT

It's probably India that she went to. (A reply to the question as to where the person has gone, or whether she went to Nepal or India. The speaker knows that she left. Basing his statement on the fact that many Tibetans go to India, he states that she went to India.)

ཁོང་རྒྱ་གར་ལ་ཕྱིན་ཡོད་ཀྱི་རེད།

b) *khong   rgya.gar - la   phyin   - yod.kyi.red*
   s/he+H India   - OBL   go (PAS) - PERF+EPI 2+FACT

She has probably gone to India. (A reply to the question as to where the person is. The speaker may know that she has departed for somewhere but not necessarily. He bases his assertion on the fact that many Tibetans go to India.)

ཁོང་མགྱོགས་པོ་རྒྱ་གར་ལ་འགྲོ་གི་ཡོད་ཀྱི་རེད།

c) *khong   mgyogs.po   rgya.gar - la   'gro   - gi.yod.kyi.red*
   s/he+H   soon   India   - OBL   go (PAS)   - IMPF+EPI 2+FACT

Probably, she will soon go to India. (A reply to the question as to when she will be going to India. The speaker knows that she was planning to go in September. It is the beginning of September now. So he infers that her departure will probably take place soon.)

---

[19] *Kyi, gi* and *gyi* are allomorphs. Their use depends on the word preceding them. In the spoken language, they are all pronounced in the same way: [*ki*]. See e.g. Kesang Gyurme 1992; Tournadre, Sangda Dorje 2003.
[20] For more details, see Section 1.2.2.1.2.

As we have seen above, the epistemic paradigm consists of three verbal endings. This is different from the evidential paradigm which consists of four endings: perfective past (aorist), perfect, imperfective and future. It is true that some epistemic types have future endings (*'gro, sa.red, a.yong, bzo.'dug*) but this is not the case for all the types of endings under consideration here. In comparison to the corresponding evidential endings, there are some differences in the tense-aspect functions and in the frequency of use of certain epistemic endings. Firstly, unlike evidential past endings, the primary epistemic endings employed to express the past tense are perfect endings, not perfective past endings. The perfective past epistemic ending is much less frequent than the perfect epistemic ending. Moreover, the perfect and perfective past epistemic endings usually differ in their scope of epistemic modality (see section 1.2.2.1.2). Secondly, the use of imperfective endings differs in both paradigms. While the evidential imperfective ending is only used in imperfective past, present and habitual contexts, the epistemic imperfective ending is also employed in future contexts (see example 40c above).

The following table shows all the epistemic types that form the epistemic paradigm. Note that there are some irregularities, mainly the existence of a future ending for several of the types, the position of the morpheme *a* in *a.yod* (**yod.a*), and the different first formant for the type *yong.nga.yod* (*yong* is used instead of *yod*):

yod.kyi.red	*pa.yin.gyi.red, yod.kyi.red, gi.yod.kyi.red*
yod.'gro	*pa.yin.'gro, yod.'gro, gi.yod.'gro* + the future ending *'gro*
yod.pa.'dra	*pa.yin.pa.'dra, yod.pa.'dra, gi.yod.pa.'dra* + the perfect ending *pa.'dra*
yod.sa.red	*pa.yin.sa.red, yod.sa.red, gi.yod.sa.red,* + the future ending *sa.red*
yod.pa.yod	*pa.yin.pa.yod, yod.pa.yod, gi.yod.pa.yod*
a.yod	The type *a.yod* differs from the other types in that the morpheme *a* does not follow the first formant but it is placed between the nominalizer (*pa, gi,* zero) and the auxiliary: *pa.a.yin, a.yod, gi.a.yod* + the future ending *a.yong*
yong.nga.yod	The type *yong.nga.yod* only consists of two forms: *yong.nga.yod, gi.yong.nga.yod,* (**pa.yong.nga.yod*)
yod.bzo.'dug	*pa.yin.bzo.'dug, yod.bzo.'dug, gi.yod.bzo.'dug* + the future ending *bzo.'dug* (This type is very rare in SST)

There are other epistemic endings in SST that are not part of the above paradigm, some of them already mentioned in the above table: *'gro, bzo.'dug, sa.red, a.yong, pa.'dra*. The others are: *pa.'dug, pa.yod, mi.yong.ngas,* and *yong*. Moreover, there is a construction with the epistemic suffix *mdog.kha.po* followed by the auxiliary *red, 'dug* or *yod* (see below).

The epistemic ending *bzo.'dug* is usually, but not exclusively, used in the future tense.
The epistemic endings *'gro, sa.red, a.yong, pa.'dug* and *mi.yong.ngas* are only used in the future tense.
The epistemic ending *pa.'dra* is used in the perfective past.
The epistemic ending *pa.yod* can, according to the context, have a past or a future meaning.
The epistemic ending *yong* can appear in all tenses.
The *mdog.kha.po* construction consists of different forms used in different tenses (For a list of all the forms with the suffix *mdog.kha.po* see 2.6)

The *mdog.kha.po*-construction is an example of an ongoing process of grammaticalization[21] of certain lexical items into an epistemic verbal ending which has not yet been completed (for more details, refer to Section 2.6). In this construction, the epistemic suffix *mdog.kha.po* is preceded by an evidential ending or directly attached to the lexical verb, and then followed by the auxiliaries *red* or *'dug*, as in example (41). Similarly, there are constructions with the morpheme *bzo* that are examples of the process of grammaticalization (for more details, refer to Section 2.11.2.2).

(41)　　　བསོད་རྣམས་གཞིས་ཀ་རྩེ་ར་འགྲོ་མདོག་ཁ་པོ་འདུག

bsod.nams　gzhis.ka.rtse - r　'gro　- mdog.kha.po　- 'dug
Sonam　　　Shigatse　　- OBL　go (PRS) - EPI 1　　　　- AUX (SENS)
It looks like Sonam is going to Shigatse. (He is a merchant and often goes to Shigatse. The speaker can see him loading up the car.)

In addition, for some past or future contexts, various combinations of the nominalizer *mkhan* and the essential epistemic auxiliaries are used in the spoken language. These combinations also demonstrate the process of incorporation of a nominalizer and an auxiliary as one suffix as well as the process of development of a new meaning of the combination. Just as in the construction employing *mdog.kha.po*, this process of grammaticalization has not yet been concluded and is generalized for these combinations (see Vokurková 2007). Although a speaker may yet be aware

---

[21] For grammaticalization, refer to Duchet 1990; Heine 1993; Hopper 1991; Steele 1981; Traugott, Heine (eds.) 1991.

of the original meaning of the nominalized construction 'a person doing an action' or 'a doer of an action', this combination has developed a new meaning. It is used to express that the agent of an event has, or had, a plan for the future. The use of this combination occurs only with controllable verbs:[22]

(42)   ཕྲུ་གུ་སང་ཉིན་སློབ་གྲྭར་འགྲོ་མཁན་ཡིན་གྱི་རེད།

phru.gu	*sang.nyin*	*slob.grwa*	*- r*	*'gro*	*- mkhan*	*: yin.gyi.red*
child	tomorrow	school	- OBL	go (PRS)	- NOM	: be (EPI 2+FACT)

The child will probably go to school tomorrow. (A reply to the question as to whether the child will go to school tomorrow. It is Monday tomorrow, so the child's intent must be to go to school.)

Another example demonstrating the process of grammaticalization is the perfective past epistemic ending, e.g. *pa.yin.gyi.red.* Whereas in the case of the previous example employing the nominalizer *mkhan* the process of grammaticalization has not yet been concluded, in the case of *pa.yin.gyi.red* (or any of the other perfective past epistemic endings), it can be stated that it has been fully grammaticalized into a verbal ending. Diachronically, the first formant consists of the nominalizer *pa* and the auxiliary *yin*, followed by the second formant *gyi.red.* It formally (but not phonetically) resembles a nominalized construction with the nominalizer *pa* followed by the essential copula *yin.gyi.red,* as in example (47). This corresponds to the difference between the evidential endings *pa.yin* or *pa.red* and their corresponding nominalized constructions, as seen in examples (43) and (44). In SST, there are combinations that can be interpreted both as nominalizations or suffixations. Let's take a look at the examples employing the evidential ending *pa.red* (example 43) and the nominalized construction V- *pa* with the essential verb *red* (example 44):

(43)   ཁོ་རང་གིས་ཁ་ལག་བཟས་པ་རེད།

a)
kho.rang	*- gis*	*kha.lag*	*bzas*	*- pa.red*
he	- ERG	food	eat (PAS)	- PFV+FACT

He ate something/had a meal.

ཁ་ལག་འདི་ཁོ་རང་གིས་བཟས་པ་རེད།

b)
kha.lag	*'di*	*kho.rang*	*- gis*	*bzas*	*- pa.red*
food	this	he	- ERG	eat (PAS)	- PFV+FACT

He ate/had this meal.

---

[22] Controllable verbs (also known as 'volitional') are verbs that indicate controllable actions, i.e. actions that depend on the agent's volition or control. On the contrary, non-controllable verbs imply actions that do not depend on the agent's volition or control.

(44)   ཁོ་རང་གིས་ཁ་ལག་བཟས་པ་འདི་རེད།

    a)   *kho.rang*   *- gis*   *kha.lag*   *bzas*   *- pa*   *'di*   *red*
        he   - ERG   food   eat (PAS)   - NOM   this   be (FACT)

        The meal that he had is this one. (This is the meal that he ate).

    འདི་ཁོ་རང་གིས་བཟས་པ་རེད།

    b)   *'di*   *kho.rang*   *- gis*   *bzas*   *- pa*   *red*
        this   he   - ERG   eat (PAS)   - NOM   be (FACT)

        This is what he ate.

And now let's see what the corresponding epistemic constructions would look like: examples (45) and (46) show the use of verbal endings, and example (47) shows nominalization:

(45)   * ཁོ་རང་གིས་ཁ་ལག་བཟས་པ་ཡིན་གྱི་རེད།

    a)   * *kho.rang*   *- gis*   *kha.lag*   *bzas*   *- pa.yin.gyi.red*
                 he   - ERG   food   eat (PAS)   - PFV+EPI 2+FACT

        Intended statement: Most likely, he ate something/had a meal.

    ཁོ་རང་གིས་ཁ་ལག་བཟས་ཡོད་ཀྱི་རེད།

    b)   *kho.rang*   *- gis*   *kha.lag*   *bzas*   *- yod.kyi.red*
        he   - ERG   food   eat (PAS)   - PERF+EPI 2+FACT

        Most likely, he ate something/had a meal.

As stated above, the primary epistemic endings for expressing the past tense in epistemic contexts are perfect, and not perfective past endings. Thus the correct translation of 'Most likely, he ate something/had a meal' is borne out by example (45b), and not example (45a) which is ungrammatical. As a result, (45b) is the corresponding epistemic utterance for the non-epistemic evidential sentence in (43a) which employs the perfective past ending *pa.red* conveying the meaning 'He ate something/had a meal.' (The speaker is 100% certain of his utterance.). On the other hand, the use of the perfective past epistemic ending is quite limited. It is only employed in sentences in which epistemic modality has a partial scope, and does not convey an epistemic scope that applies to the entire sentence, as in example (46); see Section 1.2.2.1.2 for more details:

(46)   ཁོ་རང་གིས་ཁ་ལག་འདི་བཟས་པ་ཡིན་གྱི་རེད།

    a)   *kho.rang*   *- gis*   *kha.lag*   *'di*   *bzas*   *- pa.yin.gyi.red*
        he   - ERG   food   this   eat (PAS)   - PFV+EPI 2+FACT

        It must be this meal that he ate (and not another one).

ཁ་ལག་འདི་ཁོ་རང་གིས་བཟས་པ་ཡིན་གྱི་རེད།

b) *kha.lag*   *'di*   *kho.rang*   *- gis*   *bzas*   *- pa.yin.gyi.red*
    food   this   he   - ERG   eat (PAS)   - PFV+EPI 2+FACT

It must be him who ate this meal (and not someone else).

The following is an example of a nominalized construction with the nominalizer *pa* and the epistemic verb *yin.gyi.red* which conveys the meaning '[it] is most probable', '[it] is quite likely' or '[it] must be [so]'. Example (47b) is formally identical with example (46b). However, (46b) is a sentence with a verbal ending, while (47b) contains a nominalization (Cf. example 44b, a nominalization with the evidential verb *red*).

(47)   ཁོ་རང་གིས་ཁ་ལག་བཟས་པ་འདི་ཡིན་གྱི་རེད།

    a) *kho.rang*   *- gis*   *kha.lag*   *bzas*   *- pa*   *'di*   *yin.gyi.red*
      he   - ERG   food   eat (PAS)   - NOM   this   be (EPI 2+FACT)

    The meal that he ate must be this (one).

    ཁ་ལག་འདི་ཁོ་རང་གིས་བཟས་པ་ཡིན་གྱི་རེད།

    b) *kha.lag*   *'di*   *kho.rang*   *- gis*   *bzas*   *- pa*   *yin.gyi.red*
      food   this   he   - ERG   eat (PAS)   - NOM   be (EPI 2+FACT)

    This meal must be the one that he ate.

Furthermore, just as in the case of evidential verbal endings and constructions, one can also establish a modal paradigm consisting of three forms or constructions expressing the meanings of ability/opportunity, prohibitition and obligation, respectively in the past, present and future. To convey these meanings, the lexical verb is nominalized by the nominalizer *rgyu* followed by the auxiliary *byung* (in the case of expression of a past ability/opportunity), and also by an epistemic auxiliary. These epistemic forms and constructions correspond to the evidential forms (e.g. *rgyu:byung:song, rgyu.yod.ma.red, rgyu.red*). They only differ in the epistemic meaning (100% versus <100%) and in frequency: the epistemic constructions are less common in the spoken language.

1. Epistemic ability or opportunity in past contexts is expressed by the nominalizer *rgyu* and the auxiliary *byung* followed by a perfect epistemic ending, e.g. *rgyu:byung-yod.pa.'dra*. The final perfect epistemic ending may either be affirmative (positive polarity) or negative (negative polarity). See example (48a).

rgyu:byung-yod.kyi.red, rgyu:byung-yod.'gro, rgyu:byung-yod.pa.'dra, rgyu:byung-yod.sa.red, rgyu:byung-yod.pa.yod or *rgyu:byung-a.yod, rgyu:byung-yod-mdog.kha.po-red, rgyu:byung-yod.bzo.'dug*

---

2. Epistemic prohibition in the habitual present ('probably should not do') is expressed by the nominalizer *rgyu* followed by an existential epistemic auxiliary, e.g. *rgyu:med.pa.'dra*. This form has no affirmative counterpart (e.g. **rgyu.yod.pa.'dra*). See example (48b).

rgyu:yod.kyi.ma.red, rgyu:yod.'gro'o, rgyu:med.pa.'dra, rgyu:yod.sa.ma.red, rgyu:yod.pa.med or *rgyu:med.pa.yod, rgyu:a.yod, rgyu:yod-mdog.kha.po-ma.red, rgyu:yod.bzo.mi.'dug*

---

3. Epistemic obligation or necessity in the future and the meaning of an action that has not yet been carried out and, therefore, has yet to be done ('should probably intend to', 'probably need to', 'probably have yet to') is expressed by epistemic endings consisting of the first formant *rgyu.yin* followed by a second formant, e.g. *rgyu.yin.pa.'dra*. This form has no negative counterpart (**rgyu.yin.pa.'dra*). See example (48c).

rgyu.yin.gyi.red, rgyu.yin.'gro, rgyu.yin.pa.'dra, rgyu.yin.sa.red, rgyu.yin.pa.yod, rgyu.a.yin, rgyu.yong.nga.yod, rgyu.yin-mdog.kha.po-red, rgyu.yin.bzo.'dug

---

(48)   ཁོ་རང་འགྲོ་རྒྱུ་བྱུང་མེད་པ་འདྲ།

  a) *kho.rang   'gro   - rgyu   :byung   - med.pa.'dra*
      he   go (PRS)   - NOM   : AUX   - PERF+EPI 2+SENS

  It seems he could not (was not able to) go there. (A reply to the question as to whether he went somewhere.)

  གསང་དབང་དེ་ལབ་རྒྱུ་མེད་པ་འདྲ།

  b) *gsang.dbang   de   lab   - rgyu   : med.pa.'dra*
      secret   that   tell   - NOM   : AUX+EPI 2+SENS

  It seems [we] shouldn't tell that secret. (Someone wants to share a secret. The speaker does not agree.)

42

ཁོང་རྒྱ་གར་ལ་འགྲོ་རྒྱུ་ཡིན་པ་འདྲ།

  c) *khong*   *rgya.gar*   *- la*   *'gro*   *- rgyu.yin.pa.'dra*
      s/he+H   India   - OBL   go (PAS) - FUT+EPI 2+SENS

It seems she has (yet) to leave for India. (A reply to the question as to whether she has left for India. The speaker saw some indications that leads him to think that she has probably not departed yet.)

1.2.2.1.2 Some differences between the verbal endings of the epistemic tense-aspect paradigm

In certain cases, different verbal endings of the epistemic paradigm may occur in similar contexts or in statements of a similar tense context. Their use, however, is not entirely identical. I will, therefore, compare the use of certain verbal endings with that of other verbal endings, e.g. the perfect ending with the perfective past ending, or the imperfective ending with the deontic future ending.

<u>1. The perfect ending vs. the perfective past ending</u>

The perfect ending (e.g. *yod.kyi.red*) and the perfective past ending (e.g. *pa.yin.gyi.red*) are both used in past contexts. However, unlike evidential verbal endings, the epistemic perfective past ending is generally used less frequently than the epistemic perfect ending. Certain uses of these endings have preserved a difference in aspect, but this difference is often neutralized. The perfect ending and the perfective past ending differ in the following ways:

a) The difference in aspect can be attested in present perfect tense contexts: in such contexts, only the perfect ending, and not the perfective past ending, occurs. Compare the following examples:

(49)   ཁོང་ད་ལྟ་ནང་ལ་བཞུགས་ཡོད་ཀྱི་རེད།

  a) *khong*   *da.lta*   *nang* *- la*   *bzhugs*   *- yod.kyi.red*
      s/he+H   now   home - OBL   stay+H   - PERF+EPI 2+FACT

He is probably at home now. (i.e. He has stayed at home.)

     *   ཁོང་ད་ལྟ་ནང་ལ་བཞུགས་པ་ཡིན་གྱི་རེད།

  b) * *khong*   *da.lta*   *nang* *- la*   *bzhugs*   *- pa.yin.gyi.red*
        s/he+H   Now   home - OBL   stay+H   - PFV+EPI 2+FACT

Intended statement: He is probably at home now.

b) There may be a difference in the scope of epistemic modality: in this case, perfect endings (e.g. *yod.kyi.red*) are unmarked. They usually have bearing on the entire sentence (sentence scope). In contrast, perfective past endings (e.g. *pa.yin.gyi.red*) are marked. They have a more restricted (focused) scope. They highlight only one part of the sentence (e.g. the agent, the adverbial, the predicate). As a result, perfective past endings are usually used only if one part of the sentence is focused. This is seen in examples (50) and (51): while (50b) is ungrammatical, (50c) is grammatical, as it places focus on the adverbial of time/place. Perfect endings have no such restrictions: see example (50a). Compare also the difference in scope to examples (51a) and (51b): [23]

(50) ཁོང་སླེབས་ཨ་ཡོད།

a) *khong   slebs - a.yod*
    s/he+H   arrive - PERF+EPI 1+EGO+NEG

   I doubt she has arrived (yet). (She went to Ngari. It is very far away. The speaker bases his statement on personal knowledge.)

   * ཁོང་སླེབས་པ་ཨ་ཡིན།

b) * *khong   slebs - pa.a.yin*
       s/he+H   arrive - PFV+EPI 1+EGO+NEG

   Intended statement: I doubt she arrived.

   ཁོང་ཁ་ས་ ʃ ་ལྷ་སར་སླེབས་པ་ཨ་ཡིན།

c) *khong   kha.sa / lha.sa - r   slebs - pa.a.yin*
    s/he+H   yesterday   Lhasa - OBL   arrive - PFV+EPI 1+EGO+NEG

   I doubt that she arrived yesterday/in Lhasa. (i.e. She arrived but it was probably not yesterday or probably not in Lhasa.)

(51) ང་ར་ཆམ་པ་བརྒྱབ་མེད་པ་འདྲ།

a) *nga   - r   cham.pa   brgyab - med.pa.'dra*
    I   - OBL   cold   VBZ   - PERF+EPI 2+SENS+NEG

   It seems that I haven't caught a cold. (The speaker thought he had caught a cold but now it seems he is fine.)

   ང་ར་ཆམ་པ་བརྒྱབ་པ་མིན་པ་འདྲ།

b) *nga   - r   cham.pa   brgyab - pa.min.pa.'dra*
    I   - OBL   cold   VBZ   - PFV+EPI 2+SENS+NEG

   It doesn't seem like [my illness] is a cold. (The speaker thinks he has some other element. He bases his statement on direct observation.)

---

[23] For more details and examples, see Chapter II (examples 147, 175, 200, 201, 225, 226, 254).

The difference in scope of epistemic modality produces another interesting effect. According to my Tibetan consultants, in contrast to the perfect ending, the perfective past ending may imply a sensory inference, as illustrated by example (52). This can be explained by the fact that because perfective past epistemic endings have only a limited scope, focusing on one part of the sentence, they are employed only in those sentences in which an action that happened is partially called into question: "Probably it is not him who did this work.", "Possibly this is not the book that she bought.", and so on. This is why sensory inference is implied, without regard to the original evidential meaning of the verbal ending. In the following example employing the verbal ending *pa.yin.gyi.red* the object *deb* 'book' must be determined, see example (52a). Otherwise, the sentence is ungrammatical or the perfect verbal ending *yod.kyi.red* must be used, as shown in example (52b):

(52) ཁོང་གིས་དེབ་འདི་ཉོས་པ་ཡིན་གྱི་རེད།

    a)   *khong*   *- gis*   *deb*   *'di*   *nyos*   *- pa.yin.gyi.red*
            s/he+H   - ERG   book   this   buy (PAS)   - PFV+EPI 2+FACT

            She probably bought this book. (The speaker can see the book and infers that she purchased the book, and did not borrow it.)

           ཁོང་གིས་དེབ་ཉོས་ཡོད་ཀྱི་རེད།

    b)   *khong*   *- gis*   *deb*   *nyos*   *- yod.kyi.red*
            s/he+H   - ERG   book   buy (PAS)   - PERF+EPI 2+FACT

            He probably bought some books. (He said he would go to a bookstore, so the speaker infers that he purchased some books.)

c) According to my Tibetan consultants, as opposed to the perfective past ending used in example (53b), the perfect ending implies an inference based on the speaker's knowledge of a habitual action or state: see example (53a).

(53) ཁོང་ཁ་ས་ནང་ལ་བཞུགས་བསྡད་ཡོད་ཀྱི་རེད།

    a)   *khong*   *kha.sa*   *nang*   *- la*   *bzhugs*   *bsdad*   *- yod.kyi.red*
            s/he+H   yesterday   home   - OBL   stay+H   stay   - PERF+EPI 2+FACT

            She was probably at home yesterday. (She usually stays at home. This is customary for her, so the speaker thinks that she must have been at home yesterday too.)

ཁོང་ཁ་ས་ཉི་མ་གང་ནང་ལ་བཞུགས་བསྡད་པ་ཡིན་གྱི་རེད།

b) *khong   kha.sa   nyi.ma   gang   nang   - la   bzhugs   bsdad*
    s/he+H   yesterday   day   whole   home   - OBL   stay+H   stay

    -pa.yin.kyi.red
    - PFV+EPI 2+FACT

She was probably at home yesterday. (She doesn't usually spend most of her time at home. But it was raining yesterday. So the speaker thinks that she stayed at home.)

d) When the secondary verb *myong* 'have an experience' is employed, the perfective past ending may not follow the verb *myong*, as in example (54a). This secondary verb may only be combined with the perfect ending: see example (54b):[24]

(54)   * ཁོང་བསྟན་འཛིན་ལ་དགའ་མྱོང་པ་ཡིན་ས་རེད།

    a) * *khong   bstan.'dzin   - la   dga'   myong   - pa.yin.sa.red*
          s/he+H   Tenzin   - OBL   love   have an experience   - PFV+EPI 2+SENS

        Intended statement: In all likelihood, she was in love with Tenzin.

    ཁོང་བསྟན་འཛིན་ལ་དགའ་མྱོང་ཡོད་ས་རེད།

    b) *khong   bstan.'dzin   - la   dga'   myong   - yod.sa.red*
          s/he+H   Tenzin   - OBL   love   have an experience   - PERF+EPI2+SENS

        In all likelihood, she was in love with Tenzin. (The speaker makes a guess on the basis of her behaviour when she is with Tenzin.)

2. The perfect ending vs. the imperfective ending

The perfect ending (e.g. *a.yod*) and the imperfective ending (e.g. *kyi.a.yod*) may both be used in the context of the present, but they differ in aspect. Their aspectual opposition differs in the following way: The perfect ending is used for immediate present or present actions which will not be of long duration, as in examples (55a) and (56a), whereas the imperfective ending is used for actions of long duration, repeated or generic actions: see (56b). Moreover, the imperfective ending is used as well in the context of the future.

This opposition can be illustrated by the examples below: in example (55), only the perfect ending can be used with the temporal adverb *da.lta* 'now', whereas in (56) both verbal endings can be used with the adverb *deng.sang* 'these days'. This is because the latter adverb can be interpreted as having short-term import, as with the perfect ending (perfective aspect), as well as a more durational import, as with the imperfective ending (imperfective aspect):

---

[24] For more details, refer to Section 3.2.17.

46

(55)   ཁོང་ད་ལྟ་ནང་ལ་བཞུགས་ཨ་ཡོད་ ∫ མེད་པ་འདྲ།

a) *khong   da.lta   nang.la   bzhugs   - a.yod   / med.pa.'dra*
   s/he+H   now   home   stay+H   - PERF+EPI 1+EGO / PERF+EPI 2
                                            +NEG   +SENS+NEG

I doubt she is at home now. (The speaker knows that she usually isn't at home at this time of day.)
/ She doesn't seem to be at home now. (It looks like no one is in the house right now.)

* ཁོང་ད་ལྟ་ནང་ལ་བཞུགས་ཀྱི་ཨ་ཡོད་ ∫ ཀྱི་མེད་པ་འདྲ།

b) * *khong   da.lta   nang.la   bzhugs   - kyi.a.yod   / - kyi.med.pa.'dra*
     s/he+H   now   home   stay+H   - IMPF+EPI 3   / - IMPF+EPI 2
                                              +EGO+NEG   +SENS+NEG

Intended statement: I doubt she is at home now. / She doesn't seem to be at home right now.

(56)   ཁོང་དེང་སང་ནང་ལ་བཞུགས་ཨ་ཡོད་ ∫ མེད་པ་འདྲ།

a) *khong   deng.sang   nang   - la   bzhugs   - a.yod   / - med.pa.'dra*
   s/he+H   these days   home   - OBL stay+H   - PERF+EPI 3   / - PERF+EPI 2
                                                   +EGO+NEG   +SENS+NEG

I doubt she has been at home these last few days. (The speaker knows that she wanted to go somewhere for several days.)
/ She doesn't seem to be at home these days. (The speaker observes that her house is locked up with few signs of life.)

ཁོང་དེང་སང་ནང་ལ་བཞུགས་ཀྱི་ཨ་ཡོད་ ∫ ཀྱི་མེད་པ་འདྲ།

b) *khong   deng.sang   nang   - la   bzhugs   - kyi.a.yod   / - kyi.med.pa.'dra*
   s/he+H   these days   home   - OBL stay+H   - IMPF+EPI 3   /- IMPF+EPI 2
                                                   +EGO+NEG   +SENS+NEG

I doubt she is at home these days. (She said she would go to China for a month.)
/ She doesn't seem to be at home these days. (The speaker can see that the house has been closed up for some time.)

The use of the temporal adverb *da.lta* 'now' with a perfect ending is not limited to stative verbs. It may also be employed with action verbs, such as the verb *za* 'eat', as in the following example:

(57)   ཁོང་གིས་ད་ལྟ་ཁ་ལག་བཟས་ཨ་ཡོད།

khong   - gis   da.lta   kha.lag   bzas   - a.yod
s/he+H   - ERG   now   food   eat (PAS) - PERF+EPI 2+EGO

I don't think he has had his meal yet. (Looking at his watch, the speaker considers that it is too early for the meal in question.)

3. The imperfective ending vs. the expression with the nominalizer *mkhan* + auxiliary

The imperfective ending (e.g. *gi.yod.kyi.red*) and the expression employing the nominalizer *mkhan* + auxiliary (e.g. *mkhan:yin.gyi.red*) are both used in future contexts. However, as in the case of its evidential counterpart in example (58), and as opposed to the sentence using the imperfective ending (59a), the construction with the nominalizer *mkhan* with an auxiliary conveys the meaning of an action planned for the near future (59b, see as well example (42) in Section 1.2.2.1.1). In addition, this combination may also be used for actions that were planned in the past.[25]

(58)　　ང་སང་ཉིན་ལྷ་སར་འགྲོ་མཁན་ཡིན།

nga	*sang.nyin*	*lha.sa*	*- r*	*'gro*	*- mkhan*	*: yin*
I	tomorrow	Lhasa	- OBL	go (PRS)	- NOM	: be (EGO)

I am going to Lhasa tomorrow. (This is the speaker's intent which has been decided in advance, and not at the moment of speech.)

(59)　　ཕྲུ་གུ་སང་ཉིན་སློབ་གྲྭར་འགྲོ་གི་ཡོད་ཀྱི་རེད།

a)

phru.gu	*sang.nyin*	*slob.grwa*	*- r*	*'gro*	*- gi.yod.kyi.red*
child	tomorrow	school	- OBL	go (PRS)	- IMPF+EPI 2+FACT

The child will probably go to school tomorrow. (This sentence does not indicate a planned action. It will be Monday tomorrow, so the speaker conjectures that the child will go to school.)

ཕྲུ་གུ་སང་ཉིན་སློབ་གྲྭར་འགྲོ་མཁན་ཡིན་གྱི་རེད།

b)

phru.gu	*sang.nyin*	*slob.grwa*	*- r*	*'gro*	*- mkhan*	*: yin.gyi.red*
child	tomorrow	school	- OBL	go (PRS)	- NOM	: be (EPI 2+FACT)

The child is probably going to school tomorrow. (The child was ill but has now recovered. So the speaker thinks that it is planned that the child will go to school tomorrow.)

In first person sentences, the use of the nominalizer *mkhan* is the only way of expressing doubt: see example (60). In the same context, it is impossible to use the imperfective ending, e.g. *gi.yod.pa.'dra* as in (61):

(60)　　ང་སང་ཉིན་འགྲོ་མཁན་ཡིན་པ་འདྲ།

nga	*sang.nyin*	*'gro*	*- mkhan*	*: yin.pa.'dra*
I	tomorrow	go (PRS)	- NOM	: be (EPI 2+FACT)

It seems I will be leaving tomorrow. (A reply to the question as to when the speaker is leaving. The weather looks good, so the speaker thinks he will have to depart tomorrow.)

---

[25] For more details on constructions with the nominalizer *mkhan*, see Vokurková 2007.

48

(61)   * ང་སང་ཉིན་འགྲོ་གི་ཡོད་པ་འདྲ།

             * *nga*   *sang.nyin*   *'gro*   *- gi.yod.pa.'dra*
               I   tomorrow   go (PRS)   - IMPF+EPI 2+FACT

     Intended statement: It seems I will be leaving tomorrow.

4. The imperfective ending vs. the deontic future ending

The imperfective ending (e.g. *gi.yod.kyi.red*) and the deontic future ending (e.g. *rgyu.yin.gyi.red*) can be both used in future contexts. They differ, however, both in meaning and frequency. As opposed to the imperfective ending shown in example (63a), the epistemic ending diachronically consisting of the nominalizer *rgyu* with an essential epistemic auxiliary, conveys—apart from the epistemic and evidential meanings—a deontic meaning of obligation or necessity. It denotes an action that has not yet been carried out and thus must be completed, as in examples (62) and (63b).

(62)   ལས་ཀ་ཚང་མ་རང་གིས་བྱེད་རྒྱུ་ཡིན་པ་འདྲ།

      las.ka   *tshang.ma*   *rang*   *- gis*   *byed*   *- rgyu.yin.pa.'dra*
      work   all   you   - ERG   VBZ (PRS)   - FUT+EPI 2+SENS+DEO

      It seems you have to do all the work. (The speaker bases his statement on the visual evidence that all the others have left.)

(63)   ཁོང་བོད་སྐད་སྦྱང་གི་ཡོད་ཀྱི་རེད།

     a)   *khong*   *bod.skad*   *sbyang*   *- gi.yod.kyi.red*
         s/he+H   Tibetan language   learn   - IMPF+EPI 2+FACT

      He will probably learn Tibetan. (He can speak several languages. So the speaker thinks that it is likely that he will learn Tibetan too.)

     ཁོང་བོད་སྐད་སྦྱང་རྒྱུ་ཡིན་གྱི་རེད།

     b)   *khong*   *bod.skad*   *sbyang*   *- rgyu.yin.gyi.red*
         s/he+H   Tibetan language   learn   - FUT+EPI 2+FACT+DEO

      He probably hasn't learnt Tibetan yet. Or: He probably has yet to learn Tibetan. (A reply to the question as to whether he can speak Tibetan. The person in question moved to Tibet recently. The speaker thinks that he has probably not learnt Tibetan yet.)

Compared to imperfective endings, which are more frequent in the spoken language, as well as to the deontic future evidential ending *rgyu.red* (which expresses 100% certainty), the deontic future epistemic ending is rather rare. Since its semantic scope is very limited, its combinations with various verbal classes are more restricted. It is, in general, employed only with controllable verbs in the third (and second) persons, as in examples (65a), and only exceptionally with certain non-controllable verbs (64b). Example (64a) represents an impossible combination. Use with the first person is illustrated in example (66a). Moreover, unlike the imperfective ending (*gi.yod.kyi.ma.red*) and similar to the evidential deontic future endings (**rgyu.min*, **rgyu.ma.red*), no negative counterpart of the epistemic deontic future ending exists (**rgyu.min.pa.'dra*, see example 65b):

(64) * ཁོང་ ɟ ཤི་ ɟ དགའ་རྒྱུ་ཡིན་གྱི་རེད།

a) * *khong*   *na*   / *shi* / *dga'*   - *rgyu.yin.gyi.red*
        s/he+H   be ill   / die   / love   - FUT+EPI 2+FACT

Intended statement: Probably, he has never been ill/died/been in love.

ཁོང་ལ་རག་རྒྱུ་ཡིན་གྱི་རེད།

b) *khong*   - *la*   *rag*   - *rgyu.yin.gyi.red*
       s/he+H - OBL   get   - FUT+EPI 2+FACT

Probably, he has yet to receive [it]. (The visa is usually delivered in a week's time. He applied for it four days ago.)

(65) ཁོང་ཁ་ལག་ཟ་རྒྱུ་ཡིན་པ་འདྲ།

a) *khong*   *kha.lag*   *za*   - *rgyu.yin.pa.'dra*
       s/he+H food   eat (PRS) - FUT+EPI 2+SENS

It seems she hasn't eaten yet. (Everyone else has been to the restaurant. She is still there. Someone is asking the speaker if she has eaten yet.)

* ཁོང་ཁ་ལག་ཟ་རྒྱུ་མིན་པ་འདྲ།

b) * *khong*   *kha.lag*   *za*   - *rgyu.min.pa.'dra*
         s/he+H food   eat (PRS) - FUT+EPI 2+SENS+NEG

Intended statement: It does not seem she has yet to eat.

Under certain circumstances, a deontic future ending can appear in first person sentences, as is demonstrated in example (66a) with *rgyu.yin.pa.'dra*. Nonetheless, its use with the other deontic future endings (e.g. *rgyu.yin.'gro* in example 66b) is not considered to be grammatical:

(66) ང་ཚོགས་འདུར་འགྲོ་རྒྱུ་ཡིན་པ་འདྲ།

a) *nga*   *tshogs.'du*   - *r*   *'gro*   - *rgyu.yin.pa.'dra*
       I   meeting   - OBL   go (PRS)   - FUT+EPI 2+SENS+DEO

It seems I'll have to go to the meeting. (The speaker knows that no one else is going to the meeting, but that someone definitely has to go. So he infers that he will have to be the one to go.)

50

* ང་ཚོགས་འདུར་འགྲོ་རྒྱུ་ཡིན་འགྲོ།

b) * nga   tshogs.'du - r   'gro   - rgyu.yin.'gro
     I   meeting   - OBL go (PRS) - FUT+EPI 1+FACT+DEO

Intended statement: I will probably have to go to the meeting.

As mentioned above, the imperfective ending is more frequent than the deontic future ending. It also appears in other time contexts apart from the future (imperfective past, present). Below are examples that make use of the imperfective ending *gi.yod.kyi.red* in imperfective past contexts (67a) and in future contexts (67b):

(67)   བོང་ཆུང་དུས་ཕྱུར་བ་ཟ་གི་ཡོད་ཀྱི་རེད།

   a) khong   chung   - dus   phyur.ba   za   - gi.yod.kyi.red
      s/he+H   be small - when cheese   eat (PRS) - IMPF+EPI 2+FACT

   Probably when she was little, she ate cheese. (Her family are nomads. So the speaker thinks she probably ate cheese.)

   བོང་འབྲོག་པའི་རྩ་ལ་ཕྱིན་ན་ཕྱུར་བ་ཟ་གི་ཡོད་ཀྱི་རེད།

   b) khong   'brog.pa - 'i   rtsa   - la   phyin   - na
      s/he+H   nomad   - OBL close - OBL   go (PAS)   - if

      phyur.ba   za   - gi.yod.kyi.red
      cheese   eat (PRS) - IMPF+EPI 2+FACT

   If she goes to the nomads, she will probably eat cheese. (The speaker makes this conference as nomads often eat dairy products.)

1.2.2.2 Epistemic verbal endings as markers of epistemic modality

The function common to all epistemic endings is the expression of possibility or probability. As discussed in the Introduction, epistemic modality (or epistemicity) can be defined as the expression of the speaker's evaluation of the probability of a state of affairs (Nuyts 2001) or the speaker's commitment to the truth of what he says (Palmer 1986). In this monograph, epistemic modality is defined in terms of the degree of the speaker's certainty of the actuality of his utterance. In SST, the various types of epistemic endings differ as to the degree of the speaker's certainty. I classify them according to three degrees of certainty, EPI 1, EPI 2 and EPI 3. These correspond, respectively, to the expression of weaker (>50%), stronger (+−75%) and strongest (<100%) probability on the part of the speaker. All the types of epistemic endings discussed in this work are classified below according to their epistemic degree:[26]

---

[26] This classification is based on the author's fieldwork in Tibetan communities between 2002 and 2015. The degree of certainty of each type suggested in the table may vary depending on the actual use in a given context, on the use of an epistemic adverb, as well as on the speaker's idiolect.

Epistemic scale of the epistemic endings in standard spoken Tibetan

Degree of certainty of the speaker	Gloss	Type of TAM verbal ending	
		Positive	Negative
Not certain (Weaker probability), >50%	EPI 1	*yod. 'gro* and *med. 'gro'o*, *mi.yong.ngas*, *mdog.kha.po+red/'dug*	*med. 'gro* and *yod. 'gro'o*, *mdog.kha.po-ma.red/mi. 'dug*
Quite certain (Stronger probability), +/-75%	EPI 2	*yod.kyi.red*, *yod.sa.red*, *yod.pa. 'dra*, *yod.pa.yod*, *yong*, *yong.nga.yod* *yod.bzo. 'dug*	*yod.kyi.ma.red*, *yod.sa.ma.red*, *med.pa. 'dra*, *yod.pa.med*, *med.pa.yod*, *mi.yong*, *yong.nga.med* *yod.bzo.mi. 'dug*
Almost certain (High probability), <100%	EPI 3	*pa.yod*, *pa. 'dug*	*a.yod*, *pa.med*, *pa.mi. 'dug*

Compare the three degrees of certainty expressed by epistemic verbal endings in the following examples: EPI 1 (68), EPI 2 (69), and EPI 3 (70):

Weaker probability (EPI 1):

(68) ཁོང་གིས་ཇ་སྲུབ་མ་བཏུངས་ཡོད་འགྲོ།

khong - gis   ja srub.ma   btungs   - yod. 'gro
s/he+H - ERG   Tibetan tea   drink (PAS)   - PERF+EPI 1+FACT

Maybe, she drank tea. (A reply to the question as to what beverage she was drinking. The speaker bases his assertion on the fact that this is a common drink in Tibet. She is Tibetan, so it is therefore likely that she drank it. However, the speaker cannot be sure because there are other beverages as well that she might have consumed.)

Stronger probability (EPI 2):

(69) ཁོང་གིས་ཇ་སྲུབ་མ་བཏུངས་ཡོད་ཀྱི་རེད།

khong - gis   ja srub.ma   btungs   - yod.kyi.red
s/he+H - ERG   Tibetan tea   drink (PAS)   - PERF+EPI 2+FACT

She probably drank tea. (A reply to the question as to what beverage she was drinking. Usually, she drinks tea. So the speaker assumes that it is more probable than not that on this occasion as well, she was drinking tea.)

High probability (EPI 3):

(70)   ཁོང་གིས་ཇ་སྲུབ་མ་བཏུངས་པ་ཡོད།

> *khong*   *- gis*   *ja srub.ma*   *btungs*   *- pa.yod*
> s/he+H   - ERG   Tibetan tea   drink (PAS)   - PFV-EPI 3+EGO
>
> She must have been drinking tea. (A reply to the question as to what beverage she was drinking. The speaker knows that she loves Tibetan tea. So he is almost completely positive that that's what she was drinking.)

In addition, epistemic verbal endings also mark the speaker's non-engagement or non-commitment with respect to the actuality of his utterance (see Nølke 1994; Dendale, Tasmowski 2001; for Tibetan, see Oisel 2006).

1.2.2.3 Epistemic verbal endings as markers of evidential meanings

1.2.2.3.1 Evidentiality in SST

Evidentiality is a characteristic feature of SST (see Agha 1993; DeLancey 1986, 1997, 2001, 2012; Denwood 1999; Garrett 2001; LaPolla [ed.] 2000, 2001; Mélac 2014; Sun 1993; Tournadre, Konchok Jiatso 2001; Tournadre, LaPolla 2014; as well as Tournadre, Sangda Dorje 2003). A complex system of evidentials has developed particularly in the spoken language. Its function is to mainly indicate the *source of information, access to the information,* the *time of acquisition* and the *volitionality* (or *controllability*) of the given action. These parameters are explained in the table below (Tournadre 2008: 298, it includes the category of field of knowledge):

Source	Access to information (or channel)	Field of knowledge	Time of acquisition
S° : speaker Sⁿ: other **quoted source(s)** and hearsay	•**Sensory** (visual, auditory, tactile, gustatory, olfactory , endopathic) and "extrasensory" (intuition, telepathy, medium, "6th sense") • **Inferential** (based on perception, personal knowledge, encyclopaedic knowledge, reported speech)	•**Personal**[27] (awareness of intention, personal involvement, personal experience, personal sphere) • **Non personal** (Encyclopaedic, factual)	• **Newly acquired** information (or "new knowledge") and mirative. • **Assimilated information** (or "old knowledge")

---

[27] Personal knowledge or intention are accessible to the speaker through his own awareness (and not through sensory channels).

There are several classifications of the evidentials employed in SST differing in the terminology. [28] In one classification (Tournadre 1994, 1996b; Tournadre, Sangda Dorje 2003; Mélac 2014), the SST evidential system is comprised of two main evidential types: indirect and direct. The indirect type is formed by hearsay, as, for example, when the speaker has obtained information from somebody (or something) else. It is expressed by the quotative marker *za*. This morpheme can follow either a copula or a verbal ending but never directly a lexical verb. The direct type of evidential is used when the speaker himself is an essential channel for the information in question. This type consists of four evidentials, each of them highlighting the kind of access to information that the speaker bases his utterance on: factual, sensory, inferential, and egophoric. They are expressed by various evidential verbal endings. The use of each evidential ending depends on several parameters, such as verbal aspect, tense, and the speaker's point of view. Below is an example of the indirect type (71) as well as examples of the direct evidentials (72): (a) factual, (b) sensory, (c) inferential, and (d) egophoric:

(71) ཁོང་སླེབས་བྱུང་ཟ།

khong	*slebs*	*- byung*		*za*
s/he+H	arrive	- PFV+EGO (REC)		HEARSAY

They say that she arrived.

(72) བུ་མོ་འདི་སློབ་གྲར་འགྲོ་གི་ཡོད་རེད།

a)

bu.mo	*'di*	*slob.grwa*	*- r*	*'gro*	*- gi.yod.red*
girl	this	school	- OBL	go (PRS)	- IMPF+FACT

The girl attends school. (This statement is presented as a fact or a given of the situation, with no special accesss to information; default evidential)

བུ་མོ་འདི་སློབ་གྲར་འགྲོ་གིས ྃ གི་འདུག ྃ

b)

bu.mo	*'di*	*slob.grwa*	*- r*	*'gro*	*- gis (gi. 'dug)*
girl	this	school	- OBL	go (PRS)	- IMPF+SENS

The girl is going to school [now]. (In the morning, the speaker sees her carrying her school-bag.; sensory access to information)

བུ་མོ་སློབ་གྲར་ཕྱིན་བཞག

c)

bu.mo	*slob.grwa*	*- r*	*phyin*	*- bzhag*
girl	school	- OBL	go (PAS)	- PERF+IFR

The girl has (just) left for school. (She is not at home and her school-bag is not there either.; inferred information)

---

[28] For the *conjunct* vs. *disjunct* classification, refer to DeLancey 1992.

54

ངའི་བུ་མོ་སློབ་གྲྭར་འགྲོ་གི་ཡོད།

d) *nga* -*'i*   *bu.mo*   *slob.grwa*   -*r*   *'gro*   -*gi.yod*
   girl - GEN   daughter   school   - OBL   go (PRS)   - IMPF+EGO

My daughter goes to school. (The speaker is talking about his own child, relying on personal knowledge of her habitual actions; egophoric evidential)

The direct evidentials can be defined as follows:

1. **Factual evidential**: The factual evidential is employed when the speaker judges his utterance to be based upon certain and objective information. The access to the information is not specified here: it can be indirect (general knowledge, historic facts) or direct (a particular fact). As a result, the factual can be considered as a default evidential or as Mélac (2014) terms it, not a "genuine" evidential.

2. **Sensory evidential**: The sensory evidential implies that the access to information is based upon the speaker's sensory experience. This is generally visual but it may employ any of the other senses: auditory, tactile, olfactory, or gustatory.

3. **Inferential evidential**: This evidential implies an inference or a deduction upon which the speaker's utterance is based. The speaker has observed the traces or the present result of a past action.

4. **Egophoric evidential**: The egophoric evidential implies personal knowledge or experience on the part of the speaker, or his intention. He is the source of information of the action, in which he is often directly engaged. There are several kinds of egophoric endings: intentional, receptive, habitual, allocentric.

The direct type of evidential is also sometimes classified as a three-fold system of verbal endings. These consist of the following: egophoric endings, direct evidence endings and indirect[29] evidence (or *default*) endings. To take one example, Garrett (2001: 209) speaks of three groups:

"… [in Tibetan] the evidential opposition is ternary (ego, direct, and indirect) rather than binary …"

It is important to note here that arriving at a definition of the evidential meaning of verbal endings is an extraordinarily complex process including various pragmatic and discourse interaction aspects, as Tournadre and LaPolla suggest (2014: 257):

---

[29] Note that 'direct and indirect' evidence endings and the above mentioned 'direct and indirect types' of evidential endings are in fact two different classifications.

"… in many cases the perception requires various types of senses and inferences so the use of the evidential markers is generally much more complex than can be captured by simply saying, for example, "visual sensory"… Therefore we should take into account the complexity of the cognitive processes in the description of evidential systems."

1.2.2.3.2 Evidential meanings of epistemic verbal endings

The primary function of epistemic verbal endings is not to specify evidential meaning. Nonetheless, my fieldwork has led me to the conclusion that these endings do often convey evidential meanings. For example, *yod.'gro, yod.kyi.red* and *mdog.kha.po-red* convey factual meaning, *pa.'dug, yod.pa.'dra* and *mdog.kha.po + 'dug* sensory meaning, and *pa.yod, yod.pa.yod* and *a.yod* convey egophoric meaning (personal knowledge). The fact that epistemic endings have evidential connotations was observed by Tournadre & Sangda Dorje (2003: 176, 307): this is true for several epistemic types (*yod.pa.'dra, yod.kyi.red*, and *pa.yod*). They state, in Tournadre, Sangda Dorje (2003: 176):

"The former [i.e. *yod.pa.'dra*] suggests that the speaker's inference is based on his direct observation of the evidence, while the latter [i.e. *yod.kyi.red*] indicates that the speaker's inference is based on logic or on factual information not borne out by observation.".

The evidential meaning of each type of epistemic verbal ending will be discussed in Chapter II. Compare below the differences in the evidential meaning of examples (73), (74) and (75):

(73) ཕྲུ་གུ་སློབ་གྲར་ཕྱིན་ཡོད་ཀྱི་རེད།

phru.gu	*slob.grwa*	- *r*	*phyin*	- *yod.kyi.red*
child	school	- OBL	go (PAS)	- PERF+EPI 2+<u>FACT</u>

The child probably went to school. (A reply to the question as to where the child is; the answer is based on logical inference e.g. from the fact that it is Monday morning.).

(74) དམག་མིས་ལམ་ཁག་བཀག་ཡོད་པ་འདྲ།

dmag.mi	- *s*	*lam.khag*	*bkag*	- *yod.pa.'dra*
soldier	- ERG	road	block	- PERF+EPI 2+<u>SENS</u>

Soldiers have probably blocked the road. (An answer to the question: "Why aren't there any cars on the road today?" The speaker bases his statement on the visual perception that there are no cars in the street.)

(75)　　　ཁོང་གིས་ཆང་བཟོས་ཨ་ཡོད།

khong	- gis	chang	bzos	- a.yod
s/he+H	- ERG	*chang*	make (PAS)	(PAS) - PERF+EPI 3+<u>EGO</u>+NEG

I doubt she made *chang*. (A reply to the question: "Did she make *chang*?". The speaker bases his statement on personal knowledge: he knows that she doesn't know how to make it.)

1.2.2.4 Participant perspective

Epistemic verbal endings are neutral with regard to person. Depending on the context, they can be used with any person. However, since epistemic endings are used to express the speaker's uncertainty in relation to the content of his utterance, third and second person sentences outnumber first person sentences. A speaker in any given situation is usually less certain about other people than about himself. This accounts for the fact that third person sentences are more frequent in this monograph. The following sentence provides an example of co-occurrence of the third person with an epistemic ending:

(76)　　　ཁོང་འཁྱག་གི་ཡོད་པ་འདྲ།

khong	'khyag	- gi.yod.pa.'dra
s/he+H	be cold	- IMPF+EPI 1+SENS

It seems she is cold. (The speaker can see her shivering.)

In an appropriate context that justifies the co-occurrence of the first person and the epistemic ending, it is sometimes possible to use an epistemic ending in first person sentences, as in example (77):

(77)　　　ང་ར་གསེར་གྱི་རྟགས་མ་རག་གི་ཡོད་པ་འདྲ།

nga	- r	gser	- gyi	rtags.ma	rag	- gi.yod.pa.'dra
I	- OBL	gold	- GEN	medal	get	- IMPF+EPI 2+SENS

It seems I will get the golden medal. (The speaker has seen the other competitors and he feels he is the best one.)

When expressing doubts about oneself, a speaker will often use another means of epistemic modality than one of the epistemic verbal endings, such as: epistemic adverbs (e.g. *phal.cher* 'probably' as in example 78) or other lexical means as in (79). These are often combined with evidential verbal endings (For more examples, refer to Section 1.1.2):

(78)   ང་ཕལ་ཆེར་ཁོང་ལ་ཡིད་ཆེས་ཡོད།

nga	phal.cher	khong	- la	yid.ches	yod
I	probably	s/he+H	- OBL	belief	exist (EGO)

I think I believe him. / Upon thinking it over, I (tend to) believe him. (A reply to the question as to whether the speaker believes another person.)

(79)   འདུག་སེ་བླ་དུས་ང་ཁོང་ལ་ཡིད་ཆེས་ཡོད།

'dug.se	lta	- dus	nga	khong	- la	yid.ches	yod
like this	look (PRS)	- when	I	s/he+H	- OBL	belief	exist (EGO)

I think I believe him. / Upon thinking it over, I (tend to) believe him. (A reply to the question as to whether the speaker believes another person.)

Another frequent way of expressing epistemic modality in first person sentences is the use of an affirmative epistemic ending followed by its negative counterpart. When one is talking to oneself about what one did or plans to do, it is termed autolalic.

(80)   ངས་ཁང་པའི་ནང་གི་ཆུ་འདི་བཀག་ཡོད་འགྲོའོ།   མེད་འགྲོའོ།

nga	- s	khang.pa	-'i	nang	- gi	chu	'di	bkag
I	- ERG	house	- GEN	inside	- GEN	water	this	close

- yod.'gro'o	- med.'gro'o
- PERF+EPI 1+FACT+NEG+ AUTOLALIC	- PERF+EPI 1+FACT+AUTOLALIC

I wonder if I shut off the water mains in the house. (The speaker is asking himself.)

Although first person sentences may sometimes express the speaker's doubts or hesitation as in third person sentences, they also convey other meanings, such as a lapse in memory (the speaker cannot remember something clearly), a deontic meaning (a wish or hope), a non-controlled action (in which the action described in the utterance is not contingent on the speaker's will), and so on. The various meanings of first person sentences containing an epistemic ending are illustrated by the following examples:

1) A lapse in memory: The speaker does not clearly remember, or has forgotten what he did or didn't do:

(81)   པར་འདི་ངས་བརྒྱབ་པ་ཨ་ཡིན།

par	'di	nga	- s	brgyab	- pa.a.yin
snap	this	I	- ERG	VBZ	- PFV+EPI 3+EGO+NEG

I doubt I took this picture. (It is an old picture. The speaker forgot who took it. But he tends to doubt it was him.)

(82)   གཟའ་ཟླ་བར་ངས་བརྙན་འཕྲིན་བལྟས་ཡོད་འགྲོའོ།

gza'.zla.ba	- r	nga	- s	brnyan.'phrin	bltas	- yod.'gro'o
Monday	- OBL	I	- ERG	television	watch (PAS)	- PERF+EPI 1 +FACT+NEG

I don't think I was watching TV [last] Monday. (The speaker doesn't remember if it was on Monday that he was watching TV, or if it was some other day.)

(83)   དེ་དུས་ང་ཁོང་ལ་དགའ་གི་ཡོད་པ་འདྲ།

de.dus	nga	khong	- la	dga'	- gi.yod.pa.'dra
then	I	s/he+H	- OBL	like	- IMPF+EPI 2+SENS

It seems I liked him then. (The speaker does not remember clearly.)

2) A deontic meaning of wish or hope: The speaker hopes that the content of his utterance will come about or not in the future, as the case may be:

(84)   ངར་ཕྲུ་གུ་སྐྱེས་ལ་ཡོང་།

nga	- r	phru.gu	skyes	- a.yong
I	- OBL	child	give birth	- PERF FUT+EPI 3+EGO+NEG

I wish I could have a child. (The speaker wishes to have a baby but she thinks she won't be able to. She has tried many times but it didn't work out.)

3) The action does not depend on the speaker's will:

(85)   ང་ལྷ་སར་ལས་ཀ་རག་གི་ཡོད་འགྲོ།

nga	- r	lha.sa	- r	las.ka	rag	- gi.yod.'gro
I	- OBL	Lhasa	- OBL	work	get	- IMPF+EPI 1+FACT

Maybe I will get a job in Lhasa. (Others were able to find employment there, so the speaker thinks he has a chance too.)

The first person can combine with an epistemic ending in conditional sentences to imply that the fulfilment of the content of the main clause is dependent on the condition expressed in the subordinate clause:

(86)   ང་སོག་པོའི་སྐད་སློབ་སྦྱོང་བྱེད་མཁན་ཡིན་ན་སོག་ཡུལ་ལ་འགྲོ་པ་འདུག

nga	sog.po	- 'i	skad	slob.sbyong	byed	- mkhan	yin	- na
I	Mongol	- GEN	language	study	do (PRS)	- NOM	be	- if

sog.yul	- la	'gro	- pa.'dug
Mongolia	- OBL	go (PRS)	- FUT+EPI 3+SENS

If I were studying Mongolian, I would (almost certainly) go to Mongolia. (The speaker is learning Mongolian. He asks his friend whether he should go to Mongolia. Example 86 is the friend's reply.)

(87) ང་ཆུ་ཚོད་བརྒྱད་པར་ཐོན་ན་ཆུ་ཚོད་དགུ་པར་ཁོང་གི་ནང་ལ་སླེབས་མདོག་ཁ་པོ་རེད།

nga	chu.tshod	brgyad.pa	-r	thon	-na	chu.tshod	dgu.pa	-r
I	hour	eighth	-OBL	leave	-if	hour	ninth	-OBL

khong	-gi	nang	-la	slebs	-mdog.kha.po	-red
s/he+H	-GEN	home	-OBL	arrive	-EPI 1	-AUX (FACT)

If I leave at eight, I should get to his place by nine. (The speaker is making a guess. But the time of arrival will depend on traffic.)

In addition, in first person sentences with the perfect verbal ending (e.g. *yod.pa.'dra*), the secondary verb *myong* 'have an experience' is often used after the lexical verb implying that the speaker has, in his life, probably experienced the action of the sentence. See the example below:

(88) ངས་མི་འདི་མཐོང་མྱོང་ཡོད་པ་ཡོད་ ⟋ ཡོད་པ་འདྲ།

nga	-s	mi	'di	mthong	myong	-yod.pa.yod	/yod.pa.'dra
I	-ERG	person	this	see	have an experience	-PERF+EPI 2 +EGO	/PERF+EPI 2 +SENS

As far as I can recall, I have seen this person before. / It seems I have seen this person before. (She looks familiar to the speaker.)

Certain epistemic endings, e.g. *yod.pa.yod*, *yod.pa.'dra*, combine more easily with the first person than others, e.g. *yod.kyi.red*. While it is possible to use *yod.pa.'dra* with all persons, *yod.kyi.red* can only be used in non-first person sentences: see example (89). Since the verbal ending *yod.pa.'dra* conveys a sensory meaning, the speaker may use it in a situation in which he observes something about himself, of which, nonetheless, he is not completely certain. This is not possible with the factual ending *yod.kyi.red*. Similarly, verbal endings of the type *yod.pa.yod* can be used in first person sentences implying the speaker has experienced a lapse in memory: see example (90). The following example shows the compatibility of epistemic endings with the first person (89a) and with the third person (89b):

(89) ང་ར་བཟི་ཡོད་པ་འདྲ་ ⟋ * ཡོད་ཀྱི་རེད།

a)
nga	ra.bzi	-yod.pa.'dra	/*-yod.kyi.red
I	be drunk	-PERF+EPI 2+SENS	/-PERF+EPI 2+FACT

I seem to be drunk. (The speaker can sense that he is tottering.)

ཁོ་ར་བཟི་ཡོད་པ་འདྲ་ ⟋ ཡོད་ཀྱི་རེད།

b)
kho	ra.bzi	-yod.pa.'dra	/-yod.kyi.red
he	be drunk	-PERF+EPI 2+SENS	/-PERF+EPI 2+FACT

He seems to be drunk. (The speaker can see that the person is blundering.) /He is probably drunk. (The speaker knows that the person in question has drunk two litres of *chang*. So he concludes that the person is drunk.)

(90) ང་གཙུག་ལག་ཁང་ལ་ཡོད་དུས་ཇོ་བོ་ར་མ་རྒྱལ་མོའི་ལྷ་ཁང་ལ་ཕྱིན་ཡོད་པ་ཡོད།

nga	gtsug.lag.khang	- la	yod	- dus
I	Jokhang	- OBL	exist	- when

jo.bo ra.ma rgyal.mo	- 'i	lha.khang	-la	phyin	- yod.pa.yod
Queen Goat	- GEN	chapel	-OBL	go (PAS)	- PERF+EPI 2+EGO

As far as I can recall, I did go to the Queen Goat's Chapel when I was in Jokhang. (The speaker is not 100% sure as it was a long time ago.)

In some contexts, an epistemic ending may appear in a first person plural sentence, as in example (91b), but not in a first person singular sentence (91a). This is explained by the fact that in plural sentences the action is not only dependent on the speaker but upon other people as well. The speaker, therefore, cannot be sure as to what the others will do or think. Compare the following examples with the epistemic ending *gi.yod.kyi.red*:

(91) * ང་བརྙན་འཕྲིན་ལྟ་གི་ཡོད་ཀྱི་རེད།

a) *
nga	brnyan.'phrin	lta	- gi.yod.kyi.red
I	television	watch (PRS)	- IMPF+EPI 2+FACT

Intended statement: I will probably watch TV.

ང་ཚོ་བརྙན་འཕྲིན་ལྟ་གི་ཡོད་ཀྱི་རེད།

b)
nga	- tsho	brnyan.'phrin	lta	- gi.yod.kyi.red
I	- pl	television	watch (PRS)	- IMPF+EPI 2+FACT

We will probably watch TV. (As we usually do... but it is possible the others will decide to do something else.)

The above sentence in (91a) is grammatical when interpreted in the imperfective past as 'Probably, I was watching TV.', as an answer to the question: 'What were you doing at that moment?'. The epistemic ending implies that the speaker's memory is faulty.

Similarly, it is not possible to use the verbal ending *gi.yod.pa.'dra* with the first person singular in the context shown in example (92a) but it is possible with the first person plural, as in example (92b). For the first person singular, it is possible to use the expression with the nominalizer *mkhan* combined with an epistemic auxiliary (92c):

(92) * ང་སང་ཉིན་གླིང་ག་བཏང་གར་འགྲོ་གི་ཡོད་པ་འདྲ།

a) *
nga	sang.nyin	gling.ga	btang	- gar	'gro	- gi.yod.pa.'dra
I	tomorrow	park	VBZ	- GAR	go (PRS)	- IMPF+EPI 2+SENS

Intended statement: It seems I will go on a picnic tomorrow.

ང་ཚོ་སང་ཉིན་གླིང་ག་བཏང་གར་འགྲོ་གི་ཡོད་པ་འདྲ།

b)	*nga*	*- tsho*	*sang.nyin*	*gling.ga*	*btang*	*- gar*	*'gro*	*- gi.yod.pa.'dra*
	I	- pl	tomorrow	park	VBZ	- GAR	go (PRS)	- IMPF+EPI 2+SENS

It seems we will go on a picnic tomorrow. (Tomorrow is a holiday. The decision doesn't depend on the speaker.)

ང་སང་ཉིན་གླིང་ག་བཏང་གར་འགྲོ་མཁན་ཡིན་པ་འདྲ།

c)	*nga*	*sang.nyin*	*gling.ga*	*btang*	*- gar*	*'gro*	*- mkhan*	*: yin.pa.'dra*
	I	tomorrow	park	VBZ	- GAR	go (PRS)	- NOM	AUX (EPI 2 +SENS)

It seems I will go on a picnic tomorrow. (The weather will be good.)

1.2.2.5 Geographic variation and frequency

Epistemic verbal endings can further be classified according to the parameters of geographic variation and frequency.[30] Native speakers of Lhasa and central Tibet tend to use different types of epistemic verbal endings than those located in the diaspora (for the most part India and Nepal). Below is an example with the epistemic ending *pa.'dug* (see Section 2.7.1), which generally is only used by Tibetans in central Tibet:

(93) ཁོང་ན་ཚ་མགྱོགས་པོ་དྲག་པ་འདུག

	khong	*na.tsha*	*mgyogs.po*	*drag*	*- pa.'dug*
	s/he+H	illness	fast	get better	- FUT+EPI 3+SENS

Surely, he'll be well soon. (The speaker bases his assertion on the fact that the patient is eating more than before.)

In the diaspora, epistemic endings with the morpheme *sa* (e.g. *yod.sa.red*) are the most frequent epistemic type. In contrast, they are less frequently employed in central Tibet. People from Lhasa see them as being dialectal. These endings are common in the speech of Tibetans coming from Eastern Tibet (Kham, Hor, see Section 2.5).[31] So that example (94a) is preferred in the exile community, whereas (94b) would be more preferred in Lhasa:[32]

(94) པ་སངས་ལ་དངུལ་རག་ཡོད་ས་རེད།

	a)	*pa.sangs*	*- la*	*dngul*	*rag*	*- yod.sa.red*
		Pasang	- OBL	money	get	- PERF+EPI 2+SENS

It seems Pasang got [some] money. (The speaker saw Pasang in the shop buying many items.)

---

[30] For details on each epistemic type, see Chapter II.
[31] See note 57.
[32] Nonetheless, the influence of one variant upon the other, as well as influence of the popularity of certain modes of speaking on the language change need to be both taken into consideration. Thus in Lhasa one can also hear sentences containing a verbal ending of the *sa*-type.

ཕ་སངས་ལ་དངུལ་རག་ཡོད་པ་འདྲ།

b) *pa.sangs*   *- la*   *dngul*   *rag*   *- yod.pa.'dra*
    Pasang   - OBL   money   get   - PERF+EPI 2+ SENS

It seems Pasang got [some] money. (The speaker saw Pasang in the shop buying many items.)

Geographic variation of epistemic types

Lhasa	*yod.'gro, yod.pa.'dra, pa.'dug, yod.pa.yod,* *mdog.kha.po+red/'dug, mi.yong.ngas*
Diaspora	*yod.sa.red*
Both variants	*yod.kyi.red*

Concerning negative verbal endings, there are differences in what Tibetans living in Lhasa and surrounding areas, and those from the diaspora, find acceptable. Tibetans living in the diaspora use certain negative forms that are found ungrammatical in Lhasa, e.g. *med.kyi.red, gi.med.sa.red*. The corresponding forms used in Lhasa are *yod.kyi.ma.red* and *gi.yod.sa.ma.red*. This is illustrated by example (95), which is considered to be acceptable by certain — but not all — speakers who live or used to live in the diaspora. In contrast, speakers from Lhasa would express themselves according to example (96):

(95)   ? ཁོ་ཕྱིན་མེད་ཀྱི་རེད།

   a)   *? kho*   *phyin*   *- med.kyi.red*
       he   go (PAS)   - PERF+EPI 2+FACT+NEG

He probably didn't go [there]. (The speaker bases his assertion on the fact that the person rarely goes [there, to a given location].)

? ཉི་མ་ན་གི་མེད་ས་རེད།

   b)   *? nyi.ma*   *na*   *- gi.med.sa.red*
       Nyima   be ill   - IMPF+EPI 2+SENS+NEG

It seems Nyima won't get sick. (The speaker makes an inference based on the fact that Nyima looks healthy and does a lot of sports.)

(96)   ཁོ་ཕྱིན་ཡོད་ཀྱི་མ་རེད།

   a)   *kho*   *phyin*   *- yod.kyi.ma.red*
       he   go (PAS)   - PERF+EPI 2+FACT+NEG

He probably didn't go. (The speaker bases himself on the fact that the person rarely goes [to a given location].)

ཉི་མ་ན་གི་ཡོད་ས་མ་རེད།

b) *nyi.ma*   *na*   *- gi.yod.sa.ma.red*
   Nyima   be ill   - IMPF+EPI 2+SENS+NEG

It seems Nyima won't get sick. (The speaker makes an inference based on
the fact that Nyima looks healthy and does a lot of sports.)

In addition, there are geographical differences in the epistemic paradigm of verbal endings (see
1.2.2.1.2). Certain native speakers living in the diaspora consider other future endings (than the
ones mentioned in the examples above) as grammatical, but at the same time, Tibetans from
Lhasa reject these same endings as incorrect usage. Diachronically, these endings consist of the
nominalizer *gi* and the auxiliary *yin* followed by a second formant, e.g. *gi.yin.gyi.red* or
gi.yin. 'gro.[33] Nonetheless, among those who consider these verbal endings as acceptable, some
are still hesitant about their use. Consequently, these future endings should not be considered as
part of the epistemic paradigm of SST. See example (97a) below with the questionable ending
kyi.yin.gyi.red, and (97b) with the generally acceptable ending *kyi.yod.kyi.red*:

(97)   ? བསྟན་པ་དུས་སང་ད་དུང་སློབ་སྦྱོང་བྱེད་ཀྱི་ཡིན་གྱི་རེད།

   a) *?* *bstan.pa*   *dus.sang*   *da.dung*   *slob.sbyong*   *byed*   *- kyi.yin.gyi.red*
         Tenpa   next year   still   study   VBZ (PRS)   - FUT+EPI 2+FACT

   Tenpa will probably continue [lit. do] his studies next year.

      བསྟན་པ་དུས་སང་ད་དུང་སློབ་སྦྱོང་བྱེད་ཀྱི་ཡོད་ཀྱི་རེད།

   b) *bstan.pa*   *dus.sang*   *da.dung*   *slob.sbyong*   *byed*   *- kyi.yod.kyi.red*
      Tenpa   next year   still   study   VBZ (PRS)   - IMPF+EPI 2+FACT

   Tenpa will probably continue [lit. do] his studies next year. (The speaker knows that
   Tenpa is still young.)

---

[33] My consultant suggested that the sentence with the ending *gi.yin. 'gro* (a) evoked another sentence with
the nominalizer *mkhan* and the epistemic auxiliary *yin. 'gro* (b):

   * ཁོང་ནང་ལ་འགྲོ་གི་ཡིན་འགྲོ།

a) * *khong*   *nang*   *- la*   *'gro*   *- gi.yin. 'gro*
     s/he+H   home   - OBL   go (PRS)   - FUT+EPI 1+FACT
   Intended statement: He probably intends to go home.

   ཁོང་ནང་ལ་འགྲོ་མཁན་ཡིན་འགྲོ།

b)   *khong*   *nang*   *- la*   *'gro*   *- mkhan*   *: yin. 'gro*
     s/he+H   home   - OBL   go (PRS)   - NOM   : be (EPI 1+FACT)
   He probably intends to go home.

64

The above examples confirm the hypothesis that in the exile community, there are generally fewer restrictions on the acceptability of certain linguistic items than in central Tibet. The reason is probably the fact that Tibetans living in the exile community come from all parts of Tibet, and the dialectical variations to be found there are much more common. Hence the influence of these dialects on standard Tibetan becomes more significant than the influence of such dialects in Lhasa and central Tibet.

Epistemic endings also differ as to the degree of frequency with which they are used (see the table below). Some endings are very frequent e.g. *yod.kyi.red* or *a.yod*; others are less common or rare e.g. *yong.nga.yod* or *yod.bzo.'dug*. Below are sentences with the frequently used ending *kyi.yod.kyi.red,* as well as the seldomly employed ending *pa.yin.bzo.'dug*:

(98) ཁོང་རྗེས་མར་བོད་སྐད་སྦྱང་གི་ཡོད་ཀྱི་རེད།

khong	*rjes.ma*	*bod.skad*	*sbyang*	*- gi.yod.kyi.red*
s/he+H	later	Tibetan language	learn	- IMPF+EPI 2+FACT

He will probably learn Tibetan in the future. (The speaker makes an inference from the fact that the person takes an interest in Tibet.)

(99) བུ་འདིས་དབྱིན་ཇི་སྐད་རྒྱ་གར་ནས་སྦྱངས་པ་ཡིན་བཟོ་འདུག

bu	*'di*	*- s*	*dbyin.ji.skad*	*rgya.gar*	*- nas*
boy	this	- ERG	English language	India	- ABL

sbyangs	*- pa.yin.bzo.'dug*
learn	- PFV+EPI 1+SENS

It seems this boy learnt English in India. (The speaker thinks this is the case because the boy speaks with an Indian accent.)

The division of epistemic types according to the frequency of their use

Very frequent	Relatively frequent	Rare
yod.'gro	*mi.yong.ngas*	*yod.bzo.'dug*
yod.pa.'dra	*pa.'dug*	*yong*
	pa.yod	*mi.yong*
yod.kyi.red	*yod.pa.yod*	*yong.nga.yod*
a.yod	*mdog.kha.po+red/'dug*	
yod.sa.red (exile)		

1.2.2.6 Secondary meanings of epistemic verbal endings and copulas

The core function of epistemic verbal endings and copulas is to express doubt. Nonetheless, apart from epistemic and evidential modalities, they may also convey other modal meanings. These include the communication of various derived meanings, such as hope, surprise, disagreement, and regret. These meanings are pragmatic and always contextual and situational. In determining these meanings, one has to consider illocutionary modalities and speech acts (Palmer 1986; Searle 1977; Searle, Vanderveken 1985; Tournadre 2004).[34] Prosody also has an influence on the semantic interpretation of sentences containing epistemic endings. Below are examples of the various secondary meanings of epistemic endings:

1. Desiderative

Sentences with an epistemic verbal ending or copula may sometimes have a boulic meaning: they convey the speaker's hope and expectations. The agent is often, though not always, in the first person: see the verbal ending *pa.yod* in example (100a). Such endings can be characterized as having an apprehensional function (referring to Lichtenberg's 'apprehensional epistemics', a type of mixed modality that is both epistemic and attitudinal, in Lichtenberg 1995). Another example of the desiderative function of these epistemic verbal endings is the epistemic type *a.yod* (100b):[35]

(100)   ང་ཡིག་ཚད་འདི་ལོན་པ་ཡོད།

    a)   *nga*   *yig.tshad*   *'di*   *lon*   *- pa.yod*
            I   exam   this   pass   - PFV+EPI 3+EGO

         I must have passed the exam. / Hopefully, I passed the exam. (The speaker
         answered all the questions and he thinks he provided the correct answers.)

     བསྟན་པ་སྨྱོ་ཨ་ཡོད།

    b)   *bstan.pa*   *smyo*   *- a.yod*
            Tenpa   be crazy   - PERF+EPI 3+EGO

         I hope Tenpa hasn't become insane. (The speaker knows that Tenpa has been
         behaving in a strange way recently.)

---

[34] Tournadre (2004: 52) discusses the role of illocutionary modalities and stresses the importance of the theory of speech acts in relation to the enunciative aim of the speaker: « *Le troisième domaine, celui de la visée énonciative, correspond aux modalités illocutoires et à l'objectif que poursuit le locuteur en prononçant un énoncé. Cette visée peut être analysée d'un point de vue grammatical, en types de phrases (modalités interrogatives, déclaratives, exclamatives, injonctives) mais doit aussi être plus précisément décrite dans le cadre théorique des actes de langage.* »

[35] See as well example (214) in Section 2.4. below.

66

2. Surprise and/or disagreement

Some sentences with an epistemic ending convey the speaker's surprise at what he hears and may also imply a reaction of disagreement, discontent or lack of belief. This is illustrated by the following examples with the epistemic ending *pa.yin.'gro'o* and the epistemic copulas *yin.gyi.ma.red* and *a.yin*:

(101)   དཀར་ཡོལ་འདི་ངས་བཅག་པ་ཡིན་འགྲོའོ།

dkar.yol	*'di*	*nga*	*-s*	*bcag*	*- pa.yin.'gro'o*
cup	this	I	- ERG	break	- PFV+EPI 1+FACT+NEG

What! I can't have broken the cup. (The speaker is told that he broke the cup. He is surprised and doesn't agree.)

(102)   ག༔ སྐྱེན་པ་ཐོབ་སོང་།   ཁ༔ ཡིན་གྱི་མ་རེད།

A:	*spen.pa*	*thob*	*- song*		B:	*yin.gyi.ma.red*
	Penpa	win	- PFV+SENS			be (EPI 2+FACT+NEG)

A: Penpa won.

B: Impossible./That can't be true!

(103)   ག༔ ཁོང་ལ་སྤ་སེ་རག་སོང་།   ཁ༔ ཨ་ཡིན།

A:	*khong*	*- la*	*spa.se*	*rag*	*- song*	B:	*a.yin*
	s/heH	- OBL	ticket	get	- PFV+SENS		be (EPI 3+EGO+NEG)

A: He got the tickets.

B: Are you kidding!

3. Regret

In addition, epistemic verbal endings are used in contexts implying that the speaker regrets an action carried out by him. This use is illustrated by the following example:

(104)   ངས་ཁ་ལག་འདི་མ་བཟས་ནའི་ཡོང་ང་ཡོད།

nga	*-s*	*kha.lag*	*'di*	*ma*	*bzas*	*- na'i*	*yong.nga.yod*
I	- ERG	food	this	NEG	eat (PAS)	- even if	exist (EPI 2+EGO)

If only I hadn't eaten this food. (The speaker feels too full.)

1.2.3 SYNTACTIC ANALYSIS OF THE USE OF EPISTEMIC VERBAL ENDINGS

This section deals with the use of epistemic verbal endings in various syntactic structures. First, their compatibility with various verbal constructions and verbal classes will be discussed; subsequently their use, as well as restrictions in their use in dependent clauses, questions, and so forth, will be discussed.

1.2.3.1 Compatibility of epistemic verbal endings with verbal constructions and verbal classes

Epistemic verbal endings appear in the same syntactic structures as evidential verbal endings and they usually are combined with verbs of different verbal classes. Their use is discussed in detail and illustrated by examples in Chapter II, including information about the compatibility of the epistemic ending with the following verbal classes: monovalent, ergative, possessive, affective and its use in causative constructions. Below are examples of each verbal class combined with an epistemic verbal ending: monovalent (intransitive verbs), as in example (105), ergative (transitive verbs) as in example (106), possessive (verbs expressing possession: with the first argument, the semantic owner, marked in the dative and the second argument in the absolutive) as in example (107), affective (verbs of feeling: with the first argument, the semantic receiver, marked in the absolutive and the second argument in the dative) as in example (108), and causative constructions (109):

(105)   ཉི་མ་ན་པ་ཡོད།

nyi.ma   na   - pa.yod
Nyima   be ill   - PFV+EPI 3+EGO

Nyima must have been ill. (The speaker knows that Nyima was not feeling well last night. A reply to the question as to why Nyima left early last night.)

(106)   ཁྱེད་རང་གིས་ཕ་རན་སི་ནས་དྲི་ཆབ་འདི་ཉོས་ཡོང་ང་ཡོད།

khyed.rang   - gis   pha.ran.si   - nas   dri.chab   'di   nyos
you+H   - ERG   France   - ABL   perfume   this   buy (PAS)

- yong.nga.yod
- PERF+EPI 2+EGO

You probably bought the perfume in France. (The speaker remembers that France is famous for its perfumes.)

(107)   ཁོང་ལ་ཕྲུ་གུ་སྐྱེས་པ་འདྲ།

khong   - la   phru.gu   skyes   - pa.'dra
she+H   - OBL   child   give birth   - PFV+EPI 2+SENS

It seems she's had her baby. (A reply to the question as to where she is. She was about to have a baby and she was always seen sitting in front of her house. Today, she is not there.)

(108)   ཁོང་གདུག་འདྲེ་ལ་ཞེད་ཀྱི་ཡོད་ཀྱི་མ་རེད།

> khong   gdug.'dre   - la   zhed   - kyi.yod.kyi.ma.red
> s/he+H   ghost   - OBL   be afraid   - IMPF+EPI 2+FACT+NEG

In all likelihood, she won't be afraid of ghosts. Or: She is probably not afraid of ghosts. (A reply to the question as to whether she is afraid of ghosts. The speaker knows that she is not superstitious.)

(109)   ཁོང་གིས་པད་མ་ལས་ཀ་བྱེད་རུ་བཅུག་གི་ཡོད་འགྲོ།

> khong   - gis   pad.ma   las.ka   byed   - ru   bcug   - gi.yod. 'gro
> s/he+H - ERG   Pema   work   VBZ (PRS)   - CAUS   let   - IMPF+EPI 1+FACT

She may let Pema work. (The speaker bases his statement on the fact that the person in question has come of age.)

Some epistemic endings demonstrate a more restricted use with various verbal classes.[36] From the point of view of the epistemic paradigm, the perfective past endings (e.g. *pa.yin.gyi.red*) are often subject to more restrictions than other endings (see Section 1.2.2.1.1). In the following examples, the combination of *dga'* 'love' with the epistemic ending *yod.pa.yod* is grammatical (110b), whereas with *pa.yin.pa.yod,* it is not grammatical (110a):

(110)   * མོ་རང་མི་འདིར་དགའ་པ་ཡིན་པ་ཡོད།

a)   * *mo.rang   mi   'di   - r   dga'   - pa.yin.pa.yod*
        she   person   this   - OBL   love   - PFV+EPI 2+EGO

Intended statement: I think she must have loved this man.

མོ་རང་མི་འདིར་དགའ་ཡོད་པ་ཡོད།

b)   *mo.rang   mi   'di   - r   dga'   - yod.pa.yod*
      she   person   this   - OBL   love   - PERF+EPI 2+EGO

I think she must have loved this man. (The speaker can remember how she acted when she was around the person in question.)

In addition, it is unusual to directly combine a lexical verb with the perfective past ending in first person sentences. Instead, Tibetan speakers generally prefer to use the secondary verb *myong* 'have an experience' inserted between the lexical verb and a perfect epistemic ending: e.g. *yod.'gro* in example (111b); see also other examples in Chapter II. This is explained by the fact that the speaker usually remains aware of what he or she did some time ago, and thus it is unnatural for Tibetans to say such a sentence as in example (111a). In contrast, the use of *myong*

---

[36] It appears that it is generally more difficult to use epistemic endings with affective verbs than with the other verbal classes. A number of combinations of an affective verb and an epistemic ending were judged to be incorrect usage by my consultants (e.g. the epistemic endings *gi.yong.nga.yod, pa.yin.pa.yod*).

in example (111b) implies a longer time period (possibly referring to the entire lifespan of the speaker), and thus it is more probable that he does not have complete recall concerning his actions:

(111)　　　? ངས་ཁ་ལག་དེ་བཟས་ཡོད་འགྲོ།

    a)　*? nga - s kha.lag de   bzas   - yod.'gro*
        I   - ERG food   that eat (PAS) - PERF+EPI 1+FACT
        I think I have eaten that dish. (The speaker does not recall exactly.)

    ངས་ཁ་ལག་དེ་ཟ་མྱོང་ཡོད་འགྲོ།

    b)　*nga - s kha.lag de   za   myong   - yod.'gro*
        I   - ERG food   that eat (PRS) have an experience - PERF+EPI 1+FACT
        I think I have eaten that dish. (The speaker does not recall exactly.)

Certain combinations of a verb with an epistemic ending are ungrammatical due to a prosodic or semantic reasons. Let's take an example of the egophoric auxiliary *yod* in the epistemic *mdog.kha.po*-construction. The auxiliary *yod* implies personal knowledge and experience, and thus bears the function of locating the speaker, as well as those who were in the same location as he (see, for example, the use of the egophoric verb *yod* in *zla.ba nang-la yod* 'Dawa is at home [with me].'). Consequently, *yod* may not be employed in a sentence containing the lexical verb *'gro* 'go' because this verb implies direction away from the speaker, not towards him, as in example (112b). In this example, egophoric *yod* locates the speaker in Lhasa and thus the use of the verb *'gro* 'go' would be incorrect (As, for example, in the English sentence: 'I am in Lhasa. And she said she would *go/come to see me here.', where the use of the verb 'go' is semantically incorrect.). The use of the verb *slebs* 'arrive' or *yong* 'come' (112a) in the *mdog.kha.po*-construction containing the auxiliary *yod* is possible because these lexical verbs imply the direction towards the speaker. As for the use of the verb *'gro* 'go', it is possible to combine it with the auxiliary *red:* see example (98c) above. In this case, the auxiliary *red* implies that the speaker is in a different place than Lhasa, and thus the sentence (112c) makes sense:

(112)　　　ཁོང་སང་ཉིན་ལྷ་སར་སྲེབས་ ⟨ ཡོང་མདོག་ཁ་པོ་ཡོད།

    a)　*khong sang.nyin lha.sa - r   slebs / yong - mdog.kha.po - yod*
        s/he+H tomorrow Lhasa - OBL arrive / come - EPI 1   - AUX (EGO)
        She will probably get to/come to Lhasa tomorrow. (The speaker knows that she has some time off.)

* ཁོང་སང་ཉིན་ལྷ་སར་འགྲོ་མདོག་ཁ་པོ་ཡོད།

b) * khong   sang.nyin   lha.sa   - r   'gro   - mdog.kha.po   - yod
     s/he+H   tomorrow   Lhasa   - OBL   go (PRS)   - EPI 1   - AUX (EGO)

Intended statement: She will probably go to Lhasa tomorrow.

ཁོང་སང་ཉིན་ལྷ་སར་འགྲོ་མདོག་ཁ་པོ་རེད།

c) khong   sang.nyin   lha.sa   - r   'gro   - mdog.kha.po   - red
     s/he+H   tomorrow   Lhasa   - OBL   go (PRS)   - EPI 1   - AUX (FACT)

She will probably go to Lhasa tomorrow. (Tomorrow is a day off.)

1.2.3.2 Use of epistemic verbal endings in interrogative sentences

Unlike evidential verbal endings, epistemic verbal endings are generally only used in affirmative sentences, as shown in example (113). They are not employed in interrogative sentences. When forming a question, the speaker generally uses an evidential ending instead of the epistemic ending. This is illustrated by the following example in which only the question in example (114) with the evidential verbal ending *song* or *'dug* and the interrogative particle *ngas* or *gas* is grammatical:

(113)   ཀ༔   ཁོང་ཕྱིན་ཡོད་པ་ཡོད།

     A: *khong*   *phyin*   - *yod.pa.yod*
             s/he+H   go (PAS)   - PERF+EPI 2+EGO

     He probably left. (Many people were leaving. The speaker doesn't remember well whether the person in question left as well.)

     ཁ༔   *   ཕྱིན་ཡོད་པ་ཡོད་པས།

     B: *   *phyin*   - *yod.pa.yod*   - *pas*
                 go (PAS)   - PERF+EPI 2+EGO   - Q

     Intended statement: Is it likely that he left?

(114)   ཀ༔   ཁོང་ཕྱིན་ཡོད་པ་ཡོད།

     A: *khong*   *phyin*   - *yod.pa.yod*
             s/he+H   go (PAS)   - PERF+EPI 2+EGO

     He probably left. (Many people were leaving. The speaker doesn't remember well whether the person in question left as well.)

ཁ༔ ཕྱིན་སོང་ངས་ ⌠ ཕྱིན་འདུག་གས།

B: *phyin* - *song* - *ngas* / *phyin* - *'dug* - *gas*
   go (PAS) - PFV+SENS - Q / go (PAS) - PERF+SENS - Q

Did he (leave)?

The epistemic verbal endings which are never employed with interrogative particles are: the epistemic types *a.yod*,[37] *yod. 'gro*, *yod.pa.yod* and *yod.kyi.red*, as well as the epistemic endings *pa.yod* and *yong*. Nonetheless, it is possible to employ with interrogative particles those epistemic verbal endings or copulas containing the sensory auxiliary *'dug* as their final element. See for example the verbal ending *pa. 'dug* (115), the construction *mdog.kha.po-'dug* (116a), and the copula *yin.bzo. 'dug* (116b) used with an interrogative particle. It must be, however, said that this type of questions is very rare in the spoken language. The Tibetan speakers I consulted tended to suggest that this type of questions implies a negative supposition: the speaker thinks that a certain fact or state is not the case, as in example (116a), where it is assumed that the tea is probably not hot, and in example (116b), where it is assumed that the subject of the sentence is probably not Tibetan.

(115)   ཀ༔ ཁྱེད་རང་ཟླ་བ་བཅུ་གཉིས་པར་དངུལ་འདི་ལྡང་པ་འདུག་གས།

A: *khyed.rang* *zla.ba* *bcu.gnyis.pa* - *r* *dngul* *'di*
   you+H   month   twelfth   - OBL   money   this

   ldang   - *pa. 'dug*   - *gas*
   be enough - FUT+EPI 3+SENS - Q

Will you have enough money in December?

ཁ༔ ལྡང་པ་འདུག

B: *ldang*   - *pa. 'dug*[38]
   be enough - FUT+EPI 3+SENS

For sure, I will. (The speaker still has a lot of money left.)

(116)   ཇ་འདི་ཚ་པོ་ཡོད་མདོག་ཁ་པོ་འདུག་གས།

a) *ja* *'di* *tsha.po* *yod* - *mdog.kha.po* - *'dug* - *gas*
   tea this hot   exist - EPI 1   - AUX (SENS) - Q

   Is this tea hot? (Literary: Does this tea look like it's hot?, Neither the speaker nor the addressee have tried the tea yet.)

---

[37] The morpheme *a* originally had an interrogative meaning. Cf. The use of *a* (*e*) as an interrogative particle in the Amdo dialects (See Gesang Jumian, Gesang Yangying 2002).
[38] See Thub-bStan dBang-po *et al.* (2002: 47).

72

ཁོང་བོད་པ་ཡིན་བཟོ་འདུག་གས།

b) *khong*   *bod.pa*   *yin.bzo.'dug*   - *gas*
   s/he+H   Tibetan   be (EPI 1+SENS)   - Q

   Does she look like a Tibetan? (Judging from her appearance, the speaker
   doesn't think that the person looks like a Tibetan.)

Nonetheless, in the same context, the majority of native speakers would prefer using an
evidential copula in the spoken language, not an epistemic copula, as in the following example:

(117)   ཁོང་བོད་པ་འདྲ་པོ་འདུག་གས།

   khong   *bod.pa*   *'dra.po*   *'dug*   - *gas*
   s/he+H   Tibetan   similar   exist (SENS)   - Q

   Does she look Tibetan?

Similarly, although it is possible to form a question with the epistemic ending *pa. 'dug*
followed by the interrogative particle *gas*, as in example (118), such questions are uncommon in
the spoken language. As opposed to the epistemic ending *pa. 'dug* followed by the interrogative
particle *gas*, in the same context, the evidential ending *gi.red* followed by the interrogative
particle *pas* are more frequently used in spoken Tibetan. See example (119):

(118)   ཆར་པ་བཏང་པ་འདུག་གས།

   char.pa   *btang*   - *pa.'dug*   - *gas*
   rain   VBZ   - FUT+EPI 3   - Q

   Is it going to rain?/Does it look like it's going to rain? (The speaker is asking
   somebody standing at the window as to the possibility of rain falling in the
   immediate future. He is about to leave, so he is interested in what the weather will
   be like.)

(119)   ཆར་པ་བཏང་གི་རེད་པས།

   char.pa   *btang*   - *gi.red*   - *pas*
   rain   VBZ   - FUT+FACT   - Q

   Will it rain?

Finally, let us take the example below of the epistemic copula *yin.pa. 'dra* used in an
interrogative sentence:

(120)   ཁོང་བོད་པ་ཡིན་པ་འདྲ།   འདུག་གས་ʃ རེད་པས།

khong   bod.pa   yin.pa.'dra
s/he+H   Tibetan   be (EPI 2+SENS)

'dug   - gas   / red   - pas
exist (SENS) - Q   / be (FACT)   - Q

She seems to be Tibetan. Is she? (The speaker makes a supposition, and at the same time asks someone else to confirm if he is right in his supposition.)

The above example must be interpreted as two separate clauses. The first one is an epistemic statement containing the copula *yin.pa. 'dra,* whereas the latter one is a question consisting of the copula *'dug* 'exist' or *red* 'be' and the corresponding interrogative particle. Thus, the example can be translated in English by 'She seems to be Tibetan. 'Is it like that?', 'Is she?' or even 'Am I right?'. The speaker expresses his standpoint to the actuality of his utterance and asks another person to confirm it or not.

Taking into consideration the above examples, it can be concluded that epistemic verbal endings are, in general, not used in the interrogative mood.

1.2.3.3 Use of epistemic verbal endings in dependent clauses

Epistemic verbal endings appear at the end of a complex sentence but they are generally not used in dependent clauses (examples 121, 122b, 123). This is also the case of many evidential endings, e.g. **yod.red - tsang, *red - na.* The epistemic ending *pa. 'dug* is, however, an exception since it can be used in conditional sentences in the if-clause before *na* 'if' (ex. 122a). Compare the following examples:

(121)   * ཁོང་ཕྱིན་པ་ཡོད་ཚང་···

a)   * *khong   phyin   - pa.yod   - tsang ...*
        s/he+H   go (PAS) - PFV+EPI 3+EGO - because

    Intended statement: Since he must have gone ...

      * ཆར་པ་བཏང་པ་འདུག་ཚང་···

b)   * *char.pa   btang   - pa.'dug   - tsang ...*
        rain   VBZ   - FUT+EPI 3+SENS - because

    Intended statement: Since it looks like rain ...

74

(122)   ཆར་པ་བཏང་པ་འདུག་ན་ནང་ལ་སྡོད།

a) *char.pa*   *btang*   *- pa.'dug*   *- na*   *nang*   *- la*   *sdod*
    rain   VBZ   - FUT+EPI 3+SENS   - if   home   - OBL   stay (IMP)

If it looks like rain, stay at home!

       *   ཆར་པ་བཏང་གི་ཡོད་པ་འདྲ་ན···

b) *   *char.pa*   *btang*   *- gi.yod.pa.'dra*   *- na ...*
        rain   VBZ   - IMPF+EPI 2+SENS   - if

Intended statement: If it looks like rain …

(123)   *   ཁོང་ནང་ལ་བསྡད་ཡོད་ཀྱི་རེད་དུས···

       *   *khong*   *nang*   *- la*   *bsdad*   *- yod.kyi.red*   *- dus ...*
          s/he+H   home   - OBL   stay   - PERF+EPI 2+FACT   - when

Intended statement: When (while) he was probably (staying) at home …

Epistemic verbal endings, just like evidential verbal endings, can appear at the end of a clause that is a complement of the verb *bsam* 'think'. In this case, the epistemic ending (or auxiliary) directly precedes the verb *bsam*. This construction corresponds to relative clauses in European languages (e.g. that-clauses in English) as in examples (124a) and (124b):

(124)   ཁ་པར་སྤྲད་མི་དགོས།   ངས་ཁོང་གཉིས་ཐུག་ཨ་ཡོད་བསམས་བྱུང་།

a) *kha.par*   *sprad*   *mi*   *dgos*   *nga*   *- s*   *khong*   *gnyis*
    phone   give   NEG   must   I   - ERG   s/he+H   two

    thug   *- a.yod*   *bsams*   *- byung*
    meet   - PERF+EPI 3+EGO+NEG   think   - PFV+EGO

[You] do not have to give [me] the phone. I thought the two of them had not met. (The speaker's friend is calling the speaker's sister to see if she met her niece who just arrived in Lhasa. The speaker thought that the two hadn't met, but she has been told that they actually did.)

ཁོང་སྒོ་ཕྱེ་དགོས་མེད་འགྲོའོ་བསམས་བྱུང་།

b) *khong*   *sgo*   *phye*   *dgos*   *- med.'gro'o*   *bsams*   *- byung*
    s/he+H   door   open   need   - PERF+EPI 1+FACT   think   - PFV+EGO

I thought he might need/want to open the door. (The speaker makes an inference from the fact that the person was waiting in front of the door.)

Similarly, epistemic verbal endings may be used in sentences employing both direct and indirect speech. In these sentences the epistemic verbal ending precedes the 'quotation' particle *ze,* as in the following example:

(125)   ཁོང་སྒོ་ཕྱེ་དགོས་མེད་འགྲོའོ་ཟེ་ལབ་པ་ཡིན།

khong	*sgo*	*phye*	*dgos*	*- med.'gro'o*	*ze*	*lab*	*- pa.yin*
s/he+H	door	open	need	- PERF+EPI 1+FACT	QP	say	- PFV+EGO

I said that he might want to open the door. (A reply to the question: "What did you say?")

In complex sentences, epistemic verbal endings are often used in the apodosis of conditional sentences. From the point of view of the tense-aspect paradigm (see Section 1.2.2.1.1), certain epistemic verbal endings are frequently used (perfect and imperfective), whereas others are not (deontic future and perfective). The perfect epistemic endings (e.g. *yod.kyi.red,* ex. 126) are usually used in past conditionals (past counterfactuals) and imperfective epistemic endings in present conditionals (both factual and counterfactual). See *gi.yod.kyi.red* in example (127), used with the present conditional.

(126)   ཁོང་ལ་དུས་ཚོད་ཡོད་ན་ཐུགས་སྤྲོ་ལ་ཕྱིན་ཡོད་ཀྱི་རེད།

khong	*- la*	*dus.tshod*	*yod*	*- na*	*thugs.spro*	*- la*
s/he+H	- OBL	time	exist	- if	party+H	- OBL

phyin	*- yod.kyi.red*
go (PAS)	- PERF+EPI 2+FACT

If he'd had the time, he probably would have gone to the party. (Everyone knew that it was going to be a good party. So the speaker thinks that the person in question would have gone if he had had the time.)

(127)   ཁོ་རང་ལ་རོགས་པ་མ་བྱས་ན་ཤི་གི་ཡོད་ཀྱི་རེད།

kho.rang	*- la*	*rogs.pa*	*ma*	*- byas*	*- na*
he	- OBL	help	NEG	- VBZ (PAS)	- if

shi	*- gi.yod.kyi.red*
die	- IMPF+EPI 2+FACT

If [we] don't help him, he will probably die. (A reply to the question as to what we should do with our neighbour, who is ill and poor.)

The use of epistemic endings in past conditionals is further illustrated with the non-paradigmatic past epistemic ending *pa.yod* in example (128a). This epistemic ending is the most frequently used ending in past counterfactual conditionals. Compare (128a) with example (128b), which employs another non-paradigmatic ending - the future epistemic ending *pa.'dug* - illustrating the present factual conditional:

76

(128)   ལག་རྟགས་འདིར་ཁོང་དགའ་པོ་ཡོད་ན་ངས་ཕུལ་པ་ཡོད།

a) *lag.rtags*   *'di*   *- r*   *khong*   *dga'.po*   *yod*   *- na*
    gift   this   - OBL   s/he+H   appreciative   exist   - if

    nga   *- s*   *phul*   *- pa.yod*
    I   - ERG   give+h   - PFV+EPI 3+EGO

If she liked that kind of gift, I would have certainly given it to her. (The speaker knows her very well. So he tends to think that she would not have liked to receive the gift in question.)

ལག་རྟགས་འདིར་ཁོང་དགའ་པོ་ཡོད་ན་ངས་ཕུལ་པ་འདུག

b) *lag.rtags*   *'di*   *- r*   *khong*   *dga'.po*   *yod*   *- na*
    gift   this   - OBL   s/he+H   like   exist   - if

    nga   *- s*   *phul*   *- pa.'dug*
    I   - ERG   give+h   - FUT+EPI 3+SENS

If she likes the gift, I will certainly give it to her. (If she sees the gift and seems to like it, the speaker will definitely give it to her.)

Unlike perfect epistemic endings, perfective past epistemic endings may not be used in conditional sentences (example 129a and b). (This also holds true for evidential endings, as only the perfect ending *yod.red* is employed in past conditionals, as an example 131b, but not the perfective past endings **pa.yin, *pa.red*). In example (129a), the use of the perfect ending *a.yod* is grammatical, but the perfective past ending *pa.a.yin* is not. Similarly, (129b) illustrates the impossibility of using other perfective past endings:

(129)   ཁ་ས་སྨན་བཟས་ཡོད་ན་ཁོང་ན་ཨ་ཡོད་ ʃ   *   པ་ཨ་ཡིན།

a) *kha.sa*   *sman*   *bzas*   *- yod*   *- na*   *khong*   *na*
    yesterday   medicine   eat (PAS)   - PERF   - if   s/he+H   be ill

    - a.yod   */ *- pa.a.yin*
    - PERF+EPI 3+EGO+NEG   / - PFV+EPI 3+EGO+NEG

If he had taken the medicine yesterday, he most likely would not have fallen ill. (The speaker himself has taken the medicine in question.)

*   ཁྱེད་རང་མ་ཕེབས་པ་ཡིན་ན་ ʃ ཕེབས་མེད་ན་ཁོང་ཤི་པ་ཡིན་གྱི་རེད་ ʃ པ་ཡིན་པ་ཡོད་ ʃ པ་ཡིན་པ་འདྲ།

b) ** khyed.rang*   *ma*   *- phebs*   *(- pa.yin)*   *- na*   */ phebs*   *- med*   *- na*
    you+H   NEG   - come+H   - AUX   - if   /come+H   - AUX   - if
                                                (PFV)   (PERF)

    khong   *shi*   *- pa.yin.gyi.red*   */ pa.yin.pa.yod*   */ pa.yin.pa.'dra*
    s/he+H   die   - PFV+EPI 2+FACT   / PFV+EPI 2+EGO   / PFV+EPI 2+SENS

Intended statement: If you hadn't come, he probably would have died.

In conditional sentences, the following epistemic endings and epistemic types are employed: *pa.yod, a.yod, yod.kyi.red, yod-mdog.kha.po-red, yod.'gro, yong, mi.yong.ngas.* The use of the types *yod.pa.'dra* and *yod.sa.red* (sensory meaning), and *yod.pa.yod* (egophoric meaning) is either impossible or questionable: see examples (130a) and (130b):

(130)   *   སྨན་མ་བཟས་ན་ང་ཤི་པ་འདྲ།

a)   *

sman	*ma*	*- bzas*	*- na*	*nga*	*shi*	*- pa.'dra*
medicine	NEG	- eat (PAS)	- if	I	die	- PERF+EPI 1+SENS

Intended statement: If I had not taken the medicine, I would probably have died.

    ?   ཁོང་ལ་དུས་ཚོད་ཡོད་（པ་ཡིན་）ན་ཐུགས་སྤྲོ་ལ་ཕྱིན་ཡོད་ས་རེད།

b)   *?*

khong	*- la*	*dus.tshod*	*yod*	*(- pa.yin)*	*- na*
s/he+H	- OBL	time	exist	- AUX (PFV)	- if

thugs.spro	*- la*	*phyin*	*- yod.sa.red*
party+H	- OBL	go (PAS)	- PERF+EPI 2+SENS

If he'd had the time, he would probably have gone to the party.

Although conditionals complying an epistemic verbal ending resemble conditionals with evidential verbal endings, the epistemic verbal endings partially preserve their epistemic meaning. As can be seen from the English translation, there is a slight difference in the degree of certainty between the sentence containing the epistemic verbal ending *pa.yod* (131a) and the evidential verbal ending *yod.red* (131b). The difference is between an epistemic verbal ending with certainty of <100%, as opposed to an evidential verbal ending with a certainty of 100%:

(131)   རང་གིས་ཅི་ནི་ཏེག་ཙ་མང་ཙམ་བརྒྱབ་ཡོད་ན་ཇ་འདི་ཞིམ་པོ་ཆགས་པ་ཡོད།

a)

rang	*- gis*	*ci.ni*	*teg.tsa*	*mang.tsam*	*brgyab*	*- yod*	*- na*
you	- ERG	sugar	a little bit	more	VBZ	- PERF	- if

ja	*'di*	*zhim.po*	*chags*	*- pa.yod*
tea	this	good	become	- PFV+EPI 3+EGO

If you had put just a little more sugar in the tea, it almost certainly would have tasted good. (The speaker has just tasted the tea but is not completely certain of his own utterance.)

རང་གིས་ཅི་ནི་ཏེག་ཙ་མང་ཚམ་བརྒྱབ་ཡོད་ན་ཇ་འདི་ཞིམ་པོ་ཆགས་ཡོད་རེད།

b)
rang	- gis	ci.ni	teg.tsa	mang.tsam	brgyab	- yod	- na
you	- ERG	sugar	a little bit	more	VBZ	- PERF	- if

ja	'di	zhim.po	chags	- yod.red
tea	this	good	become	- PERF+FACT

If you had put a little bit more sugar in the tea, it would have tasted good. (The speaker has just tasted the tea. Unlike (131a), he is very certain about what he is saying.)

Sometimes, a conditional sentence with an epistemic ending corresponds in English to the present hypothetical conditional (132a). A conditional sentence with an evidential ending would correspond to the present factual conditional (132b):

(132)   ངར་དངུལ་ཡོད་ན་ཡུལ་སྐོར་ལ་འགྲོ་གི་ཡོད་ཀྱི་རེད།

a)
nga	- r	dngul	yod	- na	yul.skor	- la	'gro
I	- OBL	money	exist	- if	travel	- OBL	go (PRS)

- gi.yod.kyi.red
- IMPF+EPI 2+FACT

If I had money, (probably) I would travel. (The speaker has no money, so he considers the possibility of traveling as sheer hypothesis.)

ངར་དངུལ་ཡོད་ན་ཡུལ་སྐོར་ལ་འགྲོ་གི་ཡིན།

b)
nga	- r	dngul	yod	- na	yul.skor	- la	'gro	- gi.yin
I	- OBL	money	exist	- if	travel	- OBL	go (PRS)	- FUT+EGO

If I get money, I will travel. (The possibility for the speaker to get some money is real and thus the possibility of traveling is also real.)

II. CLASSIFICATION OF EPISTEMIC VERBAL ENDINGS AND COPULAS

2.1 EPISTEMIC VERBAL ENDINGS AND COPULAS OF THE TYPE *yod.kyi.red*

2.1.1 FORMAL, SEMANTIC AND PRAGMATIC CHARACTERISTICS

This type of epistemic ending and copula consists diachronically of a nominalizer/connector combined with an auxiliary, followed by a second suffix, *kyi.red*, e.g. *kyi.yod.kyi.red*, or diachronically *kyi.yod-kyi.red* as in (133a). The negative endings of this type are formed by adding the negative particle *ma* in front of the auxiliary *red*, e.g. *kyi.yod.kyi.ma.red* (133b). In the case of *pa.yin.gyi.red*, negation may be either postverbal or preverbal. Just as in the original negation of the perfective past evidential ending *pa.red* (*ma* + V + *pa.red*, see example 134a), which is preverbal, it is possible to put the negative particle *ma* before the lexical verb which is then followed by *pa.yin.gyi.red* (as in *ma* + V + *pa.yin.gyi.red*, see example 134b). Postverbal negation, however, is preferred, and the perfect ending *yod.kyi.ma.red* is used.[39] See the following examples:

(133)   མོ་རང་ཁྱི་འདིར་ཞེད་ཀྱི་ཡོད་ཀྱི་རེད།

       a)   *mo.rang*   *khyi*   *'di*   *- r*   *zhed*   *- kyi.yod.kyi.red*
           she   dog   this   - OBL   be afraid   - IMPF+EPI 2+FACT

           She will probably be afraid of the dog. (The dog is very big.)

     མོ་རང་ཁྱི་འདིར་ཞེད་ཀྱི་ཡོད་ཀྱི་མ་རེད།

       b)   *mo.rang*   *khyi*   *'di*   *- r*   *zhed*   *- kyi.yod.kyi.ma.red*
           she   dog   this   - OBL   be afraid   - IMPF+EPI 2+FACT+NEG

           She probably won't be afraid of the dog. (The dog is very small.)

(134)   ཁོང་གིས་ལས་ཀ་འདི་མ་བྱས་པ་རེད།

       a)   *khong*   *- gis*   *las.ka*   *'di*   *ma*   *- byas*   *- pa.red*
           s/he+H   - ERG   work   this   NEG   - VBZ (PAS)   - PFV+FACT

           She didn't do the work.

---

[39] This corresponds to the use of the negative perfect evidential ending *yod.ma.red* in non-epistemic sentences.

ཁོང་གིས་ལས་ཀ་འདི་མ་བྱས་པ་ཡིན་གྱི་རེད།

b) *khong*   *- gis*   *las.ka*   *di*   *ma*   *- byas*   *- pa.yin.gyi.red*
     s/he+H   - ERG   work   this   NEG   - VBZ (PAS)   - PFV+EPI 2+FACT

Most likely, she didn't do the work. (She was very busy with other tasks.
So the speaker thinks that she probably didn't have time for it.)

Some Tibetans from the exile community also accept negative endings — formed with the negative auxiliaries *med* and *min*, e.g. *kyi.med.kyi.red, pa.min.gyi.red* — as good usage, as in example (135a). However, they still prefer negative endings formed with the negative particle *ma*, i.e. *yod.kyi.ma.red, kyi.yod.kyi.ma.red.* Verbal endings with *med* and *min* are not considered to be grammatical by Lhasa Tibetans who only consider negative endings with the negative particle *ma*, e.g. *kyi.yod.kyi.ma.red*, as correct usage; see example (135b) below:

(135)   ? མོ་ལས་ཀ་བྱེད་ཀྱི་མེད་ཀྱི་རེད།

     a)   *? mo*   *las.ka*   *byed*   *- kyi.med.kyi.red*
         she   work   VBZ (PRS)   - IMPF+EPI 2+FACT+NEG

     She probably doesn't work.

     མོ་ལས་ཀ་བྱེད་ཀྱི་ཡོད་ཀྱི་མ་རེད།

     b)   *mo*   *las.ka*   *byed*   *- kyi.yod.kyi.ma.red*
         she   work   VBZ (PRS)   - IMPF+EPI 2+FACT+NEG

     She probably doesn't work. (She is very young. So the speaker thinks that she doesn't have a job yet.)

The epistemic copulas of this type which are considered to be grammatical by both Lhasa and diaspora Tibetans are the essential copulas *yin.gyi.red* and *yin.gyi.ma.red* (136a) and the existential copulas *yod.kyi.red* and *yod.kyi.ma.red* (136b). Their use is illustrated in the following sentences:

(136)   དེབ་འདི་ཁོང་གི་ཡིན་གྱི་མ་རེད།

     a)   *deb*   *'di*   *khong*   *- gi*   *yin.gyi.ma.red*
         book   this   s/he+H   - GEN   be (EPI 2+FACT+NEG)

     This probably isn't his book. (The speaker makes an inference from the fact that the person in question usually doesn't read this kind of book.)

     བཀྲ་ཤིས་སློབ་གྲྭར་ཡོད་ཀྱི་མ་རེད།

     b)   *bkra.shis*   *slob.grwa*   *- r*   *yod.kyi.ma.red*
         Tashi   school   - OBL   exist (EPI 2+FACT+NEG)

     Tashi probably isn't at school. (The speaker makes an inference from the fact that it is noon and the school is now on lunch break.)

This type forms the following paradigm:

Affirmative endings:	Negative endings:	
	Lhasa and Diaspora	Diaspora only
yod.kyi.red	*yod.kyi.ma.red*	*med.kyi.red*
pa.yin.gyi.red	*pa.yin.gyi.ma.red*	*pa.min.gyi.red*
gi.yod.kyi.red	*gi.yod.kyi.ma.red*	*gi.med.kyi.red*

Other combinations are impossible, e.g. **gi.yin.gyi.red.*

The type *yod.kyi.red* has a factual connotation: the speaker bases his assertion on logical reasoning. This can include any kind of logical inference (excluding sensory inference), but also includes personal knowledge. The speaker makes use of his experience or feelings to infer something (see Hu 1989: 254).[40] Thus this type of verbal ending is more subjective as compared to the other types, e.g. *yod. 'gro*. The degree of certainty expressed by epistemic endings of the type *yod.kyi.red* is fairly high. Compared to the other epistemic types, it is higher than that of *yod. 'gro* and lower than *pa. 'dug*, thus corresponding to degree EPI 2. It is used very frequently in the spoken language:

(137) མོ་རང་ཕ་མ་དྲན་གྱི་ཡོད་ཀྱི་རེད།

mo.rang	*pha.ma*	*dran*	*- gyi.yod.kyi.red*
she	parent	miss	- IMPF+EPI 2+FACT

She probably misses her parents. (A reply to the question as to whether she misses her parents. She has been abroad for a long time. The speaker therefore assumes that she misses them.)

(138) མོ་རང་ལ་དངུལ་དེ་རག་ཡོད་ཀྱི་རེད།

mo.rang	*- la*	*dngul*	*de*	*rag*	*- yod.kyi.red*
she	- OBL	money	that	get	- PERF+EPI 2+FACT

She probably has got the money. (She had some money in a bank in India, but now she lives in Tibet. The speaker thinks, however, that she was somehow able to get access to her money.)

---

[40] See Hu (1989: 254): ཡོད་ཀྱི་རེད་ 表示凭个人经验或感觉推测某种情况是存在的 "*yod.kyi.red* implies that in relying on one's personal experience or feeling, [the speaker] infers a situation" [my translation]. Similarly, native speakers suggest that they use this type when they rely on *nyams.myong* 'experience' and *tshor.snang* 'feelings'.

As a general rule, the use of verbal endings of the type *yod.kyi.red* occurs less frequently in first person sentences than in third person sentences. If it does occur, the implication is often that the action expressed in the sentence is not contingent on the speaker's will. With some monovalent and ergative verbs, the implication is that the speaker does not remember the situation clearly and, therefore, he presents it in a doubtful manner. In first person sentences, the secondary verb *myong* 'have an experience' is generally used (139b):

(139) ? ང་ས་ཆ་དེར་སླེབས་ཡོད་ཀྱི་རེད།

a) ?	*nga*	*sa.cha*	*de*	*- r*	*slebs*	*- yod.kyi.red*
	I	place	that	- OBL	come	- PERF+EPI 2+FACT

I guess I've probably been to that place. (The speaker has travelled in the region but is not completely sure that he has been to that particular location.)

ང་ས་ཆ་དེར་སླེབས་མྱོང་ཡོད་ཀྱི་རེད།

b)	*nga*	*sa.cha*	*de*	*- r*	*slebs*	*myong*	*- yod.kyi.red*
	I	place	that	- OBL	come	have an experience	- PERF+EPI 2+FACT

I guess I have probably been to that place. (The speaker has travelled in the region but is not completely sure that he has been to that particular location.)

Although it is impossible to combine these endings with certain verbs (e.g. *na* 'be ill', *shi* 'die') in first person simple sentences (or even with the secondary verb *myong* 'have an experience', see example 140a), such combinations can easily appear in conditional sentences as in (140b):

(140) * ང་ན་ཚ་དེ་ན་ (མྱོང་) ཡོད་ཀྱི་རེད།

a) *	*nga*	*na.tsha*	*de*	*na*	(*myong*)	*- yod.kyi.red*
	I	ilness	that	be ill	have an experience	- PERF+EPI 2+FACT

Intended statement: I have probably got that illness (during my life).

ཁྱེད་རང་མ་ཕེབས་ན་ང་ཤི་ཡོད་ཀྱི་རེད།

b)	*khyed.rang*	*ma*	*- phebs*	*- na*	*nga*	*shi*	*- yod.kyi.red*
	you+H	NEG	- come+H	- if	I	die	- PERF+EPI 2+FACT

If you had not come, I most likely would have died. (The speaker bases his utterance on the fact that he would not have been able to survive without the help of the other person.)

In sentences containing an epistemic ending of the type *yod.kyi.red*, it is possible to use an epistemic adverb such as *gcig.byas.na* 'perhaps'and *phal.cher* 'probably', expressing possibility and probability (see Sections 1.1.1.1 and 1.1.1.2),. The epistemic adverbs expressing high probability or near-absolute certainty (see Section 1.1.1.3) are less frequently employed (*gtan.gtan* 'certainly'), or are not used at all (*brgya.cha.brgya* 'definitely'):

(141) ཁ་ལག་འདི་ཁོང་གིས་ཕལ་ཆེར་ / * བརྒྱ་ཆ་བརྒྱ་ཟ་གི་ཡོད་ཀྱི་རེད།

kha.lag	*'di*	*khong*	*- gis*	*phal.cher*	*/*brgya.cha.brgya*	*za*
meal	this	s/he+H	- ERG	probably	/ definitely	eat (PRS)

- gi.yod.kyi.red
- IMPF+EPI 2+FACT

She will probably/ *definitely eat this food. (The speaker bases himself on the fact that she usually eats this kind of food.)

2.1.2 DESCRIPTION OF THE VERBAL ENDINGS

<u>1. Verbal endings used in the perfective past</u>

The verbal endings used in the perfective past are: *yod.kyi.red, yod.kyi.ma.red, pa.yin.gyi.red* and *pa.yin.gyi.ma.red*. The endings *yod.kyi.red* and *yod.kyi.ma.red* are used in present perfect contexts, as an example (142). In addition, they are used with unreal past conditionals (past counterfactuals) in both the third and first persons, as in (143):

(142) མོ་རང་ལ་ཕྲུ་གུ་སྐྱེས་ཡོད་ཀྱི་རེད།

mo.rang	*- la*	*phru.gu*	*skyes*	*- yod.kyi.red*
she	- OBL	child	give birth	- PERF+EPI 2+FACT

She most likely had her baby. (She was pregnant when the speaker met her. He hasn't seen her for a long time so he presumes that she already gave birth to her baby.)

(143) ཁོས་སྨན་བཟས་མེད་ན་ཤི་ཡོད་ཀྱི་རེད།

kho	*- s*	*sman*	*- bzas*	*- med*	*- na*	*shi*	*- yod.kyi.red*
he	- ERG	medicine	- eat (PAS)	- PERF+NEG	- if	die	- PERF+EPI 2+ FACT

If he hadn't taken the medicine, he would most likely have died. (His illness was very serious.)

The epistemic endings *pa.yin.gyi.red* and *pa.yin.gyi.ma.red* are also employed in perfective contexts: see examples (144) and (145). However, in the spoken language they are less frequent than the perfect endings and they are not employed in conditional sentences: compare example (146) with example (143) using the perfect verbal ending *yod.kyi.red*.

(144) ཁོང་གིས་ཁ་ལག་རྙིང་པ་བཟས་པ་ཡིན་གྱི་རེད།

khong	*- gis*	*kha.lag*	*rnying.pa*	*bzas*	*- pa.yin.gyi.red*
s/he+H	- ERG	food	old	eat (PAS)	- PFV+EPI 2+FACT

She must have eaten food that had gone bad. (She felt ill. The speaker thinks that the reason for her feeling ill was that she had eaten food that had gone bad.)

(145) ང་ཆུ་ཚོད་གཉིས་པ་ཙམ་ལ་ནང་ལ་སླེབས་པ་ཡིན་གྱི་རེད།

nga	*spyir.btang*	*chu.tshod*	*gnyis.pa*	*tsam*	*- la*	*nang*	*- la*
I	generally	clock	second	about	- OBL	home	- OBL
slebs	*- pa.yin.gyi.red*						
arrive	- PFV+EPI 2+FACT						

I probably got back at around two o'clock. (The speaker went to a party last night. Somebody is asking him whether he came home at two o'clock. But he doesn't remember exactly.

(146) * ཁྱིས་སྨན་བཟས་མེད་ན་ཤི་པ་ཡིན་གྱི་རེད།

*	*khyi*	*- s*	*sman*	*bzas*	*- med*	*- na*	*shi*	*- pa.yin.gyi.red*
	dog	- ERG	medicine	eat (PAS)	- PERF+NEG	- if	die	- PFV+EPI 2+FACT

Intended statement: If the dog had not been given the medicine, it would probably have died.

There is a difference in aspect between the endings *yod.kyi.red* and *pa.yin.gyi.red.* This difference yields a difference in scope (see Section 1.2.2.1). Whereas the epistemic meaning of *yod.kyi.red* usually relates to the entire sentence (the actuality of the whole sentence is put into question), that of *pa.yin.gyi.red* only has relevance to one part of the sentence, e.g. the agent or the predicate (in other words, the doubt expressed only has bearing on one part of the sentence). Thus, in some contexts *pa.yin.gyi.red*, as in example (147a) appears to be more appropriate than *yod.kyi.red* as in (147b), which has full-sentence scope: in this example, the second clause implies that the speaker falling ill is not completely certain, which thus does not correspond with the first part of the sentence explaining the reason of his being ill. However, since *yod.kyi.red* may also be used in sentences with a partial scope of epistemic modality, example (147b) is also found to be grammatical by native speakers:

(147) ང་ཁ་ལག་འདི་བཟས་ཙང་ན་པ་ཡིན་གྱི་རེད།

a)	*nga*	*kha.lag*	*'di*	*bzas*	*- tsang*	*na*	*- pa.yin.gyi.red*
	I	food	this	eat (PAS)	- because	be ill	- PFV+EPI 2+FACT

It is probably because I ate this food that I fell ill. (The speaker thinks there is no other reason than the fact that he ate the food that explains his illness.)

ད་ཁ་ལག་འདི་བཟས་ཚང་ན་ཡོད་ཀྱི་རེད།

b) *nga   kha.lag 'di   bzas   - tsang   na   - yod.kyi.red*
   I   food   this   eat (PAS) - because be ill - PERF+EPI 2+FACT

* It is because I ate this food that it is probable that I fell ill.
It is probably because I ate this food that I fell ill. (The speaker's falling ill is a fact but he is not sure about the cause of his illness.)

2. Verbal endings employed in the imperfective past, the present and in the future

The epistemic endings used in imperfective contexts are *gi.yod.kyi.red* and *gi.yod.kyi.ma.red*. They combine easily with monovalent, ergative and affective verbs in third person sentences, as in example (148). Their use with possessive verbs is rather rare, though not excluded, as shown in (149). Example (149a) expresses a future action, whereas (149b) describes a present action. This verbal class is more compatible with the past endings *yod.kyi.red* and *pa.yin.gyi.red* (149c):

(148)   སྒྲོལ་མའི་ཕྲུ་གུ་སློབ་གྲྭར་འགྲོ་གི་ཡོད་ཀྱི་མ་རེད།

a) *sgrol.ma   - 'i   phru.gu   slob.grwa   - r   'gro*
   Dolma   - GEN   child   school   - OBL go (PRS)

   - gi.yod.kyi.ma.red
   - IMPF+EPI 2+FACT+NEG

   Dolma's children most likely don't go to school. (The speaker thinks this is the case because they have a farm and they have a lot of work to do there.)

ཁོང་བུ་མོ་དེར་དགའ་གི་ཡོད་ཀྱི་རེད།

b) *khong   bu.mo   de   - r   dga'   - gi.yod.kyi.red*
   s/he+H   girl   that - OBL like   - IMPF+EPI 2+FACT

   He probably loves that girl. (He always speaks nicely of her.)

(149)   ཟླ་བ་ལ་མ་འོངས་པར་དངུལ་མང་པོ་རག་གི་ཡོད་ཀྱི་རེད།

a) *zla.ba   - la   ma.'ongs.pa   - r   dngul   mang.po   rag*
   Dawa   - OBL   future   - OBL money   much   get

   - gi.yod.kyi.red
   - IMPF+EPI 2+FACT

   Dawa will probably get a lot of money in the future. (She has a good job.)

མོ་རང་ལ་པ་ཕའི་རྩ་ནས་དངུལ་རག་གི་ཡོད་ཀྱི་རེད།

b) *mo.rang   - la   pa.pha   - 'i   rtsa   - nas   dngul*
   she   - OBL   father   - GEN   close - ABL   money

   rag   - gi.yod.kyi.red
   get   - IMPF+EPI 2+FACT

   She most likely gets money from her father. (The speaker makes an inference from the fact that the person in question does not have a job.)

མོ་རང་ལ་དངུལ་མང་པོ་རག་ཡོད་ཀྱི་རེད་ ⌠ པ་ཡིན་གྱི་རེད།

c) *mo.rang*   *- la*   *dngul*   *mang.po*   *rag*   *- yod.kyi.red*
   she   - OBL   money   much   get   - PERF+EPI 2+FACT

   / pa.yin.gyi.red
   / PFV+EPI 2+FACT

She most likely got a lot of money. (The speaker bases his assertion on the fact that she has been spending a lot of money recently.)

When used in first person sentences, the verbal endings *gi.yod.kyi.red* or *gi.yod.kyi.ma.red* express a state whereby there is something that the speaker does not remember, or that the action in question does not depend on the speaker's will. In certain contexts, they may also express the speaker's hope of the (non)-realization of the content of his utterance, as shown in examples (150) and (152). It is not compatible with endopathic verbs (e.g. *zhed* 'be afraid'), as the speaker usually is aware of his own perceptions: see example (151).

(150)   ང་རོ་དགོང་དགོང་དག་ལྷ་རྩེ་ལ་བསྡད་ཀྱི་ཡོད་ཀྱི་རེད།

   nga   *gcig.byas.na*   *do.dgong dgong.dag*   *lha.rtse*   *- la*   *bsdad*
   I   maybe   tonight   Lhatse   - OBL   stay

   - kyi.yod.kyi.red
   - IMPF+EPI 2+FACT

(I presume that) I will probably stay in Lhatse tonight. (The speaker is going to the border. It depends on road conditions and the traffic, not on his own will, as to how far he will get tonight and thus where he will stay.)[41]
/Hopefully I will stay in Lhatse tonight.

(151)   * ང་ཁོ་རང་གི་ཁྱི་ལ་ཞེད་ཀྱི་ཡོད་ཀྱི་རེད།

   * *nga*   *kho.rang*   *- gi*   *khyi*   *- la*   *zhed*   *- kyi.yod.kyi.red*
     I   he   - GEN   dog   - OBL   be afraid   - IMPF+EPI 2+FACT

Intended statement: I will probably be afraid of his dog.[42]

---

[41] It is possible to use the verb *dgos byed* 'must' in the this sentence or the verb *slebs* 'arrive, come' instead of *bsdad* 'stay'.

[42] The meaning in example (151) may be expressed, for example, by the epistemic adverb *gcig.byas.na* 'perhaps' combined with an evidential ending:

གཅིག་བྱས་ན་ང་ཁོ་རང་གི་ཁྱི་ལ་ཞེད་སྣང་སྐྱེ་གི་རེད།

gcig.byas.na   *nga*   *kho.rang*   *- gi*   *khyi*   *- la*   *zhed.snang*   *skye*   *- gi.red*
perhaps   I   he   - GEN   dog   - OBL   fear   VBZ   - FUT+FACT
Maybe I will by afraid of his dog.

(152)   གཅིག་བྱས་ན་ང་ར་དངུལ་མང་པོ་རག་གི་ཡོད་ཀྱི་རེད།

> *gcig.byas.na*   *nga*   *- r*   *dngul*   *mang.po*   *rag*   *- gi.yod.kyi.red*
> maybe   I   - OBL   money   much   get   - IMPF+EPI 2+FACT

Hopefully I'll get a lot of money. (A reply to the question as to whether the business that the speaker has started will earn him some money.)

As shown above, this epistemic type may be used in conditional sentences. The verbal endings *gi.yod.kyi.red* and *gi.yod.kyi.ma.red* are used in present conditionals: a factual conditional, as in example (153), or a counterfactual conditional, as in example (154):

(153)   ང་ཚོ་ད་ལྟ་ཁྱི་འདིར་རོགས་པ་མ་བྱས་ན་ཤི་གི་ཡོད་ཀྱི་རེད།

> *nga*   *- tsho*   *da.lta*   *khyi*   *'di*   *- r*   *rogs.pa*   *ma*
> I   - pl   now   dog   this   - OBL   help   NEG
>
> *- byas*   *- na*   *shi*   *- gi.yod.kyi.red*
> - VBZ (PAS)   - if   die   - IMPF+EPI 2+FACT

If [we] don't help this dog, it will probably die. (The dog is emaciated. Emaciated dogs usually starve to death.)

(154)   ང་ཕྱི་རྒྱལ་ལ་ཡོད་ན་ཀོ་ཕི་འཐུང་གི་ཡོད་ཀྱི་རེད།

> *nga*   *phyi.rgyal*   *- la*   *yod*   *- na*   *ko.phi*   *'thung*   *- gi.yod.kyi.red*
> I   abroad   - OBL   exist   - if   coffee   drink (PRS)   - IMPF+EPI 2+FACT

If I were abroad, I would probably drink coffee. (The speaker knows that coffee is commonly drunk abroad.)

To sum up, the verbal endings and copulas of the type *yod.kyi.red* belong to the most frequently employed epistemic verbal endings in spoken Tibetan. Apart from simple sentences, they are also employed in factual and counterfactual conditionals. This type also demonstrates the geographic variation of standard spoken Tibetan: in the diaspora, the variations with negative endings may be formed in two different ways. This is considered to be unacceptable in central Tibet.

2.2 EPISTEMIC VERBAL ENDINGS AND COPULAS WITH THE FINAL AUXILIARY *'dra*

2.2.1 FORMAL, SEMANTIC AND PRAGMATIC CHARACTERISTICS

This epistemic type is characterized by the auxiliary *'dra* in the final position, e.g. *yod.pa.'dra*, *pa.yin.pa.'dra*. The *'dra*-endings and copulas indicate that the information on which the speaker bases his utterance is derived from the outside world, i.e. a sensory connotation (an inference based on direct evidence of a result or a consequence). They can be translated into English by such adverbs as 'apparently' or by the expressions 'it's likely', 'it seems' (the original meaning of the verb *'dra* is 'be like, be similar, look as if, seem, appear'). Concerning the degree of certainty, this epistemic type resembles the type *yod.kyi.red* and thus corresponds to degree EPI 2. It is very frequent in Lhasa and its environs.

(155)   ཉི་མ་སླེབས་པ་འདྲ།

nyi.ma	*slebs*	*- pa.'dra*
Nyima	come	- PFV+EPI 2+SENS

It seems Nyima has arrived. (The speaker can hear a voice similar to Nyima's, but he is not completely sure that it is Nyima's voice.)

The *'dra*-endings resemble verbal endings with the morpheme *sa* (e.g. *yod.sa.red*, see Section 2.5), which also express that the speaker's access to information is external. *Sa*-endings are, however, mainly used in the exile community and quite rarely in the Lhasa dialect. In contrast, *'dra*-endings are very common in Lhasa Tibetan.

The negative counterparts are formed by using the negative copulas *med* and *min*, as opposed to *yod* and *yin*, as shown in the example below:

(156)   ཁོང་གིས་བཟོས་པ་མིན་པ་འདྲ།

khong	*- gis*	*bzos*	*- pa.min.pa.'dra*
s/he+H	- ERG	make (PAS)	- PFV+EPI 2+SENS+NEG

It seems it wasn't he who made [this]. (It looks different when such an object as this is made by him.)

Unlike *yod.pa.'dra*, shown in example (157c), it is possible to negate sentences with the past endings *pa.'dra* and *pa.yin.pa.'dra* (though the latter usage is unusual) by placing the negative particle *ma* in front of the lexical verb (*ma* + V + *pa.'dra*, *ma* + V + *pa.yin.pa.'dra*). Preverbal negation often implies a stronger argumentation than postverbal negation. In example (157a) it is implied that the decision not to go was contingent on the agent in the sentence (she was free to decide whether to go or not to go), as opposed to the inferential statement in example (157b). Nonetheless, in the spoken language, sentences of the type found in example (157b) are more frequent:[43]

(157) ཁོང་མ་ཕྱིན་པ་འདྲ།

a) *khong   ma   - phyin   - pa.'dra*
   s/he+H   NEG   - go (PAS)   - PFV+EPI 2+SENS

   She seems not to have gone. Or: It seems she didn't want to go. (Her coat is still here.)

ཁོང་ཕྱིན་མེད་པ་འདྲ།

b) *khong   phyin   - med.pa.'dra*
   s/he+H   go (PAS)   - PERF+EPI 2+SENS+NEG

   She does not seem to have gone. (Her coat is still here.)

* ཁོང་མ་ཕྱིན་ཡོད་པ་འདྲ།

c) * *khong   ma   - phyin   - yod.pa.'dra*
   s/he+H   NEG   - go (PAS)   - PERF+EPI 2+SENS

   Intended statement: She does not seem to have gone.

The epistemic copulas of the *'dra*-type are the essential copulas *yin.pa.'dra* and *min.pa.'dra* and the existential copulas *yod.pa.'dra* and *med.pa.'dra*. Their use is illustrated in the example below:

(158) ཁོང་གྲྭ་པ་ཡིན་པ་འདྲ།

   khong   grwa.pa   yin.pa.'dra
   s/he+H   monk   be (EPI 2+SENS)

   He seems to be a monk. (The speaker makes an inference based on the fact that the person has shortly cropped hair.)

---

[43] For the use of the negative evidential past forms, see Tournadre and Sangda Dorje (2003: 130): "The simple past forms may be used to emphasize the agent's refusal to perform the action: I/he didn´t go (even though I/he was supposed to)".

This type forms the following paradigm:

Affirmative endings:	Negative endings:
pa.'dra	—
yod.pa.'dra	*med.pa.'dra*
pa.yin.pa.'dra	*pa.min.pa.'dra*
gi.yod.pa.'dra	*gi.med.pa.'dra*

Other combinations are impossible, e.g. **gi.yin.pa.'dra*, **gi.min.pa.'dra*.

It is possible to use the *'dra*-type both in first and third person sentences. As is the rule with epistemic endings, combinations of this type with the third person are subject to fewer constraints than with the first person. This is illustrated in the examples below: the non-controllable verbs *na* 'be ill' and *drag* 'recover' are compatible with the third person as in (159a) and (160a), as well as with the endings *yod.pa.'dra* and *gi.yod.pa.'dra*, but not with the first person as in (159b) and (160b):

(159)   ཁོང་ན་ /ᠨ དྲག་ཡོད་པ་འདྲ།

    a)   *khong   na   / drag   - yod.pa.'dra*
        s/he+H be ill / recover - PERF+EPI 2+SENS

    It seems he got sick. (The speaker makes an inference based on the fact that the person said he would definitely come but he hasn't.)
    / It seems he got better. (The speaker makes an effort based on the fact that the person has come to work.)

    *   ང་ན་ /ᠨ དྲག་ཡོད་པ་འདྲ།

    b) * *nga   na   / drag   - yod.pa.'dra*
          I   be ill / recover - PERF+EPI 2+SENS

    Intended statement: It seems I've fallen ill/got better.

(160)   ཁོང་ན་གི་ཡོད་པ་འདྲ།

    a)   *khong   na   - gi.yod.pa.'dra*
        s/he+H be ill - IMPF+EPI 2+SENS

    It seems he is ill. (He often puts his hand on his belly.)

    *   ང་ན་གི་ཡོད་པ་འདྲ།

    b) * *nga   na   - gi.yod.pa.'dra*
          I   be ill - IMPF+EPI 2+SENS

    Intended statement: It seems I am ill.

Similarly, The Tibetan speakers with whom I consulted found the following example to be fairly questionable:

(161)　　? ངས་རྡོ་རྗེ་རྒྱ་གར་ལ་འགྲོ་རུ་བཅུག་གི་མེད་པ་འདྲ།

> ?　*nga*　*- s*　*rdo.rje*　*rgya.gar*　*- la*　*'gro*　*- ru*
> 　　I　　- ERG　Dorje　India　　- OBL　go (PRS)　- CAUS
>
> 　　*bcug*　　*- gi.med.pa.'dra*
> 　　let　　　- IMPF+EPI 2+SENS+NEG

It seems I won't let Dorje go to India. (The speaker bases his statement on a change of the political situation that is observable by him. The political situation has got worse.)

Regarding the use of epistemic adverbs with this type of epistemic ending, it is possible to combine them with various epistemic adverbs, the most frequent being *gcig.byas.na* 'perhaps', *phal.cher* 'probably' and sometimes *gtan.gtan* 'certainly'. The adverb *brgya.cha.brgya* 'definitely' is not used with the *'dra-* type. Compare the following sentences containing the adverbs *gcig.byas.na* 'perhaps' and *gtan.gtan* 'certainly':

(162)　　ཁོང་གཅིག་བྱས་ན་ཁ་ལག་བཟོ་གི་ཡོད་པ་འདྲ།

> a)　*khong*　*gcig.byas.na*　*kha.lag*　*bzo*　　*- gi.yod.pa.'dra*
> 　　s/he+H　perhaps　　　meal　　VBZ (PRS)　- IMPF+EPI 2+SENS

Maybe she is cooking. (The speaker can smell, to a certain extent, food being prepared.)

ཁོང་གཏན་གཏན་ཁ་ལག་བཟོ་གི་ཡོད་པ་འདྲ།

> b)　*khong*　*gtan.gtan*　*kha.lag*　*bzo*　　*- gi.yod.pa.'dra*
> 　　s/he+H　certainly　　meal　　VBZ (PRS)　- IMPF+EPI 2+SENS

She must be cooking. (The speaker can clearly smell food being prepared.)

2.2.2 DESCRIPTION OF THE VERBAL ENDINGS

1. Verbal endings used in the perfective past

There are three affirmative verbal endings with the auxiliary *'dra* that are used in perfective past contexts: *pa.'dra, yod.pa.'dra* and *pa.yin.pa.'dra*. The first two endings are very frequent in the spoken language. The ending *pa.yin.pa.'dra* is less common.

The ending *pa.'dra* is by far the most frequently used past ending of this type. It is compatible with verbs of all verbal classes whether used in a third person sentence, as in examples (163) through (165), or a first person sentence (166). It sounds more natural to employ the secondary verb *myong* 'have an experience' in sentences with the first person; see example (166b). It can be used for single actions in perfective past contexts, as in example (163a), as well as in present perfect contexts (i.e., an action produced in the past but with a result still relevant to the present, as in example 163b). This epistemic ending has no negative counterpart. When used in negative contexts, negation is preverbal, as shown above in example (157a).

(163)　ཁོ་རང་ཁ་ས་ར་བཟི་པ་འདྲ།

a)

kho.rang	kha.sa	ra.bzi	- pa.'dra
he	yesterday	be drunk	- PFV+EPI 2+SENS

It seems he got drunk yesterday. (The speaker makes an inference from how the person was behaving yesterday.)

ཁོ་རང་ད་ལྟ་ར་བཟི་པ་འདྲ།

b)

kho.rang	da.lta	ra.bzi	- pa.'dra
he	now	be drunk	- PFV+EPI 2+SENS

He seems to be drunk. (The speaker makes an inference based on the fact that the person is reeling.)

(164)　ཁོང་མདང་དགོང་དགོང་དག་ཕེབས་པ་འདྲ།

khong	mdang.dgong dgong.dag	phebs	- pa.'dra
s/he+H	last night	go+H	- PFV+EPI 2+SENS

He seems to have left last night. (The speaker heard some noise last night.)

(165)　ཁོང་གིས་པད་མ་ལས་ཀ་བྱེད་རུ་བཅུག་པ་འདྲ།

khong	- gis	pad.ma	las.ka	byed	- ru	bcug
s/he+H	- ERG	Pema	work	VBZ (PRS)	- CAUS	let

- pa.'dra
- PFV+EPI 2+SENS

She seems to have let Pema get a job/made Pema get a job. (Pema has some money now.)

(166)　? ང་ས་ཆ་འདིར་སླེབས་པ་འདྲ།

a)

? nga	sa.cha	'di	- r	slebs	- pa.'dra
I	place	this	- OBL	arrive	- PFV+EPI 2+SENS

It seems I have been in this place [before]. (The location looks familiar to the speaker.)

ང་ས་ཆ་འདིར་སླེབས་མྱོང་ཡོད་པ་འདྲ།

b)

nga	sa.cha	'di	- r	slebs	myong	- yod.pa.'dra
I	place	this	- OBL	arrive	have an experience	- PERF+EPI 2+SENS

It seems I have been in this place [before]. (The place looks familiar to the speaker.)

94

Other frequently used verbal endings of this type are *yod.pa.'dra* and *med.pa.'dra*. They are generally very compatible with verbs of all verbal classes in third person sentences: see examples (167) through (169). Just as with the previous epistemic ending, these two endings can be used for one-time actions in the perfective past and present perfect contexts:

(167)   ཁོང་ར་བཟི་ཡོད་པ་འདྲ།

    khong   ra.bzi   - yod.pa.'dra
    s/he+H   be drunk   - PERF+EPI 2+SENS

    He seems to have got drunk. (The speaker makes an inference based on the fact that the person's face is red.)

(168)   ཁོང་ལ་སྤ་སེ་རག་མེད་པ་འདྲ།

    khong   - la   spa.se   rag   - med.pa.'dra
    s/he+H   - OBL   permit   get   - PERF+EPI 2+SENS+NEG

    She does not seem to have got the permit. (She planned to go to India and applied for a permit some time ago. She hasn't left yet.)

(169)   ཁོང་མདང་དགོང་དགོང་དག་ཕེབས་ཡོད་པ་འདྲ།

    khong   mdang.dgong dgong.dag   phebs   - yod.pa.'dra
    s/he+H   last night   go+H   - PERF+EPI 2+SENS

    He seems to have left last night. (He planned to go somewhere soon. Yesterday he was still at home. Now he is not.)

In first person sentences, the following verbal endings are rarely used or are incompatible with certain verbs, e.g. affective verbs such as *zhed* 'be afraid' or *dga'* 'love', as shown below in example (170):

(170)   * ང་ཁོང་ལ་དགའན་མེད་པ་འདྲ།

    * *nga   khong   - la   dga'   - med.pa.'dra*
    I   s/he+H   - OBL   love   - PERF+EPI 2+SENS+NEG
    Intended statement: I do not seem to have loved him.

The intended content of the above example may be conveyed by the expression *dga'.po* 'glad' combined with the copula *med.pa.'dra* (171a), or conversely by the involitional ergative verb *sem.pa shor* 'fall in love' and the epistemic ending *med.pa.'dra* (171b) instead of *dga'* 'love' and the epistemic ending *med.pa.'dra*:

(171)   ང་ཕྲུ་གུ་ཡིན་དུས་ནས་ཁོང་ལ་དགའ་པོ་མེད་པ་འདྲ།

     a)   *nga*   *phru.gu*   *yin*   *- dus*   *- nas*   *khong*   *- la*   *dga'.po*
          I   child   be   - when   - after   s/he+H   - OBL   glad

     med.pa.'dra
     exist (EPI 2+SENS+NEG)

It seems I haven't liked him since I was a child. (The statement is based upon the speaker's recollection.)

     ང་ཁོང་ལ་སེམས་པ་ཤོར་མེད་པ་འདྲ།

     b)   *nga*   *khong*   *- la*   *sems.pa*   *shor*   *- med.pa.'dra*
          I   s/he+H   - OBL   mind   lose   - PERF+EPI 2+SENS+NEG

I do not seem to have fallen in love with him. (The speaker states that she likes him, but tends to think that she hasn't fallen in love with him.)

Finally, the perfective past epistemic endings *pa.yin.pa.'dra* and *pa.min.pa.'dra* are used in the perfective past. However, they are much less frequent in the spoken language than the endings *pa.'dra* and *yod.pa.'dra*. In particular, the negative ending *pa.min.pa.'dra* is used very infrequently — it is not really compatible with certain monovalent and ergative verbs, and is generally incompatible with possessive and affective verbs: see example (174) with the possessive verb *rag* 'get'. Usually *med.pa.'dra* is used instead. The scope of epistemic modality of the ending *pa.yin.pa.'dra* is partial (bearing upon only one part of the sentence, e.g. the verb, as in example 173). Thus, in the following examples, sentence (172b), employing an adverbial of means, is considered to be more acceptable than (172a):

(172)   ? བློ་བཟང་ཕེབས་པ་ཡིན་པ་འདྲ།

     a)   ?   *blo.bzang*   *phebs*   *- pa.yin.pa.'dra*
             Lobzang   go+H   - PFV+EPI 2+SENS

Lobzang seems to have left.

     བློ་བཟང་མོ་ཊའི་ནང་ལ་ཕེབས་པ་ཡིན་པ་འདྲ།

     b)   *blo.bzang*   *mo.Ta*   *-'i*   *nang*   *- la*   *phebs*   *- pa.yin.pa.'dra*
          Lobzang   car   - GEN   inside   - OBL   go+H   - PFV+EPI 2+SENS

Lobzang seems to have gone <u>by car</u>. (His car was not in front of the house.)

(173)   ཀ༔   ཁོང་ན་པ་རེད་པས།   ཁ༔   ན་ཨ་ཡོད།   ར་བཟི་པ་ཡིན་པ་འདྲ།

     A: *khong*   *na*   *- pa.red*   *- pas*
          s/he+H   be ill   - PFV+FACT   - Q

     B: *na*   *- a.yod*   *ra.bzi*   *- pa.yin.pa.'dra*
          be ill   - PERF+EPI   be drunk   - PFV+EPI 2+SENS

     A: Was he ill?
     B: I doubt he was. It seems he was drunk. (He was tottering.)

(174) * ཁོང་ལ་སྤ་སེ་རག་པ་མིན་པ་འདྲ།

     * *khong*   *- la*   *spa.se*   *rag*   *- pa.min.pa.'dra*
       s/he+H   - OBL   ticket   get   - PFV+EPI 2+SENS+NEG

Intended statement: It seems he did not get the ticket. (Compare with example 155 above.)

<u>Differences among past-tense *'dra*-endings</u>

The verbal endings *pa.'dra, yod.pa.'dra* and *pa.yin.pa.'dra* differ in their scope of epistemic modality. Unlike *pa.'dra* and *pa.yin.pa.'dra*, which have a partial scope, *yod.pa.'dra* often refers to the entire sentence, although it can be employed in sentences with partial scope as well. In the pair of sentences in example (175), in sentence (175a) it is not clear if the action took place or not (though the speaker tends to think that it did not); in sentence (175b) the implication is that the meal was not cooked by the agent of the action. Other possibilities are suggested, e.g. a different agent or a different action:

(175) ཁོང་གིས་ཁ་ལག་བཟོས་མེད་པ་འདྲ།

   a)   *khong*   *- gis*   *kha.lag*   *bzos*   *- med.pa.'dra*
       s/he+H   - ERG   food   make (PAS)   - PERF+EPI 2+SENS+NEG

      She doesn't seem to have cooked [any] food. (The kitchen looks the same as when the speaker left it in the morning.)

     ཁ་ལག་འདི་ཁོང་གིས་བཟོས་པ་མིན་པ་འདྲ།

   b)   *kha.lag*   *'di*   *khong*   *- gis*   *bzos*   *- pa.min.pa.'dra*
       food   this   s/he+H   - ERG   make (PAS)   - PFV+EPI 2+SENS+NEG

      It doesn't seem he cooked this meal. (When he cooks, the food is not good but today it is delicious. Thus the speaker thinks that it was not the agent of the action who did the cooking.)[44]

The verbal endings *pa.'dra* and *pa.yin.pa.'dra* have, in general, a similar meaning. Nevertheless, *pa.yin.pa.'dra* occurs rarely in the spoken language. Sometimes these two endings convey a semantic difference: *pa.'dra* may refer to a more recent past action than *pa.yin.pa.'dra* or, as shown in example (176a), *pa.'dra* conveys an inchoative aspect, whereas *pa.yin.pa.'dra* in example (176b) corresponds to a verb of state (note that example 176b is considered to be ungrammatical by certain native speakers). Moreover, as stated above, the two endings differ in frequency: unlike *pa.yin.pa.'dra*, the ending *pa.'dra* is very frequent in spoken Tibetan.

---

[44] It is however possible to use the perfect ending *med.pa.'dra* in this context as well.

(176)　　　མོ་རང་ན་པ་འདྲ།

a)　　*mo.rang*　　*na*　　- *pa.'dra* [45]
　　　　she　　　　be ill　　- PFV+EPI 2+SENS

It seems she has fallen ill. (She doesn't look well.)

?　མོ་རང་ན་པ་ཡིན་པ་འདྲ།

b)　*?*　*mo.rang*　　*na*　　- *pa.yin.pa.'dra*
　　　　she　　　　be ill　　- PFV+EPI 2+SENS

It seems she has been ill. (She doesn't come to class.)

My Tibetan consultants who judged the sentence in (176b) as ungrammatical offered the following correction: the sentence should contain the secondary verb *bsdad* 'stay' followed by the epistemic endings *yod.pa.'dra* or *med.'gro'o*:

མོ་རང་ན་བསྡད་ཡོད་པ་འདྲ། ༼ མེད་འགྲོའོ།

c)　*mo.rang*　　*na*　　*bsdad*　- *yod.pa.'dra*　　　/ - *med.'gro'o*
　　　she　　　be ill　　stay　- PERF+EPI 2+SENS　　- PERF+EPI 1+FACT
　　It seems she has been ill./She has probably been ill.

2. Verbal endings of the imperfective past, the present and the future

The endings *gi.yod.pa.'dra* and *gi.med.pa.'dra* are employed in imperfective contexts. They are used for repeated actions in the past (example 177) and the present (examples 178 and 179) as well as for future actions. They are generally compatible with verbs of all verbal classes, although their use with certain verbs is considered to be ungrammatical, e.g. *shi* 'die', as seen in example (180), as this verb refers to a state, not to a process, and is thus incompatible with an imperfective verbal ending.[46]

(177)　　　སྔོན་མ་ཁོ་རང་ར་ཡང་སེ་བཟི་གི་ཡོད་པ་འདྲ།

sngon.ma　　*kho.rang*　*ra*　　　　*yang.se*　*bzi*　　- *gi.yod.pa.'dra*
before　　　　　he　　　(be drunk)　often　　(be drunk)　- IMPF+EPI 2+SENS

It seems he was often drunk before. (He looks like the kind of man who is often drunk.)

(178)　　　ཁོ་རང་ནམ་རྒྱུན་ནས་ར་བཟི་གི་ཡོད་པ་འདྲ།

kho.rang　　*nam.rgyun*　- *nas*　　*ra.bzi*　　- *gi.yod.pa.'dra*
he　　　　　usually　　　- ABL　　be drunk　- IMPF+EPI 2+SENS

It seems he usually gets drunk. (The speaker often sees him losing his balance while walking.)

---

[45] It is also possible to employ the verbal ending *yod.pa.'dra* in this sentence, although *pa.'dra* is more frequent in the spoken language.
[46] See Tournadre, Konchok Jiatso (2001: 101).

(179) དེང་སང་བཀྲ་ཤིས་པ་ཕའི་རྩ་ལ་འགྲོ་གི་མེད་པ་འདྲ།

deng.sang	bkra.shis	pa.pha	- 'i	rtsa	- la	'gro
these days	Tashi	father	- GEN	close	- OBL	go (PRS)

- *gi.med.pa.'dra*
- IMPF+EPI 2+SENS+NEG

Tashi does not seem to go to [his] father's [place] these days. (The speaker used to meet Tashi quite often when he was with his father, but now the speaker does not see him with his father anymore.)

(180) * ཁོ་ཤི་གི་ཡོད་པ་འདྲ།

* kho	shi	- gi.yod.pa.'dra
he	die	- IMPF+EPI 2+SENS

Intended statement: It seems he will die.

To convey the meaning expressed in example (180), it would be possible to employ a nominal construction with the noun *nyen.kha* 'danger' and the existential copula *'dug* 'exist', or the existential copula of this epistemic type:

(181) ཁོ་ཤི་ཡག་གི་ཉེན་ཁ་འདུག ∫ ཡོད་པ་འདྲ།

kho	shi	- yag	- gi	nyen.kha	'dug	/ yod.pa.'dra
he	die	- NOM	- GEN	danger	exist (SENS)	/ exist (EPI2+SENS)

It seems he will die.

The endings *gi.yod.pa.'dra* and *gi.med.pa.'dra* may be used in first person sentences, but such sentences are infrequent and their use is more restricted as compared to third person sentences. They combine more easily with certain possessive and affective verbs (182). With other verbs, such combinations are very infrequent or impossible (183, 184). In example (183), the combination is impossible because the lexical verb is volitional. In example (184a), the same constraint as seen in example (180) applies to the lexical verb *shi* 'die'.

(182) གཅིག་བྱས་ན་ང་ར་གསེར་གྱི་རྟགས་མ་རག་གི་ཡོད་པ་འདྲ།

gcig.byas.na	nga	- r	gser	- gyi	rtags.ma	rag
perhaps	I	- OBL	gold	- GEN	medal	get

- *gi.yod.pa.'dra*
- IMPF+EPI 2+SENS

It seems I will get the golden medal. (The speaker has seen the other competitors and he considers that he is the best one.)

(183)   * ང་དེབ་འབྲི་གི་མེད་པ་འདྲ།

       * *nga*   *deb*   *'bri*   - *gi.med.pa.'dra*
         I   book   write (PRS) - IMPF+EPI 2+SENS+NEG

Intended statement: It seems I will not write a book.

(184)   * ང་མགྱོགས་པོ་ཤི་གི་ཡོད་པ་འདྲ།

    a)   * *nga*   *mgyogs.po*   *shi*   - *gi.yod.pa.'dra*
          I   soon   die   - IMPF+EPI 2+SENS

Intended statement: It seems I will die soon.

To convey the meaning expressed in example (184a), the following sentence is also possible. It employs the secondary verb *'gro'o* (literary *grabs*) 'be about to [do]', followed by the auxiliary *yod.pa.'dra* (184b):[47]

        ང་མགྱོགས་པོ་ཤི་འགྲོའ་ཡོད་པ་འདྲ།

    b)   *nga*   *mgyogs.po*   *shi*   *'gro'o*   *yod.pa.'dra*
          I   soon   die   be about to   AUX (EPI 2+SENS)

    It seems I am about to die soon. (The speaker bases his statement on the fact
    that he is seriously ill.)

To conclude, the *'dra*-endings and copulas are very frequent in the spoken language in Lhasa and its environs. This type belongs to the most frequent epistemic types. As opposed to other types, it has three past endings: *pa.'dra, yod.pa.'dra* and *pa.yin.pa.'dra*. In conditional sentences, as compared to the other epistemic types, the *'dra*-endings are infrequent or not used at all (see 1.2.3.3).

---

[47] For more details on *'gro'o* (literary *grabs*), see Section 3.2.15.

2.3 EPISTEMIC VERBAL ENDINGS AND COPULAS WITH THE FINAL AUXILIARY *'gro/'gro'o*

2.3.1 FORMAL, SEMANTIC AND PRAGMATIC CHARACTERISTICS

This type of epistemic ending and copula is characterized by the final auxiliary *'gro* (short pronunciation) or *'gro'o* (rising intonation).[48] As concerns polarity, this type differs from the other epistemic types: the formally affirmative endings (as well as formally negative endings) may imply that the speaker considers his utterance as probable, or conversely, that he doubts the actuality of his utterance. Prosody plays an important role for the determination of the polarity of these endings. Affirmative endings with abbreviated pronunciation (e.g. *yod. 'gro*) and negative endings pronounced with rising intonation (e.g. *med. 'gro'o*) imply positive polarity (185). Negative endings with abbreviated pronunciation (e.g. *med. 'gro*) and affirmative endings pronounced with rising intonation (e.g. *yod. 'gro'o*) imply negative polarity (186). Compare the examples below:

(185) ནོར་བུ་ཁ་ས་ཕྱིན་ཡོད་འགྲོ་ / མེད་འགྲོའོ།

nor.bu	*kha.sa*	*phyin*	- *yod. 'gro / med. 'gro'o*
Norbu	yesterday	go (PAS)	- PERF+EPI 1+FACT

Norbu left maybe yesterday. (A reply to the question as to when Norbu left.)

(186) ནོར་བུ་ཁ་ས་ཕྱིན་ཡོད་འགྲོའོ་ / མེད་འགྲོ།

nor.bu	*kha.sa*	*phyin*	- *yod. 'gro'o / med. 'gro*
Norbu	yesterday	go (PAS)	- PERF+EPI 1+FACT+NEG

Maybe Norbu didn't leave yesterday. (A reply to the question as to when Norbu left.)

In case of the semantically positive verbal endings *pa.yin. 'gro* and *pa.min. 'gro'o,* the speaker's negative attitude concerning the probability of his utterance can also be expressed by the negative particle *ma* preceding the verb:

---

[48] *'gro* and *'gro'o* are phonetic transcriptions according to pronunciation in SST. At times they are also spelt *gro* and *gro'o,* see Zhou, Xie [eds.] (2003: 66).

(187)   ཕྲུ་གུ་འདི་སློབ་གྲྭ་ར་མ་ཕྱིན་པ་ཡིན་འགྲོ/པ་མིན་འགྲོའོ།

phru.gu   'di   slob.grwa   - r   ma   - phyin
child   this   school   - OBL   NEG   - go (PAS)

- pa.yin. 'gro/ pa.min. 'gro'o
- PFV+EPI 1+FACT

The child probably did not go to school. (A reply to the question as to why the child is here.)

The epistemic copulas of this type are the following: the essential copulas *yin. 'gro*, as shown in example (188), and *min. 'gro'o* (positive polarity); *yin. 'gro'o* and *min. 'gro* (negative polarity); and the existential copulas *yod. 'gro* and *med. 'gro'o* (positive polarity, as in example 189), and *yod. 'gro'o* and *med. 'gro* (negative polarity):

(188)   ཁོང་ལྷ་ས་ནས་ཡིན་འགྲོ།

khong   lha.sa   - nas   yin.'gro
s/he+H   Lhasa   - ABL   be (EPI 1+FACT)

She is probably from Lhasa. (A reply to the question as to where she is from. The speaker makes an inference based on the fact that she lives in Lhasa.)

(189)   ཁོང་ད་ལྟ་ལྷ་སར་མེད་འགྲོའོ།

khong   da.lta   lha.sa   - r   med. 'gro'o
s/he+H   now   Lhasa   - OBL   exist (EPI 1+FACT)

She probably is in Lhasa now. (The speaker makes an inference based on the fact that she often goes to Lhasa.)

This type forms the following paradigm:

Formally affirmative forms	
Semantically positive (the speaker considers his utterance as probable; short pronunciation):	Semantically negative (the speaker doubts the actuality of his utterance; rising intonation):
yod.'gro	*yod.'gro'o*
pa.yin.'gro	*pa.yin.'gro'o*
gi.yod.'gro	*gi.yod.'gro'o*

102

Formally negative forms	
Semantically positive (the speaker considers his utterance as probable; rising intonation):	Semantically negative (the speaker doubts the actuality of his utterance; short pronunciation):
med. 'gro'o	*med. 'gro*
pa.min. 'gro'o	*pa.min. 'gro*
gi.med. 'gro'o	*gi.med. 'gro*

Other combinations are impossible, e.g. *gi.yin. 'gro, *gi.min. 'gro, as shown in the example below:

(190)　　* ཁོང་ནང་ལ་འགྲོ་གི་ཡིན་འགྲོ།

　　　* *khong　　nang　- la　　'gro　　- gi.yin. 'gro*
　　　　s/he+H　　home　- OBL　　go (PRS)　- FUT+EPI 1+FACT

Intended statement: Maybe he will go home.

As stated above, both the affirmative and negative forms can have two meanings depending upon their prosody: they either express the speaker's positive standpoint as concerns the actuality of his utterance, or on the contrary, his uncertainty and doubt. Concerning the negative forms, those with the rising intonation (e.g. *med. 'gro'o*) are very frequent, whereas those with abbreviated pronunciation (e.g. *med. 'gro*) are less common in the spoken language. Instead, the affirmative forms with rising intonation (*yod. 'gro'o*) tend to be used. Concerning evidentiality, this type may be classified as factual; it generally doesn't imply any sensory or egophoric connotations. It may be viewed as part of the Lhasa dialect, in which its use is frequent. This type is less common in the exile community.

The endings of the type *yod. 'gro* resembles the type *yod.kyi.red*. However, unlike *yod.kyi.red*, they are more often used when the speaker is not basing his assertion on any reason in particular, as seen in example (191a). As a result, the type *yod. 'gro* implies, in general, a lower degree of probability than the type *yod.kyi.red* (191b), corresponding to EPI 1. Compare the following examples:

(191)　　ཁོ་འགྲོ་གི་ཡོད་འགྲོ།

　　a)　*kho　　'gro　　- gi.yod. 'gro*
　　　　he　　go (PRS)　- IMPF+EPI 1+FACT

　　　Maybe he will go. (The speaker doesn't know anything particular about the circumstances surrounding his departure. He is making a mere supposition.)

ཁོ་འགྲོ་གི་ཡོད་ཀྱི་རེད།

b) *kho   'gro   - gi.yod.kyi.red*
    he   go (PRS) - IMPF+EPI 2+FACT

He will probably go. (The speaker has knowledge of some reason or another, e.g. the person said he would go if he finished his work on time, which is a logical assumption. Thus, the speaker infers that it is probable that he will go.)

The affirmative endings with the rising intonation (e.g. *yod. 'gro'o*) may also have an interrogative function. This function originates from sentences containing the affirmative ending with a rising intonation followed by the negative ending with a rising intonation, which is usually abbreviated in the spoken language; *yod. 'gro'o med. 'gro'o,* for example, is abbreviated to *yod. 'gro'o*. The degree of certainty is approximately 50%. These sentences are often autolalic as seen in the following example (compare with example 80 in section 1.2.2.4):

(192) ངས་ཁང་པའི་ནང་གི་ཆུ་འདི་བཀག་ཡོད་འགྲོའོ།

       nga   - s   khang.pa -'i   nang   - gi   chu   'di   bkag
       I   - ERG   house   - GEN   inside - GEN   water   this   stof

       - yod. 'gro'o   (*= yod. 'gro'o med. 'gro'o*)
       - PERF+EPI 1+FACT+ AUTOLALIC

I wonder if I shut off the water mains in the house. (The speaker is asking himself.)

In first person sentences, epistemic endings of this type are compatible with various verbs, but their use is generally more restricted than in third person sentences (see the impossible combinations shown in example 193). To be considered grammatical, they often require a more specific context, such as a conditional clause, as shown in example (194):

(193) * ང་ཁོང་ལ་དགའ་ཡོད་འགྲོ།

    a) * *nga   khong   - la   dga'   - yod. 'gro*
           I   s/he+H   - OBL   love   - PERF+EPI 1+FACT

    Intended statement: I might have loved him.

       * ང་མིག་ཆུ་ཤོར་གྱི་མེད་འགྲོའོ།

    b) * *nga   mig.chu   shor   - gyi.med. 'gro'o*
           I   tear   lose   - IMPF+EPI 1+FACT

    Intended statement: I will probably cry. (Or: I am probably crying.)

104

* ང་ན་གི་མེད་འགྲོའོ།

c) * *nga*   *na*   - *gi.med.'gro'o*
     I   be ill   - IMPF+EPI 1+FACT

Intended statement: I will probably fall ill. (Or: I am probably ill.)

(194)   ཆུ་གྲང་མོ་བཏུངས་ན་ང་ན་གི་མེད་འགྲོའོ།

    chu   *grang.mo*   *btungs*   - *na*   *nga*   *na*   - *gi.med.'gro'o*
    water   cold   drink (PAS)   - if   I   be ill   - IMPF+EPI 1+FACT

    If I drink cold water, I will probably fall ill. (It is generally not healthy to drink cold water.)

As can be seen in the above example, certain epistemic endings of the type *yod.'gro* may appear in conditional sentences: factual and counterfactual. The following is an example of the past counterfactual conditional:

(195)   སྨན་མ་བཟས་ན་ཁོང་ཤི་ཡོད་འགྲོ།

    sman   *ma*   - *bzas*   - *na*   *khong*   *shi*   - *yod.'gro*
    medicine   NEG   - eat (PAS)   - if   s/he+H   die   - PERF+EPI 1+FACT

    If he had not taken the medicine, he probably would have died. (His illness was very serious.)

The endings with the auxiliary *'gro/'gro'o* are usually compatible with epistemic adverbs expressing possibility or probability, such as *gcig.byas.na* 'perhaps' and *phal.cher* 'probably': see example (196a). They are, however incompatible with adverbs expressing a high degree of certainty, such as *gtan.gtan* 'certainly' and *brgya.cha.brgya* 'definitely', as in example (196b):

(196)   གཅིག་བྱས་ན་ ⌠ ཕལ་ཆེར་ཁོང་ལ་ཕྲུ་གུ་སྐྱེས་མེད་འགྲོའོ།

a)   *gcig.byas.na* / *phal.cher*   *khong*   - *la*   *phru.gu*   *skyes*   - *med.'gro'o*
    perhaps   / probably   s/he+H   - OBL   child   give birth   - PERF+EPI 1+ FACT

    She possibly/probably had her baby. (The date of the birth has drawn near. The speaker hasn't seen her for some time.)

* ཁོང་ལ་གཏན་གཏན་ ⌠ བརྒྱ་ཆ་བརྒྱ་ཕྲུ་གུ་སྐྱེས་མེད་འགྲོའོ།

b) * *khong*   - *la*   *gtan.gtan* / *brgya.cha.brgya*   *phru.gu*   *skyes*   - *med.'gro'o*
    s/he+H   - OBL   certainly   / definitely   child   give birth   - PERF+EPI 1+ FACT

    Intended statement: She certainly/surely had her baby.

2.3.2 DESCRIPTION OF THE VERBAL ENDINGS

1. Verbal endings of the perfective past

In perfective past contexts, the following verbal endings of the *'gro*-type are used: *yod.'gro,*
med.'gro'o, yod.'gro'o, med.'gro, pa.yin.'gro, pa.min.'gro'o, pa.yin.'gro'o and *pa.min.'gro.*
The verbal endings *yod.'gro* and *med.'gro'o* (semantically positive) and *yod.'gro'o* and *med.'gro*
(semantically negative) are used in the present perfect. The sentence is viewed as positive and it
corresponds to 'possibly did' when the endings *yod.'gro* and *med.'gro'o* are used, as in example
(197). When the endings *yod.'gro'o* and *med.'gro* are used, the attitude of the speaker as to the
possibility of his utterance is negative, corresponding to 'possibly did not (do)'. These endings
are compatible with all verbal classes in third person sentences. The ending *med.'gro* is
infrequent in the spoken language as compared to *yod.'gro'o.*

(197)   ནོར་བུ་རྒྱ་གར་ལ་ཕྱིན་མེད་འགྲོའོ།

nor.bu	*rgya.gar*	*- la*	*phyin*	*- med.'gro'o*
Norbu	India	- OBL	go (PAS)	- PERF+EPI 1+FACT

Norbu probably went to India. (The speaker bases his statement on the fact
that Norbu was planning to go to India.)

In first person sentences, these verbal endings are usually not compatible with affective and
possessive verbs (see example 193a with the affective verb *dga'* 'love' above). If combined with
these endings, the secondary verb *myong* 'have an experience' is usually inserted between the
lexical verb and a perfect epistemic ending (*yod.'gro/med.'gro'o* or *yod.'gro'o/med.'gro,* see
example 198). Although the direct combination of the lexical verb with an epistemic ending of
this type without using the secondary verb *myong* is not excluded, such combinations are
infrequent. According to the Tibetans I consulted, these combinations imply that the speaker can
hardly remember what happened, e.g. as in a dream (example 199).

(198)   ང་ས་ཆ་དེར་འགྲོ་མྱོང་ཡོད་འགྲོ།

nga	*sa.cha*	*de*	*- r*	*'gro*	*myong*	*- yod.'gro*
I	place	that	- OBL	go (PRS)	have an experience	- PERF+EPI 1+FACT

I have probably been to that place. (The speaker makes a statement based on some
kind of sense or feeling, but he is not sure.)

(199)   ངའི་རྨི་ལམ་ལ་ས་ཆ་དེར་ཕྱིན་ཡོད་འགྲོ།

nga   - *'i*   *rmi.lam*   - *la*   *sa.cha*   *de*   - *r*   *phyin*
I   - GEN   dream   - OBL   place   that   - OBL   go (PAS)

- *yod.'gro*
- PERF+EPI 1+FACT

I probably went to that place in my dream. (The speaker tries to recall his dream.)

The verbal endings *pa.yin.'gro* and *pa.min.'gro'o* and *pa.yin.'gro'o* and *pa.min.' gro* are employed in the perfective past. The endings *pa.yin.'gro* and *pa.min.'gro'o* imply positive polarity, whereas *pa.yin.'gro'o* and *pa.min.'gro* imply negative polarity. In the spoken language, these endings are infrequent as compared to the perfective past endings (e.g. *yod.'gro*). The ending *pa.min.'gro* is very infrequent. In third person sentences, these endings can combine with verbs of all verbal classes. They usually have only partial scope, depending on the stress (see examples 200b and 201b), as opposed to the endings *yod.'gro/med.'gro'o* and *yod.'gro'o/med.'gro* (see examples 200a and 201a) with full-sentence scope:

(200)   ཁོང་ལ་ཚིག་མཛོད་བརྙེད་ཡོད་འགྲོའོ།

a)   *khong*   - *la*   *tshig.mdzod*   *brnyed*   - *yod.'gro'o*
    s/he+H   - OBL   dictionary   find   - PERF+EPI 1+FACT+NEG

    She probably didn't find the dictionary. (She said she would bring it if she found it. But she has not returned.)

    ཁོང་ལ་ཚིག་མཛོད་འདི་བརྙེད་པ་ཡིན་འགྲོའོ།

b)   *khong*   - *la*   *tshig.mdzod*   *'di*   *brnyed*   - *pa.yin.'gro'o*
    s/he+H   - OBL   dictionary   this   find   - PFV+EPI 1+FACT+NEG

    She probably didn't <u>find</u> this dictionary. (The dictionary looks brand-new. So the speaker tends to think that she purchased it, as opposed to finding it somewhere.)[49]

(201)   ཁོས་ཕྲུ་གུར་ཨ་རག་འཐུང་རུ་བཅུག་ཡོད་འགྲོའོ།

a)   *kho*   - *s*   *phru.gu*   - *r*   *a.rag*   *'thung*   - *ru*   *bcug*
    he   - ERG   child   - OBL   alcohol   drink (PRS)   - CAUS   let

- *yod.'gro'o*
- PERF+EPI 1+FACT+NEG

    He probably did not let the child drink alcohol. (The speaker told him to give the child some alcohol, e.g. as medicine, but he has his doubts as to whether that actually happened.)

---

[49] My Tibetan consultants also suggest that perfective past endings may have sensory connotations, no matter what their type of evidential mood is. See Section 1.2.2.1.2.

ཁོས་ཕྲུ་གུར་ཨ་རག་འཐུང་དུ་བཅུག་པ་ཡིན་འགྲོའོ།

b) *kho - s   phru.gu   - r   a.rag   'thung   - ru   bcug*
    he - ERG   child   - OBL alcohol drink (PRS) - CAUS let

    - pa.yin. 'gro'o
    - PFV+EPI 1+FACT+NEG

Maybe <u>he</u> wasn't the one who let the child drink alcohol. (Whereas in
(201a), it is not sure whether the child drank alcohol or not, in (201b) there
are no doubts that the child drank alcohol, but it is not sure whether <u>he</u> was
the one who let the child drink alcohol or not.)

Or: Maybe it wasn't <u>alcohol</u> that he let the child drink. (It was perhaps
someting else.)

My Tibetan consultants were exceptionally willing to accept, as correct usage, the
combinations shown below of first person and *pa.yin. 'gro/pa.min. 'gro'o* or
pa.yin. 'gro'o/pa.min. 'gro:

(202)   ?   ངས་ཁོང་ལ་སེམས་པ་ཤོར་པ་མིན་འགྲོའོ།

    nga   - s   khong   - la   sems.pa   shor   - pa.min. 'gro'o
    I   - ERG s/he+H   - OBL   mind   lose   - PFV+EPI 1+FACT

    I've probably fallen in love with her. (The speaker didn't realize this before.
    Now that the person has left, he realizes how much he misses her.)

Nonetheless, it is more natural for the following sentences to use the evidential ending *bzhag*
(the usage in example 203a), or the epistemic ending *pa. 'dra* (example 203b):

(203)   འདུག་སེ་ལྟ་དུས་ང་ཁོང་ལ་དགའ་བཞག

    a) *'dug.se   lta   - dus   nga   khong   - la   dga'   - bzhag*
        like that look (PRS) - when   I   s/he+H   - OBL   love   - PERF+INFR

        I've probably fallen in love with her. (The speaker didn't realize this before. Now
        that the person has left, he realize how much he misses her.)

    ང་ཕལ་ཆེར་ཁོང་ལ་དགའ་བཞག ͡ པ་འདྲ།

    b) *nga   phal.cher   khong   - la   dga'   - bzhag   / - pa. 'dra*
        I   probably   s/he+H   - OBL   love   - PERF+INFR   / - PFV+EPI 2+SENS

        I've probably fallen in love with her. (The speaker didn't realize this before. Now
        that the person has left, he realize how much he misses her.)

2. Verbal endings used in the imperfective past, the present and in the future

The verbal endings *gi.yod.'gro/gi.med.'gro'o* and *gi.yod.'gro'o/gi.med.'gro* are used in imperfective contexts, i.e. the imperfective past, the present and the future. The verbal endings *gi.yod.'gro* and *gi.med.'gro'o* convey a positive meaning (204), whereas *gi.yod.'gro'o* and *gi.med.'gro* convey a negative meaning (205). They may combine with all verbal classes in third person sentences. In first person sentences, they are usually not compatible with affective and possessive verbs (206):

(204) ཁོང་ད་ལྟ་གློག་བརྙན་འདི་ལྟ་གི་ཡོད་འགྲོ།

khong	*da.lta*	*glog.brnyan*	*'di*	*lta*	- *gi.yod.'gro*
s/he+H	now	movie	this	watch (PRS)	- IMPF+EPI 1+FACT

She is probably watching the movie. (The speaker makes an inference from the fact that the movie is extremely popular.)

(205) ནོར་བུ་བལ་ཡུལ་ལ་འགྲོ་གི་ཡོད་འགྲོའོ།

nor.bu	*bal.yul*	- *la*	*'gro*	- *gi.yod.'gro'o*
Norbu	Nepal	- OBL	go (PRS)	- IMPF+EPI 1+FACT+NEG

Norbu probably won't go to Nepal. (The political situation in Nepal is not good.)

(206) * ང་ཁོང་ལ་དགའ་གི་མེད་འགྲོའོ།

* *nga*	*khong*	- *la*	*dga'*	- *gi.med.'gro'o*
I	s/he+H	- OBL	love	- IMPF+EPI 1+FACT

Intended statement: Probably I love him.

Another verbal ending of this type, sometimes employed in future contexts, is *'gro*. The verbal ending *'gro* expresses the speaker's positive attitude as to the possibility of his utterance.[50] Its meaning corresponds in English to the statement 'I guess that (someone will do something)'.[51] This verbal ending implies a high degree of certainty (high probability or likelihood, glossed as EPI 2; see Tournadre & Konchok Jiatso 2001: 96). In the spoken language, the lexical verb is in the past stem (compare examples 207a and 207b), although semantically it always indicates the

---

[50] Compare with the following example taken from Tournadre, Konchok Jiatso (2001: 96):

ཉལ་ས་འི་འཁྲིས་སུ་སྨན་ཞོག་དང་། ཁོས་འཐུང་འགྲོ།

nyal	- *sa*	- *'i*	*'khris*	- *su*	*sman*	*zhog*	- *dang*
sleep	- NOM	- GEN	near	- OBL	medicine	put (IMP)	- IMP

kho	- *s*		*'thung*	- *'gro*			
he	- ERG		drink	- FUT+EPI 2+FACT			

Put the medicine near the bed. He will certainly drink it.

[51] See also Lhakpa Tseten (1999: 202).

109

future. It is impossible to negate sentences using *'gro* with the negative particle *ma,* as in example (207c). The negative polarity is expressed by the verbal ending *'gro'o* (with rising intonation, as in example 207d). Both endings are compatible with various verbal classes in third person sentences: see examples (207a) and (208).

(207)   ཟླ་བ་ཕྱིན་འགྲོ།

    a)   *zla.ba*   *phyin*   - *'gro*
          Dawa   go (PAS)   - FUT+EPI 2+FACT

    I suppose Dawa will go [there]. (Dawa is a driver. He told the speaker that he would go to Samye. The speaker has met a friend who wants to go to Samye as well, so he tells him that Dawa will probably be going there.)

    *   ཁོང་འགྲོ་འགྲོ།

    b) * *khong*   *'gro*   - *'gro*
            s/he+H   go (PRS)   - FUT+EPI 2+FACT

    Intended statement: I guess he will go [there].

    *   ཁོང་མ་ཕྱིན་འགྲོ།

    c) * *khong*   *ma*   - *phyin*   - *'gro*
            s/he+H   NEG   - go (PAS)   - FUT+EPI 2+FACT

    Intended statement: I guess he will not go [there].

    ཟླ་བ་ཕྱིན་འགྲོའོ།

    d)   *zla.ba*   *phyin*   - *'gro'o*
          Dawa   go (PAS)   - FUT+EPI 2+FACT+NEG

    I'm guessing that Dawa will not go [there]. (The speaker thinks that Dawa is probably too busy to make the trip.)

(208)   ཁོང་གིས་བཞེས་ཐག་མཆོད་འགྲོ།

    khong   - *gis*   *bzhes.thag*   *mchod*   - *'gro*[52]
    s/he+H - ERG   cigarette+H   VBZ+H   - FUT+EPI 2+FACT

    I guess he will smoke.

In first person sentences, these epistemic endings are at times used with non-controllable verbs — see example (209a) — but not with controllable verbs, as in (209b). It should be noted though that these combinations are not very frequent, and they are not considered grammatical by all Tibetan speakers (209a):

---

[52] Taken from Lhakpa Tseten (1999: 202).

(209)   ? ཤ་ལས་ཀ་རག་འགྲོ།

a) *?*   *nga*   *- r*   *las.ka*   *rag*   - *'gro*
           I   - OBL   work   get   - FUT+EPI 2+FACT

I might get a job.

      * ཤ་ལས་ཀ་འདི་བྱས་འགྲོ།

b) *   *nga*   *las.ka*   *'di*   *byas*   - *'gro*
         I   work   this   VBZ (PAS)   - FUT+EPI 2+FACT

Intended statement: I guess I will do this work [task].

To sum up: the epistemic endings and copulas with the auxiliary *'gro* (or *'gro'o*) are another frequently used epistemic type in spoken Tibetan. It differs from other types in that both the affirmative and negative forms may designate a positive or negative meaning, as conveyed by the intonation during the utterance. This type of epistemic ending may also be used in conditional sentences. Finally, it has a verbal ending which is used in the future — the verbal ending *'gro* (and its negative counterpart *'gro'o*). This ending differs from the other verbal endings of this type in its degree of probability: *'gro* (as well as *'gro'o*) conveys a higher degree of probability than the other *'gro*-endings. Nonetheless, both (*'gro* and *'gro'o*) are relatively rare in the spoken language.

2.4 EPISTEMIC VERBAL ENDINGS AND COPULAS WITH THE MORPHEME *a*

2.4.1 FORMAL, SEMANTIC AND PRAGMATIC CHARACTERISTICS

This type of epistemic ending and copula diachronically consists of a nominalizer, the morpheme *a* (*e*)[53] and a verbal auxiliary. There are no formally negative equivalents of these endings or copulas in standard spoken Tibetan. Below is an example of this type with the future ending *a.yong*:

(210) པ་ཕས་ཆང་བཏུངས་ཨ་ཡོང་།

pa.pha	*- s*	*chang*	*btungs*	*- a.yong*
father	- ERG	*chang*	drink (PAS)	- PERF FUT+EPI 3+EGO+NEG

I strongly doubt that father will drink *chang*. (I know that father doesn't like *chang*.)

The epistemic copulas of this type are *a.yod* (existential) and *a.yin* (essential). They are very frequent in Lhasa Tibetan. Below is an example of the use of the copula *a.yod* in a polite question:

(211) ཁྱེད་རང་ལ་སྨྱུ་གུ་གཉིས་ཨ་ཡོད་ན།

khyed.rang	*- la*	*smyu.gu*	*gnyis*	*a.yod*	*- na*
you+H	- OBL	pen	two	exist (EPI 3+EGO+NEG)	- POLITE

You wouldn't happen to have two pens, would you [please]? (The speaker would like to borrow a pen.)

This epistemic type forms the following paradigm:

a.yod
pa.a.yin
gi.a.yod
a.yong

There are no negative counterparts: **a.med, *pa.a.min, *gi.a.med, *a.ma.yong,* or other grammatical endings, e.g. **gi.a.yin*:

[53] The morpheme *e* is usually pronounced [*a*] in Lhasa. In Kham and Amdo Tibetan, *e* is used to form questions, for example the question 'Has he eaten?' is formed in the following way in Kham Tibetan: *kho - gis za.ma za e tshar - thal*. In classical Tibetan, *e* is an interrogative particle. The epistemic meaning of *a*-endings in SST is therefore semantically related to the interrogative particle *e* in literary Tibetan.

(212) * ཁོང་ལས་ཀ་བྱེད་ཀྱི་ཨ་ཡིན།

        * *khong*   *las.ka*   *byed*   *- kyi.a.yin*
           s/he+H   work   VBZ (PRS)   - FUT+EPI 3+EGO+NEG

Intended statement: I doubt she will work.

The epistemic endings with the morpheme *a*, as suggested above, are diachronically interrogative and have negative polarity: they imply a high degree of the speaker's certainty of the non-actuality of the statement. The speaker has serious doubts, close to negative certainty (degree EPI 3). These endings have egophoric connotations and correspond to such English expressions as: 'I don't think that…', 'I (strongly) doubt that…'.[54] They are very common in spoken Tibetan.

Apart from the epistemic meaning, this type often conveys other secondary meanings, such as surprise ('I would be surprised if…', as in example 213b); hope (I wish I/he [did] …', as in example 214)—see as well example (100b) in Section 1.2.2.6 above; a polite request, as in example (215); fear, as in example (216), and so on.

(213) ཀ༔ ཁོ་རྒྱ་གར་ལ་ཕྱིན་སོང་།

    A: *kho*   *rgya.gar*   *- la*   *phyin*   *- song*
           he   India   - OBL   go (PAS)   - PFV+SENS

     He went to India.

     ཁ༔ ཨ་ཡིན།

    B: *a.yin*
           be (EPI 3+EGO+NEG)

     Oh, really?/[That's] impossible.

(214) ང་ཨ་ཡིན།

     nga   *a.yin*
     I   be (EPI 3+EGO+NEG)

     I hope it doesn't fall to me. (A remark made by the speaker during a meeting because someone must be chosen to do some extra work. The speaker is wishing it will not be him.)

(215) ཁོང་ནང་ལ་བཞུགས་ཨ་ཡོད་ན།

     khong   *nang*   *- la*   *bzhugs*   *- a.yod*   *- na*
     s/he+H   home   - OBL   stay+H   - PERF+EPI 3+EGO+NEG   - POLITE

     I wonder, is he in?

---

[54] See as well Tournadre, Sangda Dorje (2003: 313).

113

(216)　ཁོང་འགྲོ་ཐུབ་ཨ་ཡོང་།

> *khong*   *'gro*   *thub*   *- a.yong*[55]
> s/he+H   go (PRS)   can   - PERF FUT+EPI 3+EGO+NEG

I fear she won't be able to go.

The secondary meanings grouped under this type of epistemic ending and copula are very common in SST, with the exception of the interrogative function, as in example (215), which is relatively infrequent. Instead, evidential endings with the interrogative particles (*pas, gas*) are used, as in example (217):

(217)　ཁོང་ནང་ལ་བཞུགས་འདུག་གས།

> *khong*   *nang*   *- la*   *bzhugs*   *- 'dug*   *- gas*
> s/he+H   home   - OBL   stay+H   - PERF+SENS   - Q

Is he in?

Just as with other epistemic types, verbal endings of the type *a.yod* usually combine with the third person. First person sentences are less frequent and their use is more restricted: the first person combines more easily with perfective endings (e.g. the perfective future ending *a.yong*, as in example 218a) than with imperfective endings (see the imperfective ending *gyi.a.yod* in example 218b and *kyi.a.yod* in 218c):

(218)　ང་མིག་ཆུ་ཤོར་ཨ་ཡོང་།

> a)   *nga*   *mig.chu*   *shor*   *- a.yong*
>   I   tears   lose   - PERF FUT+EGO+EPI 3+NEG

I doubt I will cry. (The speaker is going to watch a sad movie and bases his statement on personal experience.)

* ང་མིག་ཆུ་ཤོར་གྱི་ཨ་ཡོད།

> b)   * *nga*   *mig.chu*   *shor*   *- gyi.a.yod*
>   I   tears   lose   - IMPF+EPI 3+EGO+NEG

Intended statement: I doubt I will cry.

* ང་སང་ཉིན་ལས་ཀ་བྱེད་ཀྱི་ཨ་ཡོད།

> c)   * *nga*   *sang.nyin*   *las.ka*   *byed*   *- kyi.a.yod*
>   I   tomorrow   work   VBZ (PRS)   - IMPF+EPI 3+EGO+NEG

Intended statement: I doubt I will work tomorrow.

---

[55] My consultant suggested the following translation of this sentence into Chinese: 我恐怕他不可以去, i.e. 'I fear he won't be able to go.' (The Chinese verb *kǒngpà* 'be afraid', 'fear' also has an epistemic meaning).

Although it is possible to combine first person with the verbal ending *a.yong*, Tibetan speakers prefer other ways of expressing doubt or uncertainty when talking about themselves, as for example in (219) below:

(219)   ང་སང་ཉིན་ལས་ཀ་བྱེད་དགོས་ཡིན་ན ྄ མིན་ན ྄ ྄

nga	*sang.nyin*	*las.ka*	*byed*	*dgos*	*- yin*	*- na*	*(min*	*- na)*
I	tomorrow	work	VBZ (PRS)	must	- AUX	- if	AUX (NEG)	- if

I don't think I will work tomorrow.
Or: I wonder if I will (have to) work tomorrow.

This type of epistemic ending may appear in conditional sentences. In particular, the future ending *a.yong* is frequently employed in such sentences: see example (220):

(220)   སྨན་འདི་བཟས་ན་ཁོང་གི་ན་ཚ་དྲག་ཨ་ཡོང་།

a)
sman	*'di*	*bzas*	*- na*	*khong*	*- gi*	*na.tsha*
medicine	this	eat (PAS)	- if	s/he+H	- GEN	illness

drag	*- a.yong*
recover	- PERF FUT+EPI 3+EGO+NEG

I strongly doubt she will recover if she takes this medicine. (The speaker is familiar with this medicine and thinks that it won't help.)

ཁ་ལག་འདི་བཟས་ན་ཁོང་ན་ཨ་ཡོང་།

b)
kha.lag	*'di*	*bzas*	*- na*	*khong*	*na*	*- a.yong*
meal	this	eat (PAS)	- if	s/he	be ill	- PERF FUT+EPI 3+EGO+NEG

I don't think she will be ill if she eats this meal. (The speaker has eaten this kind of food before, or has tried the meal already.)

It is possible to combine the type *a.yod* with epistemic adverbs expressing possibility or probability, e.g. *gcig.byas.na* 'perhaps' (221a) and *phal.cher* 'probably' (221b). However, sentences classified under this type of epistemic ending occur more frequently without an epistemic adverb. As concerns adverbs expressing certainty — such as *gtan.gtan* 'certainly' and *brgya.cha.rgya* 'definitely' — they are rarely used with the type *a.yod* and their combinations are often considered to be problematic to native speakers (see example 221c). As verbal endings of the type *a.yod* emphasize the speaker's high degree of certainty of the non-actuality of his utterance, Tibetan speakers prefer using other epistemic adverbs or other epistemic means.

(221)   གཅིག་བྱས་ན་ཁོང་ང་ར་དགའ་གི་འ་ཡོད།

a) *gcig.byas.na*   *khong*   *nga*   *- r*   *dga'*   *- gi.a.yod*
   perhaps   s/he+H   I   - OBL   love   - IMPF+EPI 3+EGO+NEG

   1. Maybe she doesn't love me. (The speaker makes an assessment based on
   his own feelings.)
   2. I wish she loved me. (The speaker expresses his hope or fear.)

ཀ༔ ཁོང་ནང་ལ་བཞུགས་འདུག་གས།   ཁ༔   ཕལ་ཆེར་བཞུགས་འ་ཡོད།

b) A: *khong*   *nang*   *- la*   *bzhugs*   *- 'dug*   *- gas*
      s/he+H   home   - OBL   stay+H   - PERF+SENS   - Q

   B: *phal.cher*   *bzhugs*   *- a.yod*
      probably   stay+H   - PERF+EPI 3+EGO+NEG

A: Is he at home?
B: I strongly doubt it. (The speaker bases his statement on personal
knowledge of the habits of the person in question.)

? ཁོང་གཏན་གཏན་ཡོང་འ་ཡོང་།

c) *? khong*   *gtan.gtan*   *yong*   *- a.yong*
      s/he+H   certainly   come   - PERF FUT+ EPI 3+EGO+NEG

   I strongly doubt he will come. (The speaker thinks that it is too late now.)

2.4.2 DESCRIPTION OF THE VERBAL ENDINGS

1. Verbal endings employed in the perfective past

There are two verbal endings of this type that are used in the perfective past: the perfect ending
a.yod and the perfective past ending *pa.a.yin*.

The epistemic ending *a.yod* is employed to express doubt, as well as other secondary meanings
in past contexts that are often related to the present. In third person sentences, it can combine
with verbs of different verbal classes, as in example (222a), where it combines with a possessive
verb, and in example (222b) where it combines with an affective verb. In first person sentences,
a.yod is usually not used with affective verbs; see example (223b) below and compare:

(222)   བསྟན་འཛིན་ལ་ལས་ཀ་འདི་རག་འ་ཡོད།

a) *bstan.'dzin*   *- la*   *las.ka*   *'di*   *rag*   *- a.yod*
   Tenzin   - OBL   work   this   get   - PERF+ EPI 3+EGO+NEG

   I strongly doubt Tenzin got the job. (The speaker knows Tenzin very well
   and knows that he is not qualified for it.)

116

བསྟན་འཛིན་ཁོང་ལ་ཞེད་ཨ་ཡོད།

b) *bstan.'dzin*   *khong*   *- la*   *zhed*   *- a.yod*
    Tenzin   s/he+H   - OBL   fear   - PERF+EPI 3+EGO+NEG

I strongly doubt that Tenzin was afraid of her. (The speaker knows Tenzin very well.)

(223)   ངས་ཕྲུ་གུ་ཨ་རག་འཐུང་རུ་བཅུག་ཨ་ཡོད།

a) *nga*   *- s*   *phru.gu*   *a.rag*   *'thung*   *- ru*   *bcug*   *- a.yod*
    I   - ERG   child   alcohol   drink (PRS)   - CAUS   let   - PERF+ EPI 3 +EGO+NEG

I strongly doubt I let the child drink alcohol.

    * ང་ཁོང་ལ་ཞེད་ཨ་ཡོད།

b) * *nga*   *khong*   *- la*   *zhed*   *- a.yod*
    I   s/he+H   - OBL   fear   - PERF+EPI 3+EGO+NEG

Intended statement: I strongly doubt I was afraid of her.

The epistemic ending *pa.a.yin* is quite common in SST in perfective past contexts. Apart from the epistemic meaning, it often expresses a secondary meaning of doubt, surprise, hope or fear. Since its scope is partial (highlighting one part of the sentence, often the agent), its use is subject to certain restrictions. In example (224), the noun *las.ka* 'work' must be determined, for example by the pronoun *'di* 'this', and it preferably precedes the agent of the action (224b). This is linked to the fact that the focus position in a Tibetan sentence is before the verb. If the focus is placed on the agent, it is usually moved and occupies the place of the second argument. Moreover, the scope of epistemic modality is linked to the focused element. As a result, example (224a) is ungrammatical, whereas (224b) places the focus on the agent and example (224c) on the second argument.

(224)   * ལས་ཀ་ཁོང་གིས་བྱས་པ་ཨ་ཡིན།

a) * *las.ka*   *khong*   *- gis*   *byas*   *- pa.a.yin*
    work   s/he   - ERG   do (PAS)   - PFV+EPI 3+EGO+NEG

Intended statement: I strongly doubt <u>he</u> worked.

ལས་ཀ་འདི་ཁོང་གིས་བྱས་པ་ཨ་ཡིན།

b) *las.ka*   *'di*   *khong*   *- gis*   *byas*   *- pa.a.yin*
    work   this   s/he+H   - ERG   do (PAS)   - PFV+EPI 3+EGO+NEG

I doubt it was <u>he</u> who did [completed] this work. (He usually doesn't do this [kind of] work. The speaker bases his statement on personal experience.)

ཁོང་གིས་ལས་ཀ་འདི་བྱས་པ་ཨ་ཡིན།

c) khong   - gis   las.ka   'di   byas   - pa.a.yin
    s/he+H - ERG   work   this   VBZ (PAS) - PFV+EPI 3+EGO+NEG

I strongly doubt it was <u>this work</u> that he did. (He usually doesn't do this kind of work. The speaker bases himself on personal experience.)

<u>Differences between the verbal endings a.yod and pa.a.yin</u>

1. The epistemic ending a.yod may be employed in a wider range of contexts (compare the use of a.yod in the present tense, as an example 236a below) and has fewer restrictions than pa.a.yin. On the contrary, the verbal ending pa.a.yin is usually used only with controllable verbs and has more syntactic constraints than a.yod, as shown in example (225). In this example, unlike example (226a) with a.yod, the sentence with pa.a.yin must include an adverbial of means, place or time (225b); otherwise it is ungrammatical (225a).

(225)   * ཁོང་ཕྱིན་པ་ཨ་ཡིན།

    a)   * khong   phyin   - pa.a.yin
            s/he+H   go (PAS)   - PFV+EPI 3+EGO+NEG

    Intended statement: I strongly doubt she went [there].

    ཁོང་གནམ་གྲུ་ལ་ཕྱིན་པ་ཨ་ཡིན།

    b)   khong   gnam.gru   - la   phyin   - pa.a.yin
            s/he+H   airplane   - OBL   go (PAS)   - PFV+EPI 3+EGO+NEG

    I strongly doubt that she traveled by plane. (The speaker knows she is afraid of flying.)

(226)   ཁོང་ཕྱིན་ཨ་ཡོད།

    a)   khong   phyin   - a.yod
            s/he+H   go (PAS)   - PERF+EPI 3+EGO+NEG

    I strongly doubt she went [there]. (The speaker knows that she always calls him when she goes there.)

    ཁོང་གནམ་གྲུ་ལ་ཕྱིན་ཨ་ཡོད།

    b)   khong   gnam.gru   - la   phyin   - a.yod
            s/he+H   airplane   - OBL   go (PAS)   - PERF+EPI 3+EGO+NEG

    I strongly doubt that she traveled by plane. (The speaker knows she is afraid of flying.)

Nevertheless, although it is possible to say the sentence in (225b), Tibetan speakers prefer to utter the sentence in (226b) with the verbal ending a.yod. This is explained by the fact that the scope of probability expressed by this verbal ending can be full-sentence scope (226a) as well as partial in scope (see Part 2 below for the scope of negation).

2. The scope of negation of the two verbal endings is different. The ending *pa.a.yin* negates one part of the sentence, e.g. the agent as in (227b), but not the whole sentence. The verbal ending *a.yod* may either have the same meaning as *pa.a.yin* as in (227a, Meaning 1), or, as occurs more frequently, it can refer to the entire sentence (see example 227a, Meaning 2, in which the speaker doubts the entire hypothetical action of the agent of the sentence):

(227) ཉེན་རྟོག་པས་ལམ་ཁག་བཀག་ཨ་ཡོད།

    a) *nyen.rtog.pa*   *- s*   *lam.khag*   *bkag*   *- a.yod*
        police   - ERG   road   block   - PERF+EPI 3+EGO+NEG

       1. I strongly doubt the police blocked the road. (The speaker thinks that the police would not do so as blocking the road would create traffic problems.)
       2. I strongly doubt it was the police who blocked the road. (The speaker thinks that some other entity blocked the road.)

       ཉེན་རྟོག་པས་ལམ་ཁག་བཀག་པ་ཨ་ཡིན།

    b) *nyen.rtog.pa*   *- s*   *lam.khag*   *bkag*   *- pa.a.yin*
        police   - ERG   road   block   - PFV+EPI 3+EGO+NEG

       I strongly doubt it was the police who blocked the road. (The speaker thinks that other entity blocked the road, e.g. the army.)

3. From a semantic viewpoint, the difference between these two verbal endings is in that *pa.a.yin* may imply hope (the speaker hopes that the action was not carried out, see example 228b). The ending *a.yod,* on the other hand, usually does not have such connotations (228a):

(228) ཁོང་བུ་མོ་དེ་ལ་ཚིག་པ་ཟ་ཨ་ཡོད།

    a) *khong*   *bu.mo*   *de*   *- la*   *tshig.pa*   *za*   *- a.yod*
        s/he+H   girl   that   - OBL   anger   VBZ   - PERF+EPI 3+EGO+NEG

       I don't think he was angry with that girl. (A reply to the question as to if the person was angry with that girl. The speaker knows him very well and thinks he would not get angry.)

       ཁོང་བུ་མོ་དེ་ལ་ཚིག་པ་ཟ་པ་ཨ་ཡིན།

    b) *khong*   *bu.mo*   *de*   *- la*   *tshig.pa*   *za*   *- pa.a.yin*
        s/he+H   girl   that   - OBL   anger   VBZ   - PFV+EPI 3+EGO+NEG

       I hope he did not get angry with that girl. (A reply to the question as to whether he got angry with that girl. The speaker likes the girl in question so he hopes that the person in question did not become angry with her.)

4. Although both past endings may be directly combined to a lexical verb (229a and 229c), in sentences with the secondary verb *myong* 'have an experience', this secondary verb is followed

by the verbal ending *a.yod* (see example 229b), and may not combine with the verbal ending
pa.a.yin (example 229d):

(229)   ཁོང་ཁྱི་དེ་ལ་ཞེད་ཨ་ཡོད།

a) *khong   khyi   de   - la   zhed   - a.yod*
    s/he+H dog   that - OBL   be afraid - PERF+EPI 3+EGO+NEG

I doubt she was afraid of that dog. (The dog is large, but the speaker knows
she is not afraid of dogs.)

ཁོང་ཁྱི་དེ་ལ་ཞེད་མྱོང་ཨ་ཡོད།

b) *khong   khyi   de   - la   zhed   myong   - a.yod*
    s/he+H dog   that - OBL   be afraid have an   - PERF+EPI 3+EGO
                                            experience   +NEG

I doubt she was ever afraid of that dog.

ཁོང་ཁྱི་དེ་ལ་ཞེད་པ་ཨ་ཡིན།

c) *khong   khyi   de   - la   zhed   - pa.a.yin*
    s/he+H dog   that - OBL   be afraid - PFV+EPI 3+EGO+NEG

I doubt she was afraid of <u>that</u> dog. (That dog is small. The speaker thinks she
is not afraid of small dogs.)

*   ཁོང་ཁྱི་དེ་ལ་ཞེད་མྱོང་པ་ཨ་ཡིན།

d) * *khong   khyi   de   - la   zhed   myong   - pa.a.yin*
      s/he+H dog   that - OBL   be afraid have an   - PFV+EPI 3+EGO
                                              experience   +NEG

Intended statement: I doubt she was ever afraid of that dog.

5. Both past endings can be used in first person sentences, but they convey different meanings:
whereas *a.yod* only expresses doubt, *pa.a.yin* indicates surprise, as shown in the following
example. The verbal ending *pa.a.yin* (see example 230b) is rare, however, as compared to *a.yod*
(230a):

(230)   ང་ས་ཆ་འདིར་སླེབས་ཨ་ཡོད།

a) *nga   sa.cha   'di   - r   slebs   - a.yod*[56]
    I   place   this - OBL   come   - PERF+EPI 3+EGO+NEG

I don't think I have [ever] been here [to this place]. (The location doesn't
look familiar to the speaker.)

---

[56] This sentence is similar to the sentence with the secondary verb *myong* 'have an experience' which is
more frequent in the spoken language:

ང་ས་ཆ་འདིར་སླེབས་མྱོང་ཨ་ཡོད།

nga   sa.cha   'di   - r   slebs   - myong   a.yod
I   place   this - OBL   arrive   have an experience - PERF+EPI 3+EGO+NEG
I don't think I have [ever] been here [to this place].

120

ང་ས་ཆ་འདིར་སླེབས་པ་ཨ་ཡིན།

b) *nga   sa.cha   'di   - r   slebs   - pa.a.yin*
   I   place   this - OBL come - PFV+EPI 3+EGO+NEG

[I really would be surprised if] I had ever been here [in this place] before! (The speaker is reacting to the statement of another person telling him that he has already been to this location. The speaker expresses his surprise, as he does not think so.)

6. In first person sentences, the verbal ending *a.yod* is usually not directly employed with affective verbs (see, for example, the verbs *dga'* 'love', and *zhed* 'fear', in example 231a). These verbs either combine with the ending *pa.a.yin* (231b) or they are followed by the secondary verb *myong* 'have an experience' with the ending *a.yod*. The latter implies that the speaker does not remember if something concerning him happened, or conversely, that he does not believe it happened, as in example (231c):

(231)   * ང་ཁོང་ལ་དགའ་ཨ་ཡོད།

a) * *nga   khong   - la   dga'   - a.yod*
    I   s/he+H - OBL love - PERF+EPI 3+EGO+NEG

Intended statement: I don't think I loved her.

ང་ཁོང་ལ་དགའ་པ་ཨ་ཡིན།

b) *nga   khong   - la   dga'   - pa.a.yin*
   I   s/he+H - OBL love - PFV+EPI 3+EGO+NEG

I don't think I loved her. (The speaker is thinking it over.)

ང་ཁོང་ལ་དགའ་མྱོང་ཨ་ཡོད།

c) *nga   khong   - la   dga'   myong   - a.yod*
   I   s/he+H - OBL love have an experience - PERF+EPI 3+EGO+NEG

I don't think I ever loved her. (She is not the kind of woman the speaker likes.)

2. Verbal endings used in the imperfective and in the future

There are two verbal endings of this epistemic type used in the imperfective or in the future: *gi.a.yod* and *a.yong*. Whereas *gi.a.yod* is employed in the imperfective past, the present and the future, *a.yong* is only used in the future.

The epistemic ending *gi.a.yod* is used for repeated actions: it appears in the imperfective past, in the present as in (232), and in the future as in (233). In third person sentences, *gi.a.yod* can combine with verbs of all verbal classes; it is rarely, however, used in first person sentences.

(232)   པད་མ་སློབ་སྦྱོང་བྱེད་ཀྱི་ཨ་ཡོད།

       pad.ma   *slob.sbyong*   *byed*   *- kyi.a.yod*
       Pema   study   VBZ (PRS)   - IMPF+EPI 3+EGO+NEG

       I don't think that Pema is pursuing his studies. (The speaker knows that Pema's family have no money.)

(233)   པ་ཕས་ཉི་མ་རྒྱ་གར་ལ་འགྲོ་བཅུག་གི་ཨ་ཡོད།

       pa.pha   *- s*   *nyi.ma*   *rgya.gar*   *- la*   *'gro*   *bcug*
       father   - ERG   Nyima   India   - OBL   go (PRS)   let

       - gi.a.yod
       - IMPF+EPI 3+EGO+NEG

       I strongly doubt that father will let Nyima go to India. (The speaker has this opinion because Nyima is the father's only child.)

The verbal ending *a.yong* is generally used in perfective future contexts. It can combine with verbs of all verbal classes and it is used with both the third and first persons. The lexical verb is usually in the past stem, as shown in example (234a) with the verb *'gro* 'go' in its past stem *phyin*. This epistemic ending frequently conveys a secondary connotation of hope: see example (234a) below, which conveys a similar meaning as shown in example (234b), 'I wish he wouldn't leave tomorrow':

(234)   ཁོང་སང་ཉིན་ཕྱིན་ /⸱ *   འགྲོ་ཨ་ཡོང་།

    a)   *khong*   *sang.nyin*   *phyin*   */* 'gro*   *- a.yong*
          s/he+H   tomorrow   go (PAS)   / go (PRS)   - PERF FUT+EPI 3+EGO+NEG

          1. I doubt he will leave tomorrow. (Tomorrow is a Monday. The speaker knows that his friend is usually busy on Mondays.)
          2. I wish he would not leave tomorrow. (The speaker would like for his friend not to leave tomorrow.)

          ཁོང་སང་ཉིན་མ་ཕྱིན་ན་ཡག་པ་ལ།

    b)   *khong*   *sang.nyin*   *ma*   *phyin*   *- na*   *yag*   *- pa.la*
          s/he+H   tomorrow   NEG   go (PAS)   - if   good   - ADMIRATIVE

          I wish he wouldn't leave tomorrow. (Unfortunately, however, he is going.)

Another way of expressing hope is shown in example (234c). Unlike the sentence shown in example (234b), implying that the actual situation differs from the speaker's wish, the sentence below, employing the noun *re.ba* 'hope', does not have such implications:

122

ཁོང་སང་ཉིན་མ་འགྲོ་ཡག་གི་རེ་བ་ཡོད།

c)   *khong*   *sang.nyin*   *ma*   *'gro*   *- yag*   *- gi*   *re.ba*   *yod*
       s/he+H   tomorrow   NEG   go (PRS)   - NOM   - GEN   hope   AUX (EGO)

I hope he won't leave tomorrow. (The speaker doesn't know if the person is leaving or not, but wishes he wouldn't leave.)

Similarly, in first person sentences, *a.yong* may express the meaning of hope: 'I wish I would get the money.', as in example (235):

(235)   ང་ར་དངུལ་རག་ཨ་ཡོང་།

a)   *nga*   *- r*   *dngul*   *de*   *rag*   *- a.yong*
      I   - OBL   money   that   get   - PERF FUT+EPI 3+EGO+NEG

1. I doubt I'll get the money. (The speaker's father married again and subsequently passed away. The speaker will have difficulty gaining access to his father's money.)
2. I wish I got that money. (The speaker's wish that his father's money had been bequeathed to him.)

ང་ར་དངུལ་རག་ན་ཡག་པ་ལ།

b)   *nga*   *- r*   *dngul*   *de*   *rag*   *- na*   *yag*   *- pa.la*
      I   - OBL   money   that   get   - if   (be) good   - ADMIRATIVE

I wish I got that money. Or: If only I could get that money.

<u>The differences between the verbal endings *gi.a.yod* vs. *a.yod* and *gi.a.yod* vs. *a.yong*</u>

1. The verbal endings *a.yod* and *gi.a.yod* are sometimes used in similar contexts. They both appear in present contexts, but they mark an aspectual difference of perfective vs. imperfective. Let's look at an example with the verb *bzhugs* 'stay, sit'. Although sentences in examples (236a) and (236b) convey a similar meaning, (236a) is viewed as a single perfective action, whereas (236b) is viewed as imperfective. Furthermore, unlike the perfect ending *a.yod* (237a), the imperfective ending *gi.a.yod* is also used in the future (237b) and in the imperfective past (237c):

(236)   དེང་སང་ཁོང་བཞུགས་ཨ་ཡོད།

a)   *deng.sang*   *khong*   *bzhugs*   *- a.yod*
      these days   s/he+H   stay+H   - PERF+EPI 3+EGO+NEG

I doubt he is at home these days. (lit.: 'I doubt he has stayed at home these days.' The speaker thinks that the person has gone away for several days. So he would not be at home.)

དེང་སང་ཁོང་བཞུགས་ཀྱི་ཨ་ཡོད།

b) *deng.sang* *khong* *bzhugs* - *kyi.a.yod*
   recently   s/he+H   stay+H   - IMPF+ EPI 3+EGO+NEG

I doubt he is at home these days. (Lit.: 'I doubt he stays at home these days.'
The speaker thinks that the person lives somewhere else now.)

(237) * ཁོང་མ་འོངས་པར་དགེ་རྒན་བྱས་ཨ་ཡོད།

a) * *khong* *ma.'ongs.pa* - *r* *dge.rgan* *byas* - *a.yod*
     s/he+H   future   - OBL teacher   VBZ (PAS) - PERF+EPI 3
                                                             +EGO+NEG

Intended statement: I don't think he will be a teacher in the future.

ཁོང་མ་འོངས་པར་དགེ་རྒན་བྱེད་ཀྱི་ཨ་ཡོད།

b) *khong* *ma.'ongs.pa* - *r* *dge.rgan* *byed* - *kyi.a.yod*
   s/he+H   future   - OBL teacher   VBZ (PRS) - IMPF+EPI 3+EGO+NEG

I don't think he will be a teacher in the future. (The speaker knows that the
person in question is not very studious.)

དེ་དུས་ཁོང་དགེ་རྒན་བྱེད་ཀྱི་ཨ་ཡོད།

c) *de.dus* *khong* *dge.rgan* *byed* - *kyi.a.yod*
   then   s/he+H   teacher   VBZ (PRS) - IMPF+EPI 3+EGO+NEG

I don't think he was a teacher then. (The speaker knows the person and
thinks that he was too young to be a teacher at that time.)

2. The verbal endings *gi.a.yod* and *a.yong* may both appear in future contexts, but they differ in aspect: *a.yong* implies the perfective aspect and is therefore used for perfective future actions (e.g. for expressing the speaker's doubts concerning the actuality of a single action, as seen in example 238a), whereas *gi.a.yod* conveys an imperfective aspect. Hence the latter is used for repeated and generic actions: see example (238b) below, where the speaker knows that the action in question does not usually take place, leading to his deduction that it will also not take place in the future:

(238) ཁོང་དོ་དགོང་དགོང་དག་ཡོང་ཨ་ཡོང་།

a) *khong* *do.dgong* *dgong.dag* *yong* - *a.yong*
   s/he+H   tonight   come   - PERF FUT+EPI 3+EGO+NEG

I don't think he will come tonight. (The speaker knows that the person in question is busy today.)

ཁོང་དོ་དགོང་དགོང་དག་ཡོང་གི་ཨ་ཡོད།

b) *khong   do.dgong dgong.dag   yong   - gi.a.yod*
   s/he+H   tonight   come   - IMPF+EPI 3+EGO+NEG

I don't think he is coming tonight. (The speaker knows that the person does not usually come on Mondays. Today is Monday.)

Concerning the parameter of person, as stated above, the ending *gi.a.yod* is generally used with the third person (239), whereas *a.yong* is compatible both with the third and first persons (240):

(239)   ཁོང་ཆང་འཐུང་གི་ཨ་ཡོད།

a) *khong   chang   'thung   - gi.a.yod*
   s/he+H   chang   drink (PRS)   - IMPF+EPI 3+EGO+NEG

I don't think he drinks/will drink *chang*. (The speaker knows that the person in question doesn't like alcohol.)

   * ང་ཆང་འཐུང་གི་ཨ་ཡོད།

b) * *nga   chang   'thung   - gi.a.yod*
    I   chang   drink (PRS)   - IMPF+EPI 3+EGO+NEG

Intended statement: I do not think I drink/will drink *chang*.

(240)   ཁོང་གིས་ཆང་བཏུངས་ཨ་ཡོང་།

a) *khong   chang   btungs   - a.yong*
   s/he+H   chang   drink (PAS)   - PERF FUT+EPI 3+EGO+NEG

I doubt she will drink *chang*. (The speaker knows that she was ill last night.)

   ལོ་གསར་ལ་ང་ཕལ་ཆེར་ཆང་བཏུངས་ཨ་ཡོང་།

b) *lo.gsar   - la   nga   phal.cher   chang   btungs   - a.yong*
   New year   - OBL   I   probably   chang   drink (PAS)   - PERF FUT+EPI 3
                                   +EGO+NEG

I doubt I'll drink *chang* at New Year (Losar). (The speaker doesn't like *chang*, but it's the custom to drink it at Losar. So he doesn't completely exclude the possibility of his drinking *chang*.)

To sum up, verbal endings and copulas of the type *a.yod* are very frequent in the spoken language. Apart from their core meaning of doubt and irreality, they convey a wide range of secondary meanings such as doubt, hope or fear. The copula *a.yin* used in isolation conveying a secondary meaning of surprise is especially frequent in the spoken language of Lhasa. This epistemic type, mainly the future ending *a.yong,* is often used in conditionals.

2.5 EPISTEMIC VERBAL ENDINGS AND COPULAS WITH THE MORPHEME *sa*

2.5.1 FORMAL, SEMANTIC AND PRAGMATIC CHARACTERISTICS

This type of epistemic verbal ending and copula is characterized by the morpheme *sa* appearing in the second formant after the auxiliaries *yod* or *yin* and before the auxiliary *red,* as in the perfect ending *yod.sa.red*; see example (241):

(241)　གཅིག་བྱས་ན་ཁོང་ཁ་ས་སླེབས་ཡོད་ས་རེད།

     gcig.byas.na　*khong*　*kha.sa*　*slebs*　*- yod.sa.red*
     perhaps　　　s/he+H　yesterday　arrive　- PERF+EPI 2+SENS

     It seems he arrived yesterday. (The speaker saw that his neighbour's window was open.)

Negative endings are formed by using the negative particle *ma* in front of the auxiliary *red,* e.g. *yod.sa.ma.red* (see example 242a). In the diaspora, endings with the negative auxiliaries *med* and *min* are also occasionally accepted, e.g. *med.sa.red, pa.min.sa.red* (242b) though the negation with the negative particle *ma* is generally preferred. In Lhasa, negation with *med* and *min* are considered to be ungrammatical or dialectal:[57]

(242)　ཉི་མ་སླེབས་ཡོད་ས་མ་རེད།

  a)　*nyi.ma*　*slebs*　*- yod.sa.ma.red*
     Nyima　arrive　- PERF+EPI 2+SENS+NEG

     It seems Nyima has not arrived. (The speaker makes an inference based on the fact that Nyima's car is not parked in front of the house.)

    ? ཉི་མ་སླེབས་མེད་ས་རེད།

  b)　? *nyi.ma*　*slebs*　*- med.sa.red*
      Nyima　arrive　- PERF+EPI 2+SENS+NEG

     It seems Nyima has not arrived. (The speaker makes an inference based on the fact that Nyima's car is not parked in front of the house.)

---

[57] The negative endings with the copulas *med* and *min* are used by Tibetans from the Eastern parts of historical Tibet (Kham). Thus they should be considered as dialectal. This can be illustrated by the following example: *sgo brgyab-med.sa.red* "It seems that the door is not shut." (This was uttered by a Tibetan from Kham in the taxi when he saw the driver trying to reach the handle of the back door).

The epistemic copulas of this type are the essential copulas *yin.sa.red* and *yin.sa.ma.red,* as shown in example (243), as well as the existential copulas *yod.sa.red* and *yod.sa.ma.red,* as in example (244):

(243)   ཁོ་རང་རྒྱ་མི་ཡིན་ས་རེད།

    kho.rang   rgya.mi   yin.sa.red
    he   Chinese   be (EPI 2+SENS)

He is most likely Chinese. (The speaker judges this from how he dresses.)

(244)   ཚོང་ཁང་དེར་སྨྱུ་གུ་འཚོང་ཡག་ཡོད་ས་རེད།

    tshong.khang   de - r   smyu.gu   'tshong   - yag   yod.sa.red
    shop   that - OBL   pen   sell   - NOM   exist (EPI 2+SENS)

Pens are most likely sold in that shop. Or: It seems that that shop sells pens. (The speaker makes an inference from the fact that paper and notebooks are sold in the shop.)

This epistemic type forms the following paradigm:

Affirmative endings:	Negative endings:
yod.sa.red	*yod.sa.ma.red*
pa.yin.sa.red	*pa.yin.sa.ma.red*
gi.yod.sa.red	*gi.yod.sa.ma.red*
sa.red	*sa.ma.red*

Other endings do not exist, e.g. * *gi.yin.sa.red.*

Sa-endings express a relatively high degree of certainty (higher than the construction with *mdog.kha.po,* and comparable to the type *yod.kyi.red*); they correspond, therefore, to degree EPI 2. Concerning evidentiality, in spite of the final auxiliary *red,* which usually implies the factual evidential, *sa*-endings convey sensory connotations. In implying an external (sensory) access to information: see examples (245) and (246b), they resemble the type *yod.pa. 'dra* as in (245a) or, in future contexts, to the epistemic ending *pa. 'dug* (246a); they differ, however, from the type *yod.kyi.red* which does not convey sensory connotations: see example (247).[58]

As stated above, *sa*-endings are the most frequent type of epistemic verbal ending used by the Tibetan communities of the diaspora (India, Nepal). On the contrary, they are less frequent in

---

[58] For the type *yod.pa. 'dra* see Section 2.2., for the epistemic ending *pa. 'dug,* see Section 2.7.1., and for *yod.kyi.red,* see Section 2.1.

central Tibet. Lhasa people often view them as dialectal because they are most of the time employed by Tibetans coming to Lhasa from other regions (Kham, Hor).[59] Nonetheless, they are an important part of the variety of standard Tibetan spoken in the exile community and at times they can be heard in Lhasa (see footnote 32).

(245) ཨོ། ཉི་མ་ཡིན་ས་རེད་ / ཡིན་པ་འདྲ།

a)
o	*nyi.ma*	*yin.sa.red*	/ *yin.pa. 'dra*
oh	Nyima	be (EPI 2+SENS)	/ be (EPI 2+SENS)

Oh, it seems it's Nyima. Or. It must be Nyima. (Someone has rung three times. Nyima usually rings three times, therefore the speaker thinks it is Nyima.)

ཁོང་གི་གཞས་བཏང་སྟངས་ལ་བལྟས་ན་ཁོང་གི་ཕ་ཡུལ་སྐྱིད་པོ་ཡོད་ས་རེད།

b)
khong	- *gi*	*gzhas*	*btang*	- *stangs*	- *la*	*bltas*	- *na*
s/he+H	- GEN	song	VBZ	- way	- OBL	look (PAS)	- if

khong	- *gi*	*pha.yul*	*skyid.po*	*yod.sa.red*
s/he+H	- GEN	native place	happy	exist (EPI 2+SENS)

Judging from how he sings, his native land must be a happy one.

(246) མགྱོགས་པོ་མ་ཕྱིན་ན་ཆར་པ་བཏང་པ།

a)
mgyogs.po	*ma*	- *phyin*	- *na*	*char.pa*	*btang*	- *pa*
fast	NEG	- go (PAS)	- if	rain	VBZ	- FUT+EPI 3+SENS

[We'd] better go soon. It looks like rain. (The speaker is looking at the sky.)

མགྱོགས་པོ་མ་ཕྱིན་ན་ཆར་པ་བཏང་ས་རེད།

b)
mgyogs.po	*ma*	- *phyin*	- *na*	*char.pa*	*btang*	- *sa.red*
fast	NEG	- go (PAS)	- if	rain	VBZ	- FUT+EPI 2+SENS

[We'd] better go soon. It's most likely going to rain. (The speaker is looking at the sky.)

If access to information is via sensory means, the speaker will not use the type *yod.kyi.red*:

(247) གༀ ཨོ། ཁྱེད་རང་གོ་བྱུང་ངས།

A:
o	*khyed.rang*	*go*	- *byung*	- *ngas*
oh	you+H	hear	- PFV+EGO REC	- Q

Oh, have you heard [it]?

---

[59] Compare the following sentences in Kham dialect: *kho bod.pa yin.sa.red* "He is probably Tibetan." and *kho las.ka las - bzhin.yod.sa.red* "He probably works." (*bzhin* corresponds to the connector *gi* in spoken standard Tibetan, see Gesang Jumian, Gesang Yangying 2002).

ཁཿ   ཚོགས་འཛོགས་ཀྱི་ཡོད་ས་རེད ྄ *   ཀྱི་ཡོད་ཀྱི་རེད།

B: *tshogs*   *tshogs*   *- kyi.yod.sa.red*   */ *- kyi.yod.kyi.red*
      assembly   assemble   - IMPF+EPI 2+SENS   - IMPF+EPI 2+FACT

It seems [the monks] are having a prayer assembly. (The speaker hears the sound of religious instruments.)

Sa-endings can be used with any person, although, just as other epistemic types, combinations with the first person are relatively rare as compared to those with the third person, as well as to being subject to more restrictions. The use of *sa*-endings often implies that the speaker does not remember the action clearly, or that the action is not contingent on his will. In the following example, only the third person represents grammatical use:

(248)   * ང་ར་སྤ་སེ་དོན་ཡོད་ས་རེད།

    a)   * *nga*   *- r*   *spa.se*   *don*   *- yod.sa.red*
             I   - OBL   permit   get   - PERF+EPI 2+SENS

    Intended statement: It seems I got the permit.

    སྒྲོལ་དཀར་ལ་སྤ་སེ་དོན་ཡོད་ས་རེད།

    b)   *sgrol.dkar*   *- la*   *spa.se*   *don*   *- yod.sa.red*
          Dolkar   - OBL   permit   get   - PERF+EPI 2+SENS

    Dolkar most likely got the permit. (The speaker makes an inference based on the fact that Dolkar looks happy.)

This type of epistemic ending is not frequently used in conditional sentences. Nonetheless, its use is not entirely excluded, as illustrated in example (246b). The following conditional sentence with the imperfective ending *kyi.yod.sa.red* (249a) is considered to be ungrammatical. In contrast, however, the same epistemic ending, if employed with the temporal clause *dus* 'when', is grammatical. See example (249b) below:

(249)   ང་ར་བཟི་ན་ཞབས་བྲོ་བརྒྱབ་ཀྱི་ཡོད་ས་རེད།

    a)   * *nga*   *ra.bzi*   *- na*   *zhabs.bro*   *brgyab*   *- kyi.yod.sa.red*
             I   be drunk   - if   dance   VBZ   - IMPF+EPI 2+SENS

    Intended statement: I will probably dance if I get drunk.

    ང་ར་བཟི་དུས་ཞབས་བྲོ་བརྒྱབ་ཀྱི་ཡོད་ས་རེད།

    b)   *nga*   *ra.bzi*   *- dus*   *zhabs.bro*   *brgyab*   *- kyi.yod.sa.red*
          I   be drunk   - when   dance   VBZ   - IMPF+EPI 2+SENS

    When I am drunk, I probably dance. (The speaker doesn't know what he does when he's drunk. He has some hints though, as the next day his feet usually are aching.)

Verbal endings with the morpheme *sa* can, in general, combine with various epistemic adverbs expressing different degrees of probability, such as *gcig.byas.na* 'perhaps' (see example 241 above), *spyir.btang* 'generally' and *gtan.gtan* 'certainly'.

2.5.2 DESCRIPTION OF THE VERBAL ENDINGS

1. Verbal endings of the perfective past

In the perfective past, the perfect endings *yod.sa.red* and *yod.sa.ma.red*, as well as the perfective endings *pa.yin.sa.red* and *pa.yin.sa.ma.red* are employed.

The perfect endings *yod.sa.red* and *yod.sa.ma.red* are compatible with verbs of all verbal classes when employed with the third person: see examples (250) and (251a). These verbal endings do not usually combine with the first person, as shown in examples (251b) and (252a). In first person sentences, the secondary verb *myong* 'have an experience' is inserted between the lexical verb and the verbal ending *yod.sa.red*, as seen in example (252b):

(250)   ཁོང་ཁ་ས་སླེབས་ཡོད་ས་མ་རེད།

     khong   kha.sa   slebs   - yod.sa.ma.red
     s/he+H   yesterday   arrive   - PERF+EPI 2+SENS+NEG

     It seems she didn't arrive yesterday. (The weather was very bad yesterday.)

(251)   དེབ་འདི་ཨ་མར་བརྙེད་ཡོད་ས་རེད།

   a) *deb   'di   a.ma   - r   brnyed   - yod.sa.red*
       book   this   mother   - OBL   find   - PERF+EPI 2+SENS

       It looks like Mother found the book. (The speaker saw her tidying up yesterday.)

     * དེབ་འདི་ངར་བརྙེད་ཡོད་ས་རེད།

   b) * *deb   'di   nga   - r   brnyed   - yod.sa.red*
       book   this   I   - OBL   find   - PERF+EPI 2+SENS

       Intended statement: I probably found the book.

(252)   * ངས་བོད་ཟས་འདི་བཟས་ཡོད་ས་རེད།

   a) * *nga   - s   bod.zas   'di   bzas   - yod.sa.red*
       I   - ERG   Tibetan meal   this   eat (PAS)   - PERF+EPI 2+SENS

       Intended statement: I probably ate this Tibetan meal.

ལྟོས་ཨ།   ངས་བོད་ཟས་འདི་ཟ་མྱོང་ཡོད་ས་རེད།

b) *ltos   a   nga   - s   bod.zas   'di   za*
   look (IMP) ImpP   I   - ERG   Tibetan meal   this   eat (PRS)

   myong   - yod.sa.red
   have an experience   - PERF+EPI 2+SENS

   Look! It looks like I have eaten this Tibetan meal. (It looks familiar to the speaker.)

Other verbal endings of the *sa*-type employed in past contexts are the perfective endings *pa.yin.sa.red* and *pa.yin.sa.ma.red*. Although they can be used with all verbal classes in third person sentences (see example 253), they are less frequent than the perfect endings *yod.sa.red* and *yod.sa.ma.red,* and their use with some verbs is questionable, as shown in example (254a). The perfect ending is prefered, as shown in example (254b). Just as with the corresponding verbal endings of the other epistemic types, their scope of probability generally differs from that of *yod.sa.red* and *yod.sa.ma.red.* This is illustrated in the following example, where the doubt expressed in *pa.yin.sa.ma.red* does not concern the entire action, but only the agent of the sentence:

(253)   སྐད་ཆ་འདི་བཀྲ་ཤིས་ཀྱིས་བཤད་པ་ཡིན་ས་མ་རེད།

   skad.cha   'di   bkra.shis   - kyis   bshad   - pa.yin.sa.ma.red
   speech   this   Tashi   - ERG   say   - PFV+EPI 2+SENS+NEG

   It looks like it was not Tashi who said this. (The speaker makes an inference based on the fact that the statement in question is very unlike how Tashi usually speaks. Therefore, the speaker thinks that someone else must have uttered the statement in question.)

(254)   ? པ་སངས་ལ་དངུལ་རག་པ་ཡིན་ས་རེད།

a) *? pa.sangs   - la   dngul   rag   - pa.yin.sa.red*
   Pasang   - OBL   money   get   - PFV+EPI 2+SENS

   Probably Pasang was the one who got the money.

   པ་སངས་ལ་དངུལ་རག་ཡོད་ས་རེད།

b) *pa.sangs   - la   dngul   rag   - yod.sa.red*
   Pasang   - OBL   money   get   - PERF+EPI 2+SENS

   Pasang probably got [some, a lot of] money. (The speaker saw Pasang in a shop buying many things.)

2. Verbal endings of the imperfective past, the present and the future

The following verbal endings are employed in the imperfective past, in the present or in the future: *gi.yod.sa.red, gi.yod.sa.ma.red, sa.red, sa.ma.red.*

The endings *gi.yod.sa.red* and *gi.yod.sa.ma.red* are used in imperfective contexts, i.e. in the imperfective past and the present: see example (255). They are also employed in future contexts, as shown in example (256). They combine with verbs of all verbal classes, although their use is more restricted with the first person.

(255)   སློབ་ཕྲུག་འདི་དགེ་རྒན་ལ་ཞེད་ཀྱི་ཡོད་ས་རེད།

slob.phrug	*'di*	*dge.rgan*	*- la*	*zhed*	*- kyi.yod.sa.red*
pupil	this	teacher	- OBL	be afraid	- IMPF+EPI 2+SENS

It seems this pupil is afraid of the teacher. (The speaker makes an inference based on the fact that the child does not want to go to school.)

(256)   ངར་ཆོག་མཆན་རག་གི་ཡོད་ས་མ་རེད།

nga	*- r*	*chog.mchan*	*rag*	*- gi.yod.sa.ma.red*
I	- OBL	permit	get	- IMPF+EPI 2+SENS+NEG

It seems I won't get the permit. (Many people known to the speaker were not able to get a permit.)

The endings *sa.red* and *sa.ma.red* are used only in future contexts.[60] They combine both with the third and first persons. Certain native speakers prefer the past stem of the lexical verb, whereas others employ the present-future stem.[61] The use of these epistemic endings is illustrated by the following examples:

(257)   མཚོ་མཐོང་ས་མ་རེད།

mtsho	*mthong*	*- sa.ma.red*
lake	see	- FUT+EPI 2+SENS+NEG

It seems [we] won't see the lake. (The speaker sees clouds in the sky while climbing up to the pass from where there is a view onto the lake.)

---

[60] Note that there is also a nominalized construction in SST, with the nominalizer *sa* designating the place of an action:

ཇ་ཁང་འདི་ང་འགྲོ་ས་རེད།

ja.khang	*'di*	*nga*	*'gro*	*- sa*	*red*
teahouse	this	I	go (PRS) -	NOM	be (FACT)

This tea house is where I go ([lit.: the place where I go], implying a repeated action).

[61] In the following examples, the verb *'gro* 'go' (using the past stem *phyin* or the present-future stem *'gro*) is used:

ཁོ་ཕྱིན་ས་རེད།   ཁོ་འགྲོ་ས་རེད།

a)	*kho*	*phyin*	*- sa.red*		b)	*kho*	*'gro*	*- sa.red*
	s/he+H	go(PAS)	-FUT+EPI 2+SENS			s/he+H	go (PRS)	- FUT+EPI 2+SENS
	It seems he will go.					It seems he will go.		

132

(258)　　　ང་ན་ས་རེད།

> *nga*　　*na*　　- *sa.red*[62]
> I　　　be ill　　- FUT+EPI 2+SENS

It seems I am going to fall ill. (The speaker is not feeling well.)

(259)　　　ལས་ཀ་འདི་ང་ར་རག་ས་མ་རེད།

> *las.ka*　　*'di*　　*nga*　　- *r*　　*rag*　　- *sa.ma.red*
> job　　　this　　I　　　- OBL　　get　　- FUT+EPI 2+SENS+NEG

It seems I won't get this job. (The speaker sees many other people applying for the same job.)

To conclude, epistemic endings and copulas with the morpheme *sa* demonstrate geographic variations in epistemic verbal endings and copulas: they are very frequent among Tibetan speakers in the diaspora, but rarely used by native Lhasa speakers. Apart from the imperfective ending *gi.yod.sa.red*, which appears in future contexts, this type has another verbal ending that is only used in the future: *sa.red*. Although *sa*-type endings are at times employed in conditionals, their use is infrequent, and other types are generally preferred.

---

[62] This sentence is similar to the sentence with the epistemic ending *pa.'dug* (for more detail on *pa.'dug* see section 2.7):

ང་ན་པ་འདུག

> *nga*　　*na*　　- *pa.'dug*
> I　　　be ill　　- FUT+EPI 3+SENS
> I must be falling ill.

2.6 EPISTEMIC CONSTRUCTIONS WITH THE SUFFIX *mdog.kha.po*

2.6.1 FORMAL, SEMANTIC AND PRAGMATIC CHARACTERISTICS

This construction consists of the epistemic suffix *mdog.kha.po* preceded by an evidential ending, as in example (260a); or directly attached to the lexical verb, as in example (260b), and followed by the auxiliary *red* or *'dug,* or exceptionally by *yod*.[63] As stated in section 1.2.2.1.1., this construction is in the process of grammaticalization into an epistemic verbal ending, but this process is still ongoing. As a result, it can still be broken down into three parts, as in example (260a): the first element conveys tense-aspect (*yod*), the second element conveys epistemic modality (*mdog.kha.po*), and the third conveys evidential meaning (*red*). The construction with the egophoric auxiliary *yod* stands on the periphery of standard spoken Tibetan as it is rarely used and it does not form an entire paradigm (**pa.yin-mdog.kha.po-yod*). [64] The sentences with the suffix *mdog.kha.po* are usually negated with the negative particles *ma,* as in example (260a), and *mi,* as in example (260b). These are placed in front of the auxiliaries *red* and *'dug,* respectively.

(260) ཁོང་གིས་རི་མོ་འདི་བྲིས་ཡོད་མདོག་ཁ་པོ་མ་རེད།

a) | *khong* | *- gis* | *ri.mo* | *'di* | *bris* | *- yod* |
|---|---|---|---|---|---|
| s/he+H | - ERG | picture | this | draw (PAS) | - PERF AUX |

- mdog.kha.po	*- ma.red*
- EPI 1	- AUX (FACT+NEG)

She perhaps didn't draw this picture. (She is not good at drawing.)

ཁོང་ཡོང་མདོག་ཁ་པོ་མི་འདུག

b) | *khong* | *yong* | *- mdog.kha.po* | *- mi.'dug* |
|---|---|---|---|
| s/he+H | come | - EPI 1 | - AUX (SENS+NEG) |

It looks like he isn't coming. (He was supposed to arrive at ten o'clock. It is now half past ten.)

Some non-Lhasa born Tibetans also accept sentences with the negative auxiliary *med* instead of *yod* in front of the suffix *mdog.kha.po* (see example 261) as grammatical. Nonetheless, they

---

[63] Certain native speakers also accept constructions with the auxiliary *yod.red*.

[64] The use of the suffix *mdog.kha.po* with the egophoric auxiliary *yod* should be perhaps considered as outdated due to the disagreement among native speakers on the acceptability of this construction. Sentences with this construction were for the most part accepted by the older generation, but rejected by the younger generation.

suggest that this method of negation is infrequent as such sentences are more difficult to understand. In addition, other Tibetans do not accept these negative constructions or copulas. In consequence, this method of negation—as concerns the cases listed below— should be considered as marginal or dialectal:

- constructions with *med - mdog.kha.po - red* and *gi.med - mdog.kha.po - red*
- constructions with *med - mdog.kha.po - 'dug* and *gi.med - mdog.kha.po - 'dug*
- copulas with *min - mdog.kha.po - red* and *med - mdog.kha.po - red*
- copulas with *min - mdog.kha.po - 'dug* and *med - mdog.kha.po - 'dug*

(261)　？ ཁོང་གིས་ཡི་གེ་བྲིས་མེད་མདོག་ཁ་པོ་རེད།

?	*khong*	*- gis*	*yi.ge*	*bris*	*- med*	*- mdog.kha.po*	*- red*
	s/he+H	- ERG	letter	write (PAS)	- PERF AUX (NEG)	- EPI 1	- AUX (FACT)

Maybe she wasn't writing letters.

The copulas with the suffix *mdog.kha.po* are formed in the following way: the suffix *mdog.kha.po* follows either the copula *yin* or *yod* to form the epistemic copulas listed below (either an essential copula, as seen in example 262, or an existential copula, as seen in example 263a):

- *yin-mdog.kha.po- 'dug* and *yin-mdog.kha.po-mi. 'dug*
- *yin-mdog.kha.po-red* and *yin-mdog.kha.po-ma.red*

(262)　ཁོང་དགེ་རྒན་ཡིན་མདོག་ཁ་པོ་རེད།

a)
khong	*dge.rgan*	*yin*	*- mdog.kha.po*	*- red*
s/he+H	teacher	be	- EPI 1	- AUX (FACT)

It looks like he is a teacher. (The speaker often sees him leaving the university.)

ཁོང་དགེ་རྒན་ཡིན་མདོག་ཁ་པོ་འདུག

b)
khong	*dge.rgan*	*yin*	*- mdog.kha.po*	*- 'dug*
s/he+H	teacher	be	- EPI 1	- AUX (SENS)

He looks like a teacher. (The speaker makes an inference based on the fact that the person wears glasses.)

- *yod-mdog.kha.po- 'dug* and *yod-mdog.kha.po-mi. 'dug*
- *yod-mdog.kha.po-red* and *yod-mdog.kha.po-ma.red*

(263)   འདི་ཡག་པོ་ཡོད་མདོག་ཁ་པོ་མི་འདུག

a)   *'di*   *yag.po*   *yod*   - *mdog.kha.po*   - *mi.'dug*
     this   good   exist   - EPI 1   - AUX (SENS+NEG)

This doesn't look [seem to be] good. (The speaker makes a guess based on the appearance of something.)

A similar meaning to the one expressed above in example (263a) can also be conveyed by using the short (monosyllabic) form of the adjective *yag.po* 'good', *yag* 'to be good', followed by the suffix *mdog.kha.po* and the auxiliary *'dug*:

    འདི་ཡག་མདོག་ཁ་པོ་མི་འདུག

b)   *'di*   *yag*   - *mdog.kha.po*   - *mi.'dug*
     this   be good   - EPI 1   - AUX (SENS+NEG)

This doesn't look [seem to be] good.

Mdog.kha.po-copulas with the final auxiliary *yod* are very infrequent, and generally are not accepted, as in example (264a). Instead, the corresponding copulas with *red* are used, as in example (264b):

(264)   ?   ཁོང་བོད་ཇ་རདགའ་པོ་ཡོད་མདོག་ཁ་པོ་ཡོད།

a)   ?   *khong*   *bod.ja*   - *r*   *dga'.po*   *yod*   - *mdog.kha.po*   - *yod*
       s/he+H   Tibetan tea   - OBL   like   exist   - EPI 1   - AUX (EGO)

It seems to me that he likes Tibetan tea. (The speaker is not sure but he recalls the two of them drinking Tibetan tea together.)

    ཁོང་བོད་ཇ་རདགའ་པོ་ཡོད་མདོག་ཁ་པོ་རེད།

b)   *khong*   *bod.ja*   - *r*   *dga'.po*   *yod*   - *mdog.kha.po*   - *red*
     s/he+H   Tibetan tea   - OBL   like   exist   - EPI 1   - AUX (FACT)

It's probable that he likes Tibetan tea. (The speaker infers this from the fact that the person in question likes Tibetan food.)

Below is a list of the constructions employing the suffix *mdog.kha.po*:

Evidential ending	Epistemic suffix	Affirmative or negative auxiliary	
yod	*mdog.kha.po*	*red*	*ma.red*
yod	*mdog.kha.po*	*'dug*	*mi.'dug*
pa.yin	*mdog.kha.po*	*red*	*ma.red*
pa.yin	*mdog.kha.po*	*'dug*	*mi.'dug*
gi.yod gi.yod	*mdog.kha.po*	*red*	*ma.red*
–	*mdog.kha.po*	*'dug*	*mi.'dug*
–	*mdog.kha.po*	*red*	*ma.red*
	mdog.kha.po	*'dug*	*mi.'dug*

yod	*mdog.kha.po*	*yod*	*med*
gi.yod	*mdog.kha.po*	*yod*	*med*
–	*mdog.kha.po*	*yod*	*med*

In addition, there is a construction employing the suffix *mdog*: it is *yod-mdog-'dug,* which is also sometimes used in SST.

Other combinations cannot be formed with the suffix *mdog.kha.po,* e.g.: **gi.yin-mdog.kha.po-'dug* (265)*, *gi.yin-mdog.kha.po-red,* or **gi-mdog.kha.po-red.* Similarly, combinations with the egophoric auxiliary *yin,* even in first person sentences, as seen in example (266a), are not possible. Instead, the auxiliary *red* must be used: see example (266b). Since the suffix *mdog.kha.po* cannot function as a verb, it is also impossible to combine it with past endings such as *bzhag, song* and *byung,* e.g. **mdog.kha.po - bzhag, *yod-mdog.kha.po - song.*

(265)   * ཕུར་བུ་སྐོར་བ་འགྲོ་གི་ཡིན་མདོག་ཁ་པོ་འདུག

     * *phur.bu*   *skor.ba*   *'gro*   - *gi.yin*   - *mdog.kha.po*   - *'dug*
     Phurbu   circumbulation   go (PRS)   - FUT   - EPI 1   - AUX (SENS)

Intended statement: It seems Phurbu will perform circumbulations.

(266)   * ང་ཚོ་གཅིག་བྱས་ན་སང་ཉིན་འགྲོ་མདོག་ཁ་པོ་ཡིན།

  a) * *nga* - *tsho* *gcig.byas.na* *sang.nyin* *'gro* - *mdog.kha.po*
     I - pl perhaps tomorrow go (PRS) - EPI 1

  - *yin*
  - AUX (EGO)

Intended statement: Maybe we will leave tomorrow.

137

ང་ཚོ་གཅིག་བྱས་ན་སང་ཉིན་འགྲོ་མདོག་ཁ་པོ་རེད།

b) *nga - tsho gcig.byas.na sang.nyin 'gro - mdog.kha.po*
   I - pl perhaps tomorrow go (PRS) - EPI 1

- red
- AUX (FACT)

Maybe we will leave tomorrow. (Always, at this time of year, the speaker and the others go to plant trees. Someone is asking him when they will leave.)

The final auxiliary *red* is compatible only with verbs, and not with adjectives (or adjectival verbs) used in the predicate, as seen in example (267). In the case of predicative adjectives, the short (monosyllabic) form is used (for ex. *zhim.po* 'tasty' is shortened to *zhim* 'to be tasty'); it is then followed by *mdog.kha.po* and the auxiliary *'dug*. It is also possible to place another word between *mdog.kha.po* and the copula *'dug*: note the use of the indefinite article *cig* 'a' in example (268). This is impossible when the construction *mdog.kha.po-'dug* is employed after verbs, or with the auxiliary *red*, as shown in example (269):

(267)   * ཁ་ལག་འདི་ཞིམ་མདོག་ཁ་པོ་རེད།

         * *kha.lag 'di zhim - mdog.kha.po - red*
           meal this be tasty - EPI 1 - AUX (SENS)

         Intended statement: This meal could be nice.

(268)   ཁ་ལག་འདི་ཞིམ་མདོག་ཁ་པོ་ཅིག་འདུག

         kha.lag 'di zhim - mdog.kha.po cig 'dug
         meal this tasty - EPI 1 a AUX (SENS)

         This meal could be nice. (It looks tasty.)

(269)   * ཁོང་སང་ཉིན་འགྲོ་མདོག་ཁ་པོ་ཅིག་འདུག / རེད།

         * *khong sang.nyin 'gro - mdog.kha.po cig 'dug / red*
           s/he+H tomorrow go (PRS) - EPI 1 a AUX (SENS) /AUX (FACT)

         Intended statement: It seems he will leave tomorrow.

It is also possible to use the auxiliaries *yod.red,* as in example (270a), and *yod* after a predicative adjective, although the use of the egophoric auxiliary *yod* is very restricted. Its use in this context is not accepted by all native speakers, as seen in example (270b): [65]

---

[65] Instead, the following sentence with the suffix *mdog.kha.po* sounds more natural to native speakers:

ཁ་ལག་འདི་ངས་ཞིམ་མདོག་ཁ་པོ་བཟོས་ཡོད།

kha.lag 'di nga - s zhim mdog.kha.po bzos - yod
food this I - ERG tasty EPI 1 VBZ (PAS) - PERF+EGO

It seems I cooked the meal [in such a way that it came out] tasty.

138

(270)　　　ཁ་ལག་འདི་ཞིམ་མདོག་ཁ་པོ་ཡོད་རེད།

　　a)　*kha.lag*　*'di*　*zhim*　*- mdog.kha.po*　*- yod.red*
　　　　meal　　　this　　be tasty　- EPI 1　　　　- AUX (FACT)

　　The meal should be nice. (Statement of general fact)

　　　?　ཁ་ལག་འདི་ཞིམ་མདོག་ཁ་པོ་ཡོད།

　　b)　*?*　*kha.lag*　*'di*　*zhim*　*- mdog.kha.po*　*- yod*
　　　　meal　　　this　　be tasty　- EPI 1　　　　- AUX (EGO)

　　The meal should be nice. (The speaker cooked the meal.)

The degree of certainty of the speaker using a *mdog.kha.po*-construction is similar to that conveyed by the type *yod.'gro*, corresponding to degree EPI 1. It is used when the speaker utters an assumption based on the external appearance of things and situations.[66] Moreover, *mdog.kha.po*-constructions differ in evidential modality, depending on the final auxiliary employed: *red* is factual, *'dug* sensory, and *yod* egophoric. These constructions are quite frequent in the spoken language in Lhasa. They are, in general, not used in the diaspora.

Difference between the constructions *mdog.kha.po-red* and *mdog.kha.po-'dug*

Concerning combinations of the suffix *mdog.kha.po* with verbs, there is a difference between the use of the final auxiliaries *'dug* and *red*. The first variation, *mdog.kha.po-'dug,* is generally used when the speaker has discovered something for the first time; it is related to the present moment, as seen in example (271a). This construction resembles the type *yod.bzo.'dug* (see Section 2.11). The other auxiliary, *red*, conveys a more general impact. It is used for repeated actions, implying that the speaker has general knowledge of the situation: he has not discovered it just at the moment of his utterance, as in example (271b).[67]

(271)　　　ཆར་པ་བཏང་མདོག་ཁ་པོ་འདུག

　　a)　*char.pa*　*btang*　*- mdog.kha.po*　*- 'dug*
　　　　rain　　　VBZ　　- EPI 1　　　　- AUX (SENS)

　　　It looks like it is going to rain. (Looking at the sky, the speaker makes an
　　　inference based on the fact that the sky is cloudy.)

---

[66] The words *mdog* and *mdog.kha* (or *kha.dog*) originally mean 'colour' (figuratively, 'outer appearance'), *kha.po* corresponds to 'appearance', 'form'. *Mdog* also appears in the verb *mdog byed* 'pretend'. The expression *mdog.kha.po* became grammaticalized and now functions as a means of expressing probability. The *mdog.kha.po*-construction is translated into Chinese by *kàn yàngzi kěnéng* 'looking at the appearance, it seems …' or *wàibiǎo hǎoxiàng* 'the exterior seems…' See *Bod-rgya shan-sbyar gyi lha-sa-'i kha-skad tshig-mdzod* (1983: 518).

[67] Some Tibetan speakers suggest that constructions with *mdog.kha.po* and the auxiliary *red* are more common in the spoken language than constructions with *'dug*.

ཆར་པ་བཏང་མདོག་ཁ་པོ་རེད།

b) *char.pa*   *btang*   *- mdog.kha.po*   *- red*
    rain   VBZ   - EPI 1   - AUX (FACT)

It is likely that it will rain. (The speaker thinks this because it is May, and it usually rains in May.)

Difference between the constructions *mdog.kha.po-red* and *mdog.kha.po-yod*

The constructions *mdog.kha.po-red* and *mdog.kha.po-yod* differ in tense and evidential meaning. Whereas *mdog.kha.po-red* is usually used for actions following the moment of utterance and is factual, *mdog.kha.po-yod* is used for actions preceding the moment of utterance and is egophoric.

If there is no indication of time, sentences with *mdog.kha.po-red* are generally interpreted as being in the future tense (272a). The construction *mdog.kha.po-red* can also be used with the adverb *da.lta* 'now'. Its use in past contexts is questionable; Tibetan speakers disagree on the acceptability of this construction in past contexts: see its use with the adverb *kha.sa* 'yesterday' in example (272b). Certain native speakers instead suggest the usage shown in example (272c):

(272)   ཁོང་(སང་ཉིན་ / ད་ལྟ་) འགྲོ་མདོག་ཁ་པོ་རེད།

a) *khong*   *(sang.nyin / da.lta)*   *'gro*   *- mdog.kha.po*   *- red*
    s/he+H   (tomorrow / now)   go (PRS)   - EPI 1   - AUX (FACT)

She will probably leave (tomorrow/now). (The speaker makes an inference based on the fact that tomorrow/the present moment is favourable for departure.)

?   ཁོང་ཁ་ས་འགྲོ་ / ཕྱིན་མདོག་ཁ་པོ་རེད།

b) *?*   *khong*   *kha.sa*   *'gro /phyin*   *- mdog.kha.po*   *- red*
          s/he+H   yesterday   go (PRS)/(PAS)   - EPI 1   - AUX (FACT)

She probably left yesterday.

ཁོང་ཁ་ས་ཕྱིན་ཡོད་མདོག་ཁ་པོ་རེད།

c) *khong*   *kha.sa*   *phyin*   *- yod*   *- mdog.kha.po*   *- red*
    s/he+H   yesterday   go (PAS)   - PERF   - EPI 1   - AUX (FACT)

She probably left yesterday. (It was Saturday.)

It should be emphasized that, as stated above, constructions with the egophoric auxiliary *yod* are not considered grammatical by certain native speakers. If a specific time period is not designated, *mdog.kha.po-yod* refers to a past action; in example (273a) it designates the perfective past. When the adverb *da.lta* 'now' is used, it implies the present perfect tense, as an example (273b).

140

(273)   ཁོང་ལྷ་སར་འགྲོ་མདོག་ཁ་པོ་ཡོད།

a)

khong	*lha.sa*	*- r*	*'gro*	*- mdog.kha.po*	*- yod*
s/he+H	Lhasa	- OBL	go (PRS)	- EPI 1	- AUX (EGO)

She perhaps went to Lhasa. (A reply to the question as to where she has gone. She had told the speaker she would go to Lhasa.)

ཁོང་ད་ལྟ་ལྷ་སར་འགྲོ་མདོག་ཁ་པོ་ཡོད།

b)

khong	*da.lta*	*lha.sa*	*- r*	*'gro*	*- mdog.kha.po*	*- yod*
s/he+H	now	Lhasa	- OBL	go (PRS)	- EPI 1	- AUX (EGO)

She has perhaps left for Lhasa by now. (She told the speaker that she would leave at noon. It is now half past twelve.)

Although it is possible to employ *mdog.kha.po*-constructions with any person, first person sentences are less frequent. The final auxiliary *red* is usually used with the first person: see example (274) with *gi.yod-mdog.kha.po-red*, and example (275) with *yod-mdog.kha.po-red*. Constructions that employ final auxiliaries *yod* and *'dug* are either incompatible or infrequently used with the first person, as in example (275).

(274)   ངར་ལྡེ་མིག་བརྙེད་ཀྱི་ཡོད་མདོག་ཁ་པོ་རེད།

nga	*- r*	*lde.mig*	*de*	*brnyed*	*- ki.yod*	*- mdog.kha.po*	*- red*
I	- OBL	key	that	find	- IMPF	- EPI 1	- AUX (FACT)

I might find the key. (The speaker lost his key while he was going somewhere. But he has not gone far, so there is a chance of finding the key.)

(275)   ང་ཆུང་དུས་གདུག་འདྲེར་ཞེད་ཡོད་མདོག་ཁ་པོ་རེད་ ⌠? འདུག ⌠* ཡོད།

nga	*chung*	*- dus*	*gdug.'dre*	*- r*	*zhed*	*- yod*
I	be small	- when	demon	- OBL	be afraid	- PERF

- mdog.kha.po	*- red*	*/ ? - 'dug*	*/* - yod*
- EPI 1	- AUX (FACT)	/ - AUX (SENS)	/ - AUX (EGO)

When I was a child, I was perhaps afraid of demons.

It is possible to use constructions with the suffix *mdog.kha.po* in conditional sentences. Below are two examples of past counterfactual conditions with the third person, as seen in example (276a), and the first person, as seen in example (276b):

(276)   མི་གཞན་དག་གིས་རོགས་པ་མ་བྱས་ན་བཀྲ་ཤིས་ཤི་ཡོད་མདོག་ཁ་པོ་རེད།

a)

mi	*gzhan.dag*	*- gis*	*rogs.pa*	*ma*	*- byas*	*- na*
person	other	- ERG	help	NEG	- VBZ (PAS)	- if

bkra.shis	*shi*	*- yod*	*- mdog.kha.po*	*- red*
Tashi	die	- PERF	- EPI 1	- AUX (FACT)

If others hadn't helped him, Tashi probably would have died. (Tashi was wounded and he was bleeding a lot.)

སྨན་མ་བཟས་ན་ང་ཤི་ཡོད་མདོག་ཁ་པོ་རེད།

b)
sman	*ma*	*- bzas*	*- na*	*nga*	*shi*	*- yod*
medicine	NEG	- eat (PAS)	- if	I	die	- PERF

- mdog.kha.po	*- red*
- EPI 1	- AUX (FACT)

If I hadn't taken the medicine, I would have probably died. (My illness was serious.)

Generally speaking, it is possible to use various epistemic adverbs with *mdog.kha.po*-constructions, with the exception of *mdog.kha.po-yod*. This is illustrated in an example (277), employing the adverb *phal.cher* 'probably'. Other adverbs such as *gcig.byas.na* 'perhaps', *gtan.gtan* 'certainly', and *brgya.cha.brgya* 'definitely' may also be used.

(277) བྱམས་པ་ཕལ་ཆེར་གཞིས་ཀ་རྩེར་འགྲོ་མདོག་ཁ་པོ་རེད།

byams.pa	*phal.cher*	*gzhis.ka.rtse*	*- r*	*'gro*	*- mdog.kha.po*
Champa	probably	Shigatse	- OBL	go (PRS)	- EPI 1

- red
- AUX (FACT)

Champa will probably go to Shigatse. (The speaker makes an inference based on the fact that Champa's wife is from Shigatse.)

2.6.2 DESCRIPTION OF *mdog.kha.po*-CONSTRUCTIONS

2.6.2.1 Use of *mdog.kha.po*-constructions with the final auxiliaries *red* and *'dug* in the perfective past

In the perfective past, the following constructions are employed: *yod-mdog.kha.po-red* and *yod-mdog.kha.po-ma.red, yod-mdog.kha.po-'dug* and *yod-mdog.kha.po-mi.'dug, yod-mdog-'dug* and *yod-mdog-mi.'dug, pa.yin-mdog.kha.po-red* and *pa.yin-mdog.kha.po-ma.red, pa.yin-mdog.kha.po-'dug* and *pa.yin-mdog.kha.po-mi.'dug.*

1. a) Constructions with *yod-mdog.kha.po-red* and *yod-mdog.kha.po-ma.red*

   b) Constructions with *yod-mdog.kha.po-'dug* and *yod-mdog.kha.po-mi.'dug*

The constructions *yod-mdog.kha.po-red / yod-mdog.kha.po-ma.red*, as in example (278a), and *yod-mdog.kha.po-'dug / yod-mdog.kha.po-mi.'dug,* as in example (278b), are used in perfective contexts. They are generally compatible with verbs of all verbal classes of all persons: see example (279) for third person use, and example (280) for first person use. The lexical verb is in the past stem.

142

(278) འབྲོག་པས་གཡག་བསད་ཡོད་མདོག་ཁ་པོ་རེད།

a)
'brog.pa	- s	g.yag	bsad	- yod	- mdog.kha.po	- red
nomad	- ERG	yak	kill	- PERF	- EPI 1	- AUX (FACT)

The nomads perhaps killed a yak. (The speaker makes an inference based on the fact that it will be winter soon.)

འབྲོག་པ་འདི་ཚོས་གཡག་བསད་ཡོད་མདོག་ཁ་པོ་འདུག

b)
'brog.pa	'di	- tsho	- s	g.yag	bsad	- yod	- mdog.kha.po
nomad	this	- pl	- ERG	yak	kill	- PERF	- EPI 1

- 'dug
- AUX (SENS)

It looks like these nomads killed a yak. (A reply to the question as to what the nomads were doing in the city. The speaker makes an inference based on the fact that he saw them in the city with a huge load, which was probably yak meat.)

(279) ད་ལྟ་ཁོང་ལྷ་སར་བསྡད་ཡོད་མདོག་ཁ་པོ་རེད།

da.lta	khong	lha.sa	- r	bsdad	- yod	- mdog.kha.po
now	s/he+H	Lhasa	- OBL	stay	- PERF	- EPI 1

- red
- AUX (FACT)

Maybe she is staying in Lhasa now. (The speaker infers from the fact that she usually resides in Lhasa at the beginning of the month.)

(280) ང་ར་བཟི་ཡོད་མདོག་ཁ་པོ་རེད།

nga	ra.bzi	- yod	- mdog.kha.po	- red
I	be drunk	- PERF	- EPI 1	- AUX (FACT)

I was perhaps drunk. (The speaker is told by someone else that he said something he does not remember. The speaker therefore infers that he must have been drunk.)

Just as with other epistemic types, in first person sentences Tibetan speakers usually prefer the secondary verb *myong* 'have an experience' to follow the lexical verb and precede the *mdog.kha.po-* construction: this is demonstrated in example (281a). This kind of sentence is preferred to that shown in example (281b) which does not employ the secondary verb:

(281) ང་ཆུང་དུས་ཕྱག་དབང་རག་མྱོང་ཡོད་མདོག་ཁ་པོ་རེད།

a)
nga	chung	- dus	phyag.dbang	rag	myong	- yod
I	be small	- when	blessing	get	have an experience	- PERF

- mdog.kha.po	- red
- EPI 1	- AUX (FACT)

When I was a child, supposedly I got a blessing (from a lama). (The speaker doesn't recall clearly as he was a child at the time.)

? ང་ཆུང་དུས་ཕྱག་དབང་རག་ཡོད་མདོག་ཁ་པོ་རེད།

b) *? nga   chung   - dus   phyag.dbang   rag   - yod   -mdog.kha.po*
     I   be small - when   blessing   get   - PERF   -EPI 1

- red
- AUX (FACT)

When I was a child, I supposedly got a blessing (from a lama).

2. Constructions with *yod-mdog-'dug* and *yod-mdog-mi.'dug*

The constructions *yod-mdog-'dug* and *yod-mdog-mi.'dug* are also used in perfective contexts. In general, they resemble the constructions *yod-mdog.kha.po-'dug / yod-mdog.kha.po-mi.'dug*. Nonetheless, native speakers suggest that they express a higher degree of certainty and are less frequent than constructions containing the suffix *mdog.kha.po*.[68] Below is an example of the use of *yod-mdog-'dug*:

(282)   ཁོང་གིས་ཤ་བཟས་ཡོད་མདོག་འདུག

            khong   - gis   sha   bzas   - yod   - mdog   - 'dug
            s/he+H - ERG   meat   eat (PAS) - PERF - EPI 2   - AUX (SENS)

            It looks like he ate some meat. (The speaker sees shreds of meat around the person's mouth.)

3. a) Constructions with *pa.yin-mdog.kha.po-red* and *pa.yin-mdog.kha.po-ma.red*
b) Constructions with *pa.yin-mdog.kha.po-'dug* and *pa.yin-mdog.kha.po-mi.'dug*

These constructions are less frequent than constructions using *yod-mdog.kha.po-red /ma.red* and *yod-mdog.kha.po-'dug /mi.'dug,* and their scope of probability is also different, as shown in example (283). They are employed in the perfective past and are compatible with all verbal classes. The lexical verb is in the past stem. They are used only infrequently in first person sentences, as shown in example (284):

(283)   ཁོང་གིས་ཀུ་ཤུ་བཟས་པ་ཡིན་མདོག་ཁ་པོ་མ་རེད།

            khong   - gis   ku.shu   bzas   - pa.yin   - mdog.kha.po
            s/he+H - ERG   apple   eat (PAS) - PFV   - EPI 1
            - ma.red
            - AUX (FACT+NEG)

            It pehaps wasn't apples she was eating. (The speaker has been asked if she was eating apples. He makes his inference based on the fact that she usually doesn't eat apples and similar fruit.)

---

[68] Tibetan consultants suggest that this construction is mostly used by the older generation.

(284)   དེབ་འདི་ངས་ཉོས་པ་ཡིན་མདོག་ཁ་པོ་རེད།

> *deb   'di   nga   -s   nyos   -pa.yin   -mdog.kha.po*
> book   this   I   -ERG   buy (PAS)   -PFV   -EPI 1
>
> *-red*
> -AUX (FACT)

> I perhaps bought this book. (The speaker tends to purchase many books about history. The book in question is also a book about history, so he thinks that he may have bought it himself, as opposed to someone else. He isn't sure, though.)

2.6.2.2 Use of *mdog.kha.po*-constructions with the final auxiliaries *red* and *'dug* in the imperfective and in the future

In the imperfective and in the future, the following constructions are used: *gi.yod-mdog.kha.po-red* and *gi.yod-mdog.kha.po-ma.red, gi.yod-mdog.kha.po-'dug* and *gi.yod-mdog.kha.po-mi.'dug, mdog.kha.po-red* and *mdog.kha.po-ma.red, mdog.kha.po-'dug* and *mdog.kha.po-mi.'dug.*

1. a) Constructions with *gi.yod-mdog.kha.po-red* and *gi.yod-mdog.kha.po-ma.red*
   b) Constructions with *gi.yod-mdog.kha.po-'dug* and *gi.yod-mdog.kha.po-mi.'dug*

The constructions *gi.yod-mdog.kha.po-red / gi.yod-mdog.kha.po-ma.red,* shown in example (285), and *gi.yod-mdog.kha.po-'dug / gi.yod-mdog.kha.po-mi.'dug,* shown in example (286), are compatible with verbs of all verbal classes in the imperfective past, as in example (285a), the present (example 286), and the future (example 285b). As stated above, when used without any specific time indication, constructions with the auxiliary *red* are generally interpreted as taking place in the future; see example (285b).

(285)   དེ་དུས་ཁོང་བོད་སྐད་སྦྱང་གི་ཡོད་མདོག་ཁ་པོ་མ་རེད།

> a) *de.dus   khong   bod.skad   sbyang   -gi.yod   -mdog.kha.po*
>   then   s/he+H   Tibetan language   learn   -IMPF   -EPI 1
>
>   *-ma.red*
>   -AUX (FACT+NEG)

> It looks like she was not learning Tibetan then. (The speaker makes an inference based on the fact that she was only ten at that time.)

ཁློ་བཟང་ཁོ་དང་སྐད་ཆ་བཤད་ཀྱི་ཡོད་མདོག་ཁ་པོ་རེད།

b) *blo.bzang*   *kho*   *dang*   *skad.cha*   *bshad*   *- kyi.yod*
    Lobzang   he   ASSOC   speech   say   - IMPF

    - mdog.kha.po   *- red*
    - EPI 1   - AUX (FACT)

Lobzang will probably talk to him. (Lobzang hasn't been speaking to the person in question, because they had quarreled. A long time has elapsed since the quarrel, however, so the speaker thinks Lobzang will talk to the person again.)

(286)   མོ་རང་དུག་ལོག་འདི་གོན་གྱི་ཡོད་མདོག་ཁ་པོ་མི་འདུག

    mo.rang   *dug.log*   *'di*   *gon*   *- gyi.yod*   *- mdog.kha.po*   *- mi.'dug*
    she   clothes   this   wear   - IMPF   - EPI 1   - AUX
                                                                             (SENS+NEG)

It looks like she doesn't wear this dress. (The speaker has not seen her wearing it.)

2. a) Constructions with *mdog.kha.po-red* and *mdog.kha.po-ma.red*

These constructions are generally used in a prospective context (the present inference of a future action forecast as an expected outcome, as shown in example 287); they may, however, appear as well in a present context. These constructions are frequent in the spoken language and are compatible with all verbal classes. The lexical verb is in the present-future stem.

(287)   བསྟན་པར་དངུལ་རག་མདོག་ཁ་པོ་མ་རེད།

    a) *bstan.pa*   *- r*   *dngul*   *rag*   *- mdog.kha.po*   *- ma.red*
        Tenpa   - OBL   money   get   - EPI 1   - AUX (FACT+NEG)

    Tenpa won't probably get [any] money. (Tenpa bet in a lottery. But the chances of winning are very small.)

    ཁོང་ཁམས་ལ་འགྲོ་མདོག་ཁ་པོ་རེད།

    b) *khong*   *khams*   *- la*   *'gro*   *- mdog.kha.po*   *- red*
        s/he+H   Kham   - OBL   go (PRS)   - EPI 1   - AUX (FACT)

    She will probably go to Kham. (The speaker knows that she has been thinking of going there for a long time.)

Although *mdog.kha.po-red* may appear in first person sentences, its use is more restricted than with the third person. Its preferred combination is with non-controllable verbs, as it is more natural to use an epistemic ending with the first person when the action cannot be controlled by the speaker, or when it is not contingent upon his will. See example (288) below with the non-controllable verb *slebs* 'get to, arrive':

146

(288) གཅིག་བྱས་ན་ང་རྗེས་མ་རྒྱ་གར་ལ་སླེབས་མདོག་ཁ་པོ་རེད།

gcig.byas.na	nga	rjes.ma	rgya.gar	- la	slebs	- mdog.kha.po
perhaps	I	later	India	- OBL	arrive	- EPI 1

- red
- AUX (FACT)

It seems I will get to India one day. (The speaker thinks he has a chance of getting a visa.)

b) Constructions with *mdog.kha.po-'dug* and *mdog.kha.po-mi.'dug*

The constructions *mdog.kha.po-'dug* and *mdog.kha.po-mi.'dug* are usually used in a present context, as shown in example (289a), or a near future context, as shown in example (289b). In both cases, the speaker hazards a guess based on appearance (the sensory evidential):

(289) ཁོང་དབྱིན་ཇི་སྐད་ཤེས་མདོག་ཁ་པོ་མི་འདུག

a)

khong	dbyin.ji.skad	shes	- mdog.kha po	- mi.'dug
s/he+H	English language	know	- EPI 1	- AUX (SENS+NEG)

It looks like she does not know English. (The speaker infers from the fact that she is not talking to anyone.)

ཁོང་སང་ཉིན་ང་ཚོ་མཉམ་པོ་འགྲོ་མདོག་ཁ་པོ་མི་འདུག

b)

khong	sang.nyin	nga	- tsho	mnyam.po	'gro	- mdog.kha.po
s/he+H	tomorrow	I	- pl	together	go (PAS)	- EPI 1

- mi.'dug
- AUX (SENS+NEG)

It looks like he is not going with us tomorrow. (The speaker has been to the person's room and has seen that he isn't packing up.)

2.6.2.3 *Mdog.kha.po*-constructions with the final auxiliary *yod*

As stated above, most combinations with the *mdog.kha.po-* construction and the final auxiliary *yod* are problematic: some Tibetan consultants consider them to be grammatical, whereas others do not. These constructions imply that the speaker bases his statement on some kind of personal knowledge or personal experience (the egophoric evidential).

1. Constructions with *mdog.kha.po-yod* and *mdog.kha.po-med*

The default use of *mdog.kha.po-yod* and *mdog.kha.po-med* constructions is in past-context statements, although they may also occur with other tenses. Although it is possible to combine them with various verbal classes, this usage is infrequent. The lexical verb is in the present-future stem. Compare the following: in example (290), which is considered to be grammatical by certain

Tibetan speakers, the controllable verb *'gro* 'go' is used, whereas the use of the affective verb *dga'* 'love', as shown in example (291) is refused by all consultants:

(290)   ? ཁོང་ཡུལ་སྐོར་ལ་འགྲོ་མདོག་ཁ་པོ་མེད།

?	*khong*	*yul.skor*	*- la*	*'gro*	*- mdog.kha.po*	*- med*
	s/he+H	travel	- OBL	go (PRS)	- EPI 1	- AUX (EGO+NEG)

She does not seem to have gone for a trip. (The speaker knows she was very busy.)

(291)   * མོ་བུ་དེར་དགའ་མདོག་ཁ་པོ་ཡོད།

*	*mo*	*bu*	*de*	*- r*	*dga'*	*- mdog.kha.po*	*- yod*[69]
	she	boy	that	- OBL	love	- EPI 1	- AUX (EGO)

Intended statement: It seems she loved that guy.

2. Constructions with *yod-mdog.kha.po-yod* and *yod-mdog.kha.po-med*

The constructions *yod-mdog.kha.po-yod* and *yod-mdog.kha.po-med* are usually used in past contexts (perfective past). They are much less frequent than *yod-mdog.kha.po-red* and *yod-mdog.kha.po-ma.red*, although they are compatible with various verbal classes. The lexical verb is in the past stem. The following sentences illustrate the use of these constructions, although they are considered to be problematic by some consultants.

(292)   ? ཁོང་གིས་ལས་ཀ་འདི་བྱས་ཡོད་མདོག་ཁ་པོ་ཡོད།

?	*khong*	*- gis*	*las.ka*	*'di*	*byas*	*- yod*	*- mdog.kha.po*	*- yod*
	s/he+H	- ERG	work	this	VBZ (PAS)	- PERF	- EPI 1	- AUX (EGO)

It looks like he did the work. (The speaker wanted him to do the work.)

(293)   ཁོང་ཁ་ས་ཕྱིན་ཡོད་མདོག་ཁ་པོ་ཡོད།

	khong	*kha.sa*	*phyin*	*- yod*	*- mdog.kha.po*	*- yod*
	s/he+H	yesterday	go (PAS)	- PERF	- EPI 1	- AUX (EGO)

It looks like she left yesterday. (They live together in one flat. She told the speaker yesterday she would soon be going away. She is not in now, so the speaker thinks she has already left. It is also possible, however, that she just went out to buy something.)

3. Constructions with *gi.yod-mdog.kha.po-yod* and *gi.yod-mdog.kha.po-med*

The constructions *gi.yod-mdog.kha.po-yod* and *gi.yod-mdog.kha.po-med* are used in imperfective contexts. These include the imperfective past, the present and the future (implied as a secondary

---

[69] It is possible to use the construction *yod-mdog.kha.po-red* in this sentence.

meaning), as shown in example (294). Just as with the other constructions with the auxiliary *yod*, they are considered to be problematic and are infrequent in the spoken language. The lexical verb is in the present-future stem.

(294)　　？ ལྟོས་ཨཱ། ཡེ་ཤེས་རྒྱ་གར་ལ་འགྲོ་གི་ཡོད་མདོག་ཁ་པོ་མེད།

> ？ *ltos*　　*a*　　*ye.shes*　　*rgya.gar*　　*- la*　　*'gro*　　*- gi.yod*
> look (IMP)　ImpP　Yeshe　　India　　　- OBL　go (PRS)　- IMPF
>
> *- mdog.kha.po*　　*- med*
> - EPI 1　　　　　　- AUX (EGO+NEG)

Look! Yeshe probably won't go to India. (The speaker was asked if, in his opinion, Yeshe will be going to India and he is now thinking it over. He knows that Yeshe has already been to India and so considers it to be unlikely.)

In conclusion, constructions with the epistemic suffix *mdog.kha.po* form the same tense-aspect paradigm as most types of epistemic endings. Nonetheless, they have not yet undergone the entire process of suffixation and, therefore, may still be broken down into three parts: the tense-aspect, the degree of certainty and the evidential meaning. Constructions with the auxiliaries *red* and *'dug*, unlike those with *yod*, are frequent in the spoken language of central Tibet. *Mdog.kha.po*-constructions may be used in conditional sentences.

2.7 EPISTEMIC VERBAL ENDINGS *pa.'dug* AND *pa.yod*

The epistemic endings *pa.'dug* and *pa.yod* [70] convey a very high degree of certainty of the speaker towards the actuality of his utterance; it is, in general, higher than the degree of certainty of most of the other verbal endings. Their epistemic meaning corresponds in English to such adverbs as 'certainly', 'surely', 'undoubtedly' or to the epistemic meaning of the verb 'must'. Unlike other epistemic types, these two epistemic endings do not form a tense-aspect paradigm (see Section 1.2.2.1.1). See the examples below:

(295)   གཅིག་བྱས་ན་ཁོང་གིས་ཁ་ལག་བཟོས་པ་འདུག

   a) *gcig.byas.na*   *khong*   *- gis*   *kha.lag*   *bzos*   *- pa.'dug*
       perhaps   s/he+H   - ERG   food   VBZ (PAS)   - FUT+EPI 3+SENS

   She must be going to cook. (The speaker just saw her going into the kitchen.)

        ཁོང་གིས་ཁ་ལག་བཟོས་པ་ཡོད།

   b) *khong*   *- gis*   *kha.lag*   *bzos*   *- pa.yod*
       s/he+H   - ERG   food   VBZ (PAS)   - PFV+EPI 3+EGO

   As far as I know, she was cooking. Or: She must have cooked. (She told the speaker that she would be cooking.)

2.7.1 EPISTEMIC ENDINGS *pa.'dug* AND *pa.mi.'dug*

Semantic, pragmatic and syntactic characteristics

The epistemic ending *pa.'dug* expresses a high degree of certainty of the speaker towards the actuality of his utterance, corresponding to degree EPI 3 of the epistemic scale presented in Section 1.2.2.2. It implies a present inference of an action that will take place in the near future. It is used for prospective actions when the speaker is almost 100% sure that the action will take place, as in example (296). In addition, *pa.'dug* conveys information obtained on a sensory basis. This verbal ending is very frequent in the spoken language of central Tibet but is generally not used in the diaspora.

(296)   ཆར་པ་བཏང་པ་འདུག

   char.pa   *btang*   *- pa.'dug*
   rain   VBZ   - FUT+EPI 3+SENS

   It looks like rain. (The speaker can see clouds in the sky.)

---

[70] In standard spoken Tibetan, no corresponding factual epistemic ending exists: **pa.yod.red*.

Nevertheless, it is possible that the predicted action will not take place (although the speaker views such a possibility as minimal), as can be seen in example (297) below:

(297)   ངའི་བསམ་པར་ཆར་པ་བཏང་པ་འདུག་བསམས་བྱུང་ཡིན་ནའི་ད་ལྟ་གནམ་དྭངས་སོང་།

nga	- i	bsam.pa	- r	char.pa	btang	- pa.'dug
I	- GEN	thought	- OBL	rain	VBZ	- FUT+EPI 3+SENS

bsams	- byung	yin.na'i	da.lta	gnam	dwangs	- song
think	- PFV+EGO	but	now	sky	clear up	- PFV+SENS

I thought it was definitely going to rain, but then the sky cleared up.

In the spoken language, *'dug* is often omitted in affirmative sentences (*pa.'dug > pa*):

(298)   ཉི་མ་ཤར་པ།

nyi.ma	shar	- pa
sun	shine	- FUT+EPI 3+SENS

The sun is (surely) about to rise. (The speaker is looking out of the window.)

The epistemic ending *pa.'dug* is compatible with verbs of all verbal classes; the lexical verb preceding it is usually in the past stem, but the use of the present-future stem is possible as well, as an example (299) below:

(299)   བསྟན་པ་གཅིག་བྱས་ན་རྒྱ་ནག་ལ་མགྱོགས་པོ་ཕྱིན྾འགྲོ་པ་འདུག

bstan.pa	gcig.byas.na	rgya.nag	- la	mgyogs.po
Tenpa	perhaps	China	- OBL	quickly

phyin	/ 'gro	- pa.'dug
go (PAS)	/ go (PRS)	- FUT+EPI 3+SENS

Tenpa must be going to China soon. (The speaker has just met another friend who told him he wanted to meet Tenpa. The speaker informs him that Tenpa will be leaving soon.)

Sentences employing this epistemic ending cannot be interpreted as taking place in the past tense:

(300)   * ཁོང་ཟླ་ཉིན་རྒྱ་ནག་ལ་ཕྱིན་པ་འདུག

b)   * | khong | zla.nyin | rgya.nag | - la | phyin | - pa.'dug |
|---|---|---|---|---|---|
| s/he+H | last year | China | - OBL | go (PAS) | - * PFV+EPI 3+SENS |

Intended statement: She must have gone to China last year.

In ergative constructions, the object of the verb is often determined and the ergative particle usually marks the agent:

(301) གཅིག་བྱས་ན་ཁོང་གིས་དེབ་མང་པོ་ / ཁ་ཤས་ / དེ་ཉོས་པ་འདུག

gcig.byas.na	*khong*	*- gis*	*deb*	*mang.po*	*/ kha.shas*	*/ de*
perhaps	s/he+H	- ERG	book	many	some	that

nyos	*- pa.'dug*
buy (PAS)	- FUT+EPI 3+SENS

He certainly is going to buy many books/several books/that book. (The speaker has met the person in question in front of a bookshop.)

The negative counterpart of *pa.'dug* is *pa.mi.'dug*. It expresses a high degree of the speaker's certainty of the non-actuality of his utterance (<100%). Otherwise, it has the same characteristics as *pa.'dug*:

(302) ཆར་པ་བཏང་པ་མི་འདུག

a)
char.pa	*btang*	*- pa.mi.'dug*
rain	VBZ	- FUT+EPI 3+SENS+NEG

It doesn't look like rain. (The speaker bases his statement on his visual perception that the sky is clear.)

ཁོང་ཚོ་སྤོ་ལོ་ཤོར་པ་མི་འདུག

b)
khong	*- tsho*	*spo.lo*	*shor*	*- pa.mi.'dug*
s/he+H	- pl	ball	lose	- FUT+EPI 3+SENS+NEG

They can't lose the game. (The speaker can see that they have improved their score, and the game is almost over.)

The epistemic endings *pa.'dug* and *pa.mi.'dug* are frequently used with the third person. In first person sentences, they are usually combined with non-controllable verbs, as in examples (303) and (304); but not with controllable verbs, as in example (305a). They may, though, be employed in the apodosis with controllable verbs in statements of predictions or prophesy, as seen in example (305b). In this case, the epistemic ending does not necessarily relate to the near future, but to a moment at an unspecified time in the future:

(303) ང་ར་བཟི་པ།

a)
nga	*ra.bzi*	*- pa*
I	be drunk	- FUT+EPI 3+SENS

I am certainly going to get drunk. (The speaker is drinking too much *chang*.)

152

ན་ཚ་འདི་ངར་འགོས་པ་མི་འདུག

b) na.tsha   'di   nga   - r   'gos   - pa.mi.'dug
    illness   this   I   - OBL   catch   - FUT+EPI 3+SENS+NEG

I can't catch this illness. (The speaker often meets a friend who suffers from
a given illness. Someone is warning him to be careful, or he will catch it
too.)

(304)   གྲོད་ཁོག་ཞེ་པོ་ཅིག་ལྟོགས་ཀྱིས། ང་ཤི་པ།

grod.khog   zhe.po.cig   ltogs   - kyis   nga   shi
stomach   very   be hungry - IMPF+SENS   I   die

- pa[71]
- FUT+EPI 3+SENS

I'm dying of hunger. (lit.: I'm hungry [to the point that] I will certainly die.)

(305)   * ང་རྒྱ་གར་ལ་ཕྱིན་པ་འདུག

a)   * nga   rgya.gar   - la   phyin   - pa.'dug
        I   India   - OBL   go (PAS) - FUT+EPI 3+SENS

Intended statement: I will certainly go to India.

སློབ་གྲྭ་ཐོན་ནས་ང་གཅིག་བྱས་ན་དགེ་རྒན་བྱས་པ་འདུག

b)   slob.grwa   thon   - nas   nga   gcig.byas.na   dge.rgan   byas
     school   graduate   - after   I   perhaps   teacher   VBZ (PAS)

- pa.'dug
- FUT+EPI 3+SENS

After graduating from school, I will almost certainly become a teacher. (The
speaker is predicting his own future.)

The endings *pa.'dug* and *pa.mi.'dug* may be employed in the apodosis of conditional
sentences; for a factual statement, see example (306a); for a hypothetical statement, see example
(306b):

(306)   གཟབ་གཟབ་མ་བྱས་ན་མོ་ཊ་བརྡུངས་པ་འདུག

a)   gzab.gzab   ma   - byas   - na   mo.Ta - s   brdungs
     attention   NEG   - VBZ (PAS) - if   car   - INSTR   hit

- pa.'dug
- FUT+EPI 3+SENS

If [we] are not careful, we'll definitely get into an accident (in [lit.:with] the
car). (The road is very dangerous and there are many cars on this road.)

---

[71] This combination is a metaphoric expression used to convey an extreme feeling of hunger, tiredness,
etc. corresponding to "I am dying of hunger."

153

ང་སོག་པོའི་སྐད་སློབ་སྦྱོང་བྱེད་མཁན་ཡིན་ན་སོག་ཡུལ་ལ་ཕྱིན་པ་འདུག

b) | *nga* | *sog.po* | *-'i* | *skad* | *slob.sbyong* | *byed* | *- mkhan* |
|---|---|---|---|---|---|---|
| I | Mongol | - GEN | language | study | VBZ (PRS) | - NOM |

yin	*- na*	*sog.yul*	*- la*	*phyin*	*- pa. 'dug*	
be	- if	Mongolia	- OBL	go (PAS)	- FUT+EPI 3+SENS	

If I studied Mongolian, I would (almost certainly) go to Mongolia. (The speaker has a friend who studies Mongolian, and he is asking the speaker if he should go to Mongolia.)

The endings *pa. 'dug* and *pa.mi. 'dug* are generally compatible with various epistemic adverbs expressing different degrees of probability: see example (305b) above with *gcig.byas.na* 'perhaps', as well as example (305b), similarly above, and example (307) with *gtan.gtan* 'certainly', below. *Phal.cher* 'probably' and *brgya.cha.brgya* 'definitely' are also used.

(307)   ང་གཏན་གཏན་ན་པ་མི་འདུག

nga	*gtan.gtan*	*na*	*- pa.mi. 'dug*
I	certainly	be ill	- FUT+EPI 3+SENS+NEG

Surely I will not fall ill. (The speaker has a robust health.)

2.7.2 EPISTEMIC ENDINGS *pa.yod* AND *pa.med*

Semantic, pragmatic and syntactic characteristics

The epistemic ending *pa.yod* has two distinct meanings depending on the time context of the statement. In general, the epistemic meaning of probability occurs mainly in the past. In past contexts, it expresses a very high degree of certainty on the part of the speaker — degree EPI 3, corresponding to 80% certainty and more, as in example (308a). In future contexts, in sentences with a controllable verb, *pa.yod* implies previous agreement between the speaker and other person(s), as in example (308b). Since the action in question has been previously discussed, the speaker considers it as agreed upon. Therefore, my consultants tend to interpret future-tense sentences containing a controllable verb and *pa.yod* as expressing the speaker's absolute certainty. Both uses of *pa.yod* are frequent in the spoken language.

(308)   ཁོང་ཆུ་ཚོད་དགུ་པར་ཕེབས་པ་ཡོད།

a) | *khong* | *chu.tshod* | *dgu.pa* | *- r* | *phebs* | *- pa.yod* |
|---|---|---|---|---|---|
| s/he+H | o'clock | ninth | - OBL | go+H | - PFV+EPI 3+EGO |

Interpretation in a past context: He must have left at nine. (He told the speaker he would leave at nine, but the speaker has not seen him leave.)

154

ཁོང་ཆུ་ཚོད་དགུ་པར་ཕེབས་པ་ཡོད།

b) *khong*   *chu.tshod*   *dgu.pa*   *- r*   *phebs*   *- pa.yod*
   s/he+H   o'clock   ninth   - OBL   go+H   - FUT+EGO

Interpretation in a future context: As far as I know, he is leaving at nine.
(The speaker has spoken with the other person who said he would leave at nine.)

The ending *pa.yod* has egophoric connotations: "the speaker is privy to certain information" (see Tournadre & Sangda Dorje 2003: 307), for instance, he might have discussed the matter with someone else beforehand. Thus, it is possible to translate sentences with *pa.yod* by such expressions as 'I know that in principle' or 'from what I know', and 'as far as I know' (see Tournadre & Sangda Dorje 2003: 307).

(309)   རང་ཞེ་པོ་ཅིག་ན་པ་ཡོད།

rang   *zhe.po.cig*   *na*   *- pa.yod*
you   very   hurt   - PFV+EPI 3+EGO
[From what I know], this must have hurt. (The speaker has himself experienced a similar injury, thus, he can imagine the pain the injured person would be feeling.)

Alhough in a future statement, *pa.yod* implies a previous agreement of the speaker with another person on a given topic, there is an inherent difference in the use of controllable or non-controllable verbs. With controllable verbs, the emphasis is on the speaker's certainty, as in example (308b) above, whereas with non-controllable verbs (e.g. *'gos* 'infect') there is still room left for doubt, as in example (310) below:

(310)   ང་ན་ཚ་འདི་འགོས་པ་མེད།

nga   *na.tsha*   *'di*   *'gos*   *- pa.med*
I   illness   this   infect   - FUT+EPI 3+EGO+NEG
(I know that in principle) I won't catch this illness. (The speaker is vaccinated and is thus fairly sure of not catching the illness in question. He leaves room, however, for doubt.)

When *pa.yod* is used with a controllable verb in a future context, its use is close to the use of an evidential ending. Compare the sentence given in example (308b) above with the sentence below, containing the evidential ending *kyi.red,* example (311). In a future context, both sentences express certainty. But unlike example (311) below, the sentence in example (308b) implies previous agreement with another person or emphasis placed upon the speaker's knowledge (as in the expression 'I know that in principle' or 'as far as I know'):

(311)　　　ཁོང་ཆུ་ཚོད་དགུ་པར་ཕེབས་ཀྱི་རེད།

> *khong*　　*chu.tshod*　　*dgu.pa*　　*- r*　　*phebs*　　*- kyi.red*
> s/he+H　　o'clock　　ninth　　- OBL　　go+H　　- FUT+FACT
>
> He will go at nine. (Factual information, with no special details.)

The verbal ending *pa.yod* is compatible with verbs belonging to all verbal classes. The lexical verb preceding *pa.yod* is most of the time in the past stem, whether the sentence in question is interpreted in a past or future context, as seen in example (312a). The present-future stem can also be used, but this is less frequent in the spoken language as shown in example (312b) below.[72] According to *Bod-kyi lha.sa-'i skad-kyi brda.sprod* (2003: 135), when the verb is in the present-future stem, the speaker may be referring to the future or the past. As a result, both sentences, (312a) and (312b), may thus have two interpretations: in a past context as well as in a future context. See the examples below with the verb *'gro* 'to go': the past stem is *phyin,* and the present-future stem is *'gro*:

(312)　　　ཁོང་ཁ་ལག་ཉོ་གར་ཕྱིན་པ་ཡོད།

> a)　　*khong*　　*kha.lag*　　*nyo*　　*- gar*　　*phyin*　　*- pa.yod*
> 　　　s/he+H　　food　　buy (PRS)　　- GAR　　go (PAS)　　- PFV+EPI 3+EGO /FUT+EGO
>
> 　　1. She must have gone to buy food. (The speaker saw her leaving with her shopping bag.)
> 　　2. As far as I know, she is going to buy food. (The speaker discussed this with her. She said she would go and buy food, thus relieving the addressee of this sentence of the task.)

　　　ཁོང་ཁ་ལག་ཉོ་གར་འགྲོ་པ་ཡོད།

> b)　　*khong*　　*kha.lag*　　*nyo*　　*- gar*　　*'gro*　　*- pa.yod*
> 　　　s/he+H　　food　　buy (PRS)　　- GAR　　go (PRS)　　- PFV+EPI 3+EGO /FUT+EGO
>
> 　　1. As far as I know, she is going to buy food. (The speaker discussed this with her. She said she would go and buy food, thus relieving the addressee of this sentence of the task.)
> 　　2. She must have gone to buy food. (The speaker saw her leaving with her shopping bag.)

Furthermore, unlike Tibetan consultants who tend to suggest that *pa.yod* conveys an epistemic meaning only in past contexts, *Bod-kyi lha.sa-'i skad-kyi brda.sprod* (2003: 135) claims that *pa.yod* expresses probability in past and future contexts both, as can be seen from the Chinese translations below in example (313a):

---

[72] Tibetan consultants suggest that the present-future stem of a lexical verb is primarily used in literary Tibetan. In the spoken language the past stem is preferred.

(313)   ཁ་ལག་ཁོང་གིས་བཟོ་བ་ཡོད།

a) *kha.lag   khong   - gis   bzo   - ba.yod (i.e. pa.yod)*
    meal   s/he+H   - ERG   VBZ (PRS)   - FUT+EPI 3+EGO/PFV+EPI 3+EGO

1. It must be he who is going to cook. (cf. the Chinese translation: 饭<u>大概</u>是她
来做[73] 'It is <u>probably</u> he who is going to cook the meal.')
2. It must have been he who did the cooking. (cf. the Chinese translation: 饭<u>大</u>
<u>概</u>他已经做了 'It is <u>probably</u> he who has cooked the meal.')

As suggested above, the present-future stem is mainly used in literary Tibetan. In the spoken
language, the past stem of the lexical verb *bzo,* i.e. *bzos,* is preferred in the above sentence, as
shown as well in the following example (313b). As opposed to arguments made in *Bod-kyi
lha.sa-'i skad-kyi brda.sprod* (2003: 135),[74] Tibetan consultants state that both past and future
interpretations are possible:

ཁ་ལག་ཁོང་གིས་བཟོས་པ་ཡོད།

b) *kha.lag   khong   - gis   bzos   - pa.yod*
    meal   s/he+H   - ERG   VBZ (PAS)   - PFV+EPI 3+EGO / FUT+EGO

1. He must have cooked the meal. (The speaker saw him in the kitchen, but he
did not actually see him cooking. The speaker knows that he usually does the
cooking.)
2. (As far as) I know, he is the one who will cook the meal. (The speaker
agreed with him that he would do the cooking. The speaker is therefore
convinced that he is the one who will cook.)

Consequently, other means, such as adverbials of time, temporal clauses or the context of the
statement itself are important for sentence-tense determination with the epistemic ending *pa.yod*:

(314)   པ་ཕས་ཟླ་བ་དུས་སང་རྒྱ་ནག་ལ་འགྲོ (རུ) བཅུག་པ་ཡོད།

a) *pa.pha   - s   zla.ba   dus.sang   rgya.nag   - la   'gro*
    father   - ERG   Dawa   next year   China   - OBL   go (PRS)

    (- ru)   bcug   - pa.yod
    - CAUS   let   - FUT+EGO

As far as I know, Father will let Dawa go to China next year. (The speaker
and father have spoken about it, and so the decision has been made.)

---

[73] Tibetan consultants disagree with this Chinese translation.
[74] In Zhou, Xie, eds. (2003: 135) example (313b) is interpreted only in a past context.

157

ཁོང་གིས་ཟླ་བ་ཟླ་ཉིན་རྒྱ་ནག་ལ་འགྲོ་（རུ）བཅུག་པ་ཡོད།

b) khong   - gis   zla.ba   zla.nyin   rgya.nag   - la   'gro
    s/he+H   - ERG   Dawa   last year China   - OBL   go (PRS)

    (- ru)   bcug   - pa.yod
    - CAUS   let   - PFV+EPI 3+EGO

He must have let Dawa go to China last year. (The person in question made a
statement about it last year, and the speaker hasn't seen him or Dawa since.)

The negative counterpart of *pa.yod* is *pa.med*. It expresses the speaker's conviction of the high improbability of the actuality of his utterance, corresponding to 'certainly not'. Otherwise it has the same characteristics as *pa.yod*; it can be used for past actions (<100% certainty) or future actions (near 100% certainty):

(315)   ཁ་ལག་འདི་ཁོང་གིས་བཟོས་པ་མེད།

    kha.lag   'di   khong   - gis   bzos   - pa.med
    meal   this   s/he+H - ERG   make (PAS) - PFV+EPI 3+EGO+NEG

    As far as I can tell, she can't have cooked this meal. (When she does the
    cooking, the food tastes good; this time the food doesn't taste good.)

Since the object of the verb is determined (*'di*), the above example is interpreted as having occurred in the past tense. The following example, without *'di*, demonstrates a future interpretation:

(316)   དེ་རིང་ཁོང་གིས་ཁ་ལག་བཟོས་པ་མེད།

    de.ring   khong   - gis   kha.lag   bzos   - pa.med
    today   s/he+H - ERG   food   make (PAS) - FUT+EGO+NEG

    I think she isn't going to cook today. (She had told the speaker she had no
    time to cook, so someone else will have to do it.)

With some verbs, only the past interpretation is possible, as an example (317a). See as well example (317b) with the possessive verb *rag* 'get'; this may only be interpreted in the past tense, and not in the future:

(317)   སྒྲོལ་དཀར་ལ་སྤ་སེ་རག་པ་མེད།

    a) sgrol.dkar   - la   spa.se   rag   - pa.med
        Dolkar   - OBL   ticket   get   - PFV+EPI 3+EGO+NEG

    As far as I know, Dolkar did not get a ticket. Or: There's no way that Dolkar
    got a ticket. (The speaker also went to buy tickets and there were only a few
    left. Dolkar went to get the tickets later.)

* སྒྲོལ་དཀར་ལ་སང་ཉིན་སྤ་སེ་རག་པ་མེད།

b) * *sgrol.dkar*   *- la*   *sang.nyin*   *spa.se*   *rag*   *- pa.med*
    Dolkar   - OBL   tomorrow   ticket   get   - PFV+EPI 3+EGO+NEG

Intended statement: Dolkar certainly won't get a ticket.

The corresponding future negative interpretation of example (317a) can be expressed by means of the epistemic ending *a.yong* (see Section 2.4), as shown in example (317c) below:

སྒྲོལ་དཀར་ལ་སང་ཉིན་སྤ་སེ་རག་ལ་ཡོང་།

c) *sgrol.dkar*   *- la*   *sang.nyin*   *spa.se*   *rag*   *- a.yong*
   Dolkar   - OBL   tomorrow   ticket   get   - PERF FUT+EPI 3+EGO+NEG

I doubt Dolkar will [be able to] get a ticket tomorrow. (The speaker knows that as of today, there were few tickets left.)

The endings *pa.yod* and *pa.med* are usually used with the third person. It is, however, possible to use them in sentences with the first person. These combinations mostly appear in conditional sentences, as shown below in example (318):

(318)   ང་ར་ཟླ་ཉིན་དུས་ཚོད་ཡོད་ན་ཡུལ་སྐོར་ལ་ཕྱིན་པ་ཡོད།

nga   *- r*   *zla.nyin*   *dus.tshod*   *yod*   *- na*   *yul.skor*   *- la*
I   - OBL   last year   time   exist   - if   travel   - OBL

phyin   *- pa.yod*
go (PAS)   - PFV+EPI 3+EGO

If I had had time last year, I (almost certainly) would have travelled.

These epistemic endings are often used in conditional sentences to express unreal past conditions (the past counterfactual), as in example (319). See as well Section 1.2.3.3. At times, they also express the present counterfactual, as shown below in example (320):

(319)   ཁ་ལག་གང་བྱུང་མང་བྱུང་མ་བཟས་ན་བཀྲ་ཤིས་ན་པ་མེད།

kha.lag   *gang.byung mang.byung*   *ma*   *- bzas*   *- na*   *bkra.shis*
food   carelessly   NEG   - eat (PAS)   - if   Tashi

na   *- pa.med*
be ill   - PFV+EPI 3+EGO+NEG

If Tashi had not eaten carelessly [eaten too fast, eaten the wrong thing, etc.], he (almost certainly) wouldn't have got sick.

159

(320) ཁོང་གིས་ང་ར་རོགས་པ་མ་བྱས་ན་ང་ད་ལྟ་སློབ་གྲྭ་ཆེན་མོར་འགྲོ་ཐུབ་པ་མེད།

khong	*- gis*	*nga*	*- r*	*rogs.pa*	*ma*	*- byas*	*- na*	*nga*
s/he+H	- ERG	I	- OBL	help	NEG	- VBZ (PAS)	- if	I

da.lta	*slob.grwa chen.mo*	*- r*	*'gro*	*thub*	*- pa.med*
now	university	- OBL	go (PRS)	be able	- PFV+EPI 3+EGO+NEG

If he hadn't helped me, I wouldn't be able to attend university now.

The endings *pa.yod* and *pa.med* can combine with various epistemic adverbs (e.g. *gcig.byas.na* 'perhaps', *phal.cher* 'probably', or *gtan.gtan* 'certainly'):

(321) མདང་དགོང་གཅིག་བྱས་ན་ཁོང་ན་པ་ཡོད།

mdang.dgong	*gcig.byas.na*	*khong*	*na*	*- pa.yod*
last night	perhaps	s/he+H	be ill	- PFV+EPI 3+EGO

Maybe he got sick last night. (The speaker knows that the person in question was very cold last night.)

2.8 EPISTEMIC VERBAL ENDINGS AND COPULAS OF THE TYPE *yod.pa.yod*

2.8.1 FORMAL, SEMANTIC AND PRAGMATIC CHARACTERISTICS

The epistemic endings and copulas of the type *yod.pa.yod* diachronically consist of the same auxiliaries (*yin, yod*) and nominalizers/connectors (*pa, gi, rgyu*) as evidential verbal endings; they do not contain other morphemes. Negative endings may be formed by the final auxiliary *med* (e.g. *yod.pa.med*), or by the initial auxiliary *med* (e.g. *med.pa.yod*), as in example (322). Similarly, example (323) illustrates the negative copulas *yod.pa.med* and *med.pa.yod*:[75]

(322)　　སྒྲོལ་མ་གྲོད་ཁོག་ལྟོགས་ཡོད་པ་མེད ∫ མེད་པ་ཡོད།

sgrol.ma	*grod.khog*	*ltogs*	*- yod.pa.med*
Dolma	stomach	be hungry	*/ - med.pa.yod*
			- PERF+EPI 2+EGO+NEG
			/ - PERF+EPI 2+EGO+NEG

Dolma is probably not hungry. (The speaker recalls that she ate in the morning.)

(323)　　དཔེ་ཆ་འདི་ངག་དབང་ལ་ཡོད་པ་ཡོད།　　རྡོ་རྗེ་ལ་ཡོད་པ་མེད ∫ མེད་པ་ཡོད།

dpe.cha	*'di*	*ngag.dbang*	*- la*	*yod.pa.yod*
Tibetan book	this	Ngagwang	- OBL	exist (EPI 2+EGO)
rdo.rje	*- la*	*yod.pa.med*	*/ med.pa.yod* [76]	
Dorje	- OBL	exist (EPI 2+EGO+NEG)	/ exist (EPI 2+EGO+NEG)	

As far as I can remember, Ngagwang has this Tibetan book, [but] Dorje doesn't.

The copulas of this type are *yin.pa.yod/yin.pa.med* (or *min.pa.yod*) and *yod.pa.yod/yod.pa.med* (or *med.pa.yod*). Since this type conveys a mnemic meaning (see below), they are often, although not exclusively, used in a past context conveying a sense of 'As far as I (can) remember', or 'As far as I (can) recall' (324):

(324)　　ཁོང་སྔ་མ་ཁ་ལོ་པ་ཡིན་པ་ཡོད།

khong	*snga.ma*	*kha.lo.pa*	*yin.pa.yod*
s/he+H	before	driver	be (EPI 2+EGO)

As far as I remember, he was a driver before. (The speaker remembers vaguely that the person worked as a driver before.)

---

[75] See Zhou, Xie, eds. (2003: 78). Nonetheless, some native speakers prefer the negative ending *yod.pa.med* and reject *med.pa.yod*, others suggest using *med.pa.yod* and reject *yod.pa.med*.
[76] Taken from Zhou, Xie, eds. (2003: 78).

(325)   ཀཿ ལྡེ་མིག་ཡོད་པས།   ཁཿ ཕལ་ཆེར་ཡོད་པ་ཡོད།

A: *lde.mig*   *yod*   *- pas*   B: *phal.cher*   *yod.pa.yod*
     key   exist   - Q   probably   exist (EPI 2+EGO)

A: Have you got the key?
B: As far as I can recall, I do have it.

This epistemic type forms the following paradigm:

Affirmative endings	Negative endings
yod.pa.yod	*yod.pa.med* or *med.pa.yod*
pa.yin.pa.yod	*pa.yin.pa.med*
gi.yod.pa.yod	*gi.yod.pa.med* or *gi.med.pa.yod*

Other combinations are impossible, e.g.:

* *gi.yin.pa.yod*:   * *bzo - gi.yin.pa.yod*   Intended: '… will probably make'

* *yod.pa.'dug*:   * *bzos - yod.pa.'dug*   Intended: '… probably made'

* *med.pa.med*:   * *bzos - med.pa.med*   Intended: '… probably did not make'

The epistemic endings of the type *yod.pa.yod* imply a high degree of certainty on the part of the speaker (degree EPI 2). They have egophoric connotations and frequently convey a mnemic[77] meaning as well: the speaker remembers something but he is not absolutely sure, as, for example, some time has elapsed since the event in question. These endings can therefore be translated into English by such expressions as 'I recall (perhaps) that …', 'I remember that (perhaps)'or 'I think this was the case (but do not recollect clearly)'. This type of ending is employed in the spoken language of Lhasa but less frequently so than some other epistemic endings (e.g. *yod. 'gro*, *yod.pa. 'dra*).[78] Below is an example of the use of this epistemic type:

(326)   གྲི་ངས་ཁྱེར་ཡོད་པ་ཡོད།

     gri   *nga*   *- s*   *khyer*   *- yod.pa.yod*
     knife   I   - ERG   bring   - PERF+EPI 2+EGO

     I'm pretty sure I have brought a knife. (The speaker has brought many items
     to a picnic, although he is not absolutely sure if he has brought a knife or
     not. Although he is quite sure when uttering the above sentence, he may then
     state: "Oh, I didn't bring the knife, I am wearing another jacket today. It's in
     the other one.")

---

[77] Tournadre, Sangda Dorje (2003: 339) call these verbal endings 'mnemic auxiliaries' and translate them the following way: 'I seem to remember', 'I vaguely remember'.

[78] Some native speakers have difficulties accepting some of the examples given in Section 2.8.

Verbal endings of the type *yod.pa.yod* can be used both in third and first person sentences. Unlike other types of epistemic endings, this type is easily compatible with the first person due to its mnemic meaning:

(327)　　ང་ལྷ་སར་ཉི་མ་གསུམ་བསྡད་དགོས་ཀྱི་ཡོད་པ་ཡོད།

nga	*lha.sa*	*- r*	*nyi.ma*	*gsum*	*bsdad*	*dgos*	*- kyi.yod.pa.yod*
I	Lhasa	- OBL	day	three	stay	need	- IMPF+EPI 2+EGO

As far as I can remember, I will stay in Lhasa for three days. (The speaker will be going to many places, and thus does not recall his exact itinerary and how long he will stay in each place.)

The type *yod.pa.yod* is generally compatible with various epistemic adverbs (e.g. *phal.cher* 'probably', *gcig.byas.na* 'perhaps', *spyir.btang* 'generally', or *gtan.gtan* 'certainly'):

(328)　　མོ་གཏན་གཏན་སློབ་གྲྭར་འགྲོ་གི་ཡོད་པ་ཡོད།

mo	*gtan.gtan*	*slob.grwa*	*- r*	*'gro*	*- gi.yod.pa.yod*
she	certainly	school	- OBL	go (PRS)	- IMPF+EPI 2+EGO

She certainly attends school. (The speaker recalls that she is the same age as his daughter.)

2.8.2 DESCRIPTION OF THE VERBAL ENDINGS

1. Verbal endings of the perfective past

The following verbal endings of this type are used in the perfective past: *yod.pa.yod* and *yod.pa.med/med.pa.yod* and *pa.yin.pa.yod* and *pa.yin.pa.med*.

The endings *yod.pa.yod* and *yod.pa.med* are used in present perfect contexts, usually when the speaker reminds himself of something but not in a very clear manner. In third person sentences, they are compatible with all verbal classes: see examples (329) and (330). With the first person, these verbal endings are usually not used with affective verbs because the speaker generally is aware of what his feelings are or were, as shown in example (331):

(329)　　ཁོང་གིས་ཁ་ལག་བཟས་ཡོད་པ་ཡོད།

khong	*- gis*	*kha.lag*	*bzas*	*- yod.pa.yod*
s/he+H	- ERG	food	eat (PAS)	- PERF+EPI 2+EGO

She probably had her meal. (The speaker can vaguely remember her talking about going to a restaurant.)

(330) ཁོང་ད་ལྟ་བཞུགས་ཡོད་པ་ཡོད།

khong   da.lta   bzhugs   - yod.pa.yod
s/he+H   now   stay+H   - PERF+EPI 2+EGO

Probably he's in now. (The speaker cannot clearly remember what the person told him.)

(331) * ང་ཁོང་ལ་ཡིད་ཆེས་ / དགའ་ཡོད་པ་ཡོད།

*   nga   khong   - la   yid.ches   / dga'   - yod.pa.yod
    I   s/he+H - OBL   believe   / love   - PERF+EPI 2+EGO

Intended statement: As far as I can recall, I believed/loved him.

According to some native speakers, *yod.pa.yod* and *yod.pa.med/med.pa.yod* may also be employed in conditional counterfactual sentences (unreal past conditions). Other Tibetans, however, reject this usage, as shown in example (332):

(332) ? ཁྱེད་རང་མ་ཕེབས་ན་ང་ཤི་ཡོད་པ་ཡོད།

a) ? khyed.rang   ma   - phebs   - na   nga   shi   - yod.pa.yod
      you+H   NEG   - come+H   - if   I   die   - PERF+EPI 2+EGO

If you hadn't come, I would have probably died.

? ཁྱེད་རང་མ་ཕེབས་ན་ཁོང་ཤི་ཡོད་པ་ཡོད།

b) ? khyed.rang   ma   - phebs   - na   khong   shi   - yod.pa.yod
      you+H   NEG   - come+H   - if   s/he+H   die   - PERF+EPI 2+EGO

If you hadn't come, she would have probably died.

The verbal endings *pa.yin.pa.yod* and *pa.yin.pa.med* also indicate that the speaker is reminding himself of a past action, but these kinds of sentences are less frequent than sentences with the perfect endings of this type and their use with varying verbs is more restricted. They are usually employed with controllable verbs in third person sentences. The scope of probability is often aimed at the agent or the predicate (the action of the verb). In other words, the verbal ending and the agent or the action of the verb are closely connected, as can be seen in the following example:

(333) རི་མོ་འདི་ཁོང་གིས་བྲིས་པ་ཡིན་པ་ཡོད།

ri.mo   'di   khong   - gis   bris   - pa.yin.pa.yod
painting this   s/he+H - ERG   draw (PAS)   - PFV+EPI 2+EGO

I seem to remember it is probably he who drew the picture. (i.e. Looking at the picture the speaker is not sure whether it was the person in question who drew it or not.)

164

The verbal endings *pa.yin.pa.yod* and *pa.yin.pa.med* are, in general, not used with non-controllable verbs, as shown in example (334a). Instead, the perfect endings *yod.pa.yod* and *yod.pa.med* are employed: see example (334b).

(334) * ཁོང་མི་འདིར་ཞེད་པ་ཡིན་པ་ཡོད།

    a)   * *khong   mi   'di - r   zhed   - pa.yin.pa.yod*
            s/he+H   person   this - OBL be afraid - PFV+EPI 2+EGO

        Intended statement: I think she must have been afraid of that person.

        ཁོང་མི་འདིར་ཞེད་ཡོད་པ་ཡོད།

    b)   *khong   mi   'di - r   zhed   - yod.pa.yod*
            s/he+H   person   this - OBL be afraid - PERF+EPI 2+EGO

        I think she must have been afraid of that person. (The speaker remembers how she acted around the person in question.)

Moreover, the endings *pa.yin.pa.yod* and *pa.yin.pa.med* are combined only infrequently with the first person. This restriction, coupled with the one above, illustrate the fact that perfective endings are in general less frequently used than perfect endings. Examples of the use of perfective endings with the first person are considered grammatical only by some native speakers, whereas others consider them to be ungrammatical:

(335) ? རི་མོ་འདི་ངས་བྲིས་པ་ཡིན་པ་ཡོད / པ་ཡིན་པ་མེད།

     ? *ri.mo   'di   nga - s   bris   - pa.yin.pa.yod / pa.yin.pa.med*
       picture this I - ERG draw (PAS) - PFV+EPI 2+EGO / PFV+EPI 2
                                              +EGO+NEG

        As far as I can remember, I drew/didn't draw this picture. (The speaker compares the picture with his own style of drawing.)

2. Verbal endings of the imperfective past, the present and the future

The verbal endings of this type employed in the imperfective past, the present and the future are *gi.yod.pa.yod* and *gi.yod.pa.med/gi.med.pa.yod.*

The endings *gi.yod.pa.yod* and *gi.yod.pa.med/gi.med.pa.yod* are used in the imperfective past: see example (336a), the present: as in example (336b); the future: as in example (336c); or in those contexts when the speaker does not remember the action clearly. They are compatible with verbs belonging to all verbal classes and may appear both in the third and first persons:

(336) ཁོང་སླེབས་དུས་ང་ཡི་གི་འབྲི་གི་ཡོད་པ་ཡོད།

a) *khong   slebs - dus   nga   yi.ge   'bri   - gi.yod.pa.yod*
   s/he+H   come - when   I   letter   write (PRS)   - IMPF+EPI 2+EGO

   I'm pretty sure I was writing letters when he came. (The speaker bases
   his statement on a hazy recollection.)

ཁོང་བོད་སྐད་ཤེས་ཀྱི་ཡོད་པ་མེད།

b) *khong   bod.skad   shes   - gi.yod.pa.med*
   s/he+H   Tibetan language   know   - IMPF+EPI 2+EGO+NEG

   As far as I know, he has no knowledge of Tibetan. (The speaker seems
   to remember that he and the person spoke Chinese together.)

ཁོང་ཆུ་ཚོད་གཉིས་པར་ཡོང་གི་ཡོད་པ་ཡོད།

c) *khong   chu.tshod   gnyis.pa   - r   yong   - gi.yod.pa.yod*
   s/he+H   o'clock   second   - OBL   come   - IMPF+EPI 2+EGO

   She is expected at two o'clock. (She called and said she would come to
   that place. The speaker thinks she will be arriving at 2 o'clock.)

In present-future contexts, the verbal endings *gi.yod.pa.yod* and *gi.yod.pa.med/gi.med.pa.yod*
imply habitual or iterative actions, as an example (337a). A single (perfective) action is expressed
via a construction with the nominalizer *mkhan*, as shown in example (337b; see as well Section
1.2.2.1.2):

(337) ཁོང་ཕྱི་ལོགས་ལ་ཁ་ལག་ཟ་གི་ཡོད་པ་ཡོད།

a) *khong   phyi.logs   - la   kha.lag   za   - gi.yod.pa.yod*
   s/he+H   outside   - OBL   meal   eat (PRS)   - IMPF+EPI 2+EGO

   As far as I know, he (usually) eats out. (The speaker never sees him in
   the canteen.)

ཁོང་དོ་དགོང་ཕྱི་ལོགས་ལ་ཁ་ལག་ཟ་གར་འགྲོ་མཁན་ཡིན་པ་ཡོད།

b) *khong   do.dgong   phyi.logs   - la   kha.lag   za   - gar*
   s/he+H   tonight   outside   - OBL   meal   eat (PRS)   - GAR

   'gro   - mkhan   : yin.pa.yod
   go (PRS)   - NOM   : AUX (EPI 2+EGO)

   As far as I can recall, he is eating out tonight. (The speaker seems to
   remember hearing him talk about going out to dinner earlier in the day.)

To conclude, since the type *yod.pa.yod* conveys a mnemic meaning, it appears to be easier to
combine its verbal endings in first person sentences implying faulty recollection on the part of the
speaker. There is some disagreement among native speakers concerning the acceptability of the
past endings *yod.pa.yod* and *yod.pa.med/med.pa.yod* in past counterfactual conditionals, as well
as of other sentences employing this type of epistemic ending.

166

2.9 EPISTEMIC VERBAL ENDINGS AND COPULAS OF THE TYPE *yong.nga.yod*

2.9.1 FORMAL, SEMANTIC AND PRAGMATIC CHARACTERISTICS

This type of verbal ending and copula diachronically consists of the auxiliary *yong*, followed by the connector *ba,* pronounced *nga*[79] in the spoken language, and the auxiliary *yod*. Negative endings are formed by using the negative final auxiliary *med,* e.g. *yong.nga.med*. This is illustrated in the following example:

(338)　　ཁོང་ཕྱི་ལོགས་ལ་ཕྱིན་ཡོང་ང་མེད།

> *khong*　*phyi.logs*　*- la*　*phyin*　*- yong.nga.med*
> s/he+H　outside　- OBL　go (PAS)　- PERF+EPI 2+EGO+NEG
>
> She most likely didn't go out. (The speaker knows that she usually stays home.)

Unlike other epistemic types, there are only two copulas corresponding to this type of epistemic ending. These are *yong.nga.yod* and *yong.nga.med*. Certain Tibetan consultants employ them as existential copulas (more common), others as essential copulas. Compare the following examples: (339a) employs *yong.nga.yod* as an existential copula, while (339b) illustrates its use as an essential copula:

(339)　　? ཁོང་བལ་ཡུལ་ལ་ཡོང་ང་ཡོད།

> a)　? *khong*　*bal.yul*　*- la*　*yong.nga.yod*
> 　　s/he+H　Nepal　- OBL　exist (EPI 2+EGO)
>
> She is probably in Nepal. (The speaker met her in India. She told him she would go to Nepal soon: now he is back in Tibet and people are inquiring as to her location.)

　　? ཁོང་དགེ་རྒན་ཡོང་ང་ཡོད།

> b)　? *khong*　*dge.rgan*　*yong.nga.yod*
> 　　s/he+H　teacher　be (EPI 2+EGO)
>
> She is probably a teacher.

---

[79] The pronunciation is influenced by the preceding auxiliary *yong*.

This type forms the following paradigm:

Affirmative endings:	Negative endings:
yong.nga.yod	yong.nga.med
gi.yong.nga.yod	gi.yong.nga.med

Other endings do not exist, e.g. *yong.nga. 'dug, *yong.nga.yod.red, *pa.yong.nga.yod, as shown in the example below:

(340)   * ཁོང་ཁ་ལག་བཟོས་པ་ཡོང་ང་ཡོད།

* khong	- gis	kha.lag	bzos	- pa.yong.nga.yod
s/he+H	- ERG	meal	VBZ (PAS)	- PERF+EPI 2+EGO

Intended statement: She probably did the cooking.

Semantically, the verbal endings and copulas of the type *yong.nga.yod* are similar to the type *yod.pa.yod.* They express a fairly high degree of certainty of the speaker, corresponding to degree EPI 2, and they convey egophoric connotations. This type appears to illustrate generational differences in the use of certain language items. The older generation of Tibetans prefer to employ it, whereas the younger generation does not. In addition, Sangda Dorje[80] suggests that this type is mostly used by Tibetans who do not speak Chinese. Consequently, some of the examples given here are not considered grammatical by all the native speakers with whom I conducted interviews.[81]

Just as with other epistemic types, the verbal endings of the type *yong.nga.yod* can be used with the third person, as in example (341a), and the first person, as in example (341b), although unsurprisingly sentences with the third person are more frequent:

(341)   གྲི་དེ་ཁོང་གིས་ཁྱེར་ཡོང་ང་ཡོད།

a) gri	de	khong	- gis	khyer	- yong.nga.yod
knife	that	s/he+H	- ERG	bring	- PERF+EPI 2+EGO

Probably he brought the knife. (The speaker knows that the person in question is responsible for the kitchen utensils.)

---

[80] Personal communication by Sangda Dorje (professor at Tibet university).
[81] This has bearing on examples (341b), (344), and (346).

? ཁྱི་དེ་ངས་ཁྱེར་ཡོང་ང་ཡོད།

b) *? gri   de   nga   - s   khyer   - yong.nga.yod*
    knife   that   I   - ERG   bring   - PERF+EPI 2+EGO

I'm pretty sure I have the knife. (The speaker has brought many things for the picnic, but he is not completely sure if he has brought the knife.)

As a rule, the type *yong.nga.yod* is compatible with various epistemic adverbs, such as *phal.cher* 'probably', *gcig.byas.na* 'perhaps' and *gtan.gtan* 'certainly': these modify the degree of certainty the speaker has towards his utterance. Compare the examples below: (342b) implies a higher degree of certainty than (342a) because the adverb *gtan.gtan* 'certainly' implies a higher degree of certainty than *phal.cher* 'probably':

(342)   སྒྲོལ་མ་ཕལ་ཆེར་དབྱིན་ཇི་སྐད་སྦྱང་གི་ཡོང་ང་ཡོད།

a) *sgrol.ma   phal.cher   dbyin.ji.skad   sbyang   - gi.yong.nga.yod*
    Dolma   probably   English language   learn   - IMPF+EPI 2+EGO

Dolma is probably studying English. (The speaker met Dolma, and she told him she was planning to buy an English textbook.)

སྒྲོལ་མ་གཏན་གཏན་དབྱིན་ཇི་སྐད་སྦྱང་གི་ཡོང་ང་ཡོད།

b) *sgrol.ma   gtan.gtan   dbyin.ji.skad   sbyang   - gi.yong.nga.yod*
    Dolma   certainly   English language   learn   - IMPF+EPI 2+EGO

Dolma is certainly studying English. (The speaker met Dolma and she told him she was going to pay for English classes in a language school.)

2.9.2 DESCRIPTION OF THE VERBAL ENDINGS

1. Verbal endings of the perfective past

The verbal endings *yong.nga.yod* and *yong.nga.med* are primarily used in perfective past contexts, and in immediate present contexts. They are compatible with all verbal classes in third person sentences: see example (343). Just as with other epistemic types, their use is more restricted in first person sentences. These endings can also be employed in past conditional sentences though this use is not accepted by all Tibetans, as shown in example (344):

(343)   ཕལ་ཆེར་མོ་ལོ་ཉི་ཤུ་ལ་སླེབས་ཡོང་ང་ཡོད།

a) *phal.cher   mo   lo   nyi.shu   - la   slebs   - yong.nga.yod*
    probably   she   year   twenty   - OBL   come   - PERF+EPI 2+EGO

She is probably twenty years old. (When the speaker first met the person's daughter she was about ten years old. That occurred approximately ten years ago.)

169

ཁོང་ད་ལྟ་ནང་ལ་བཞུགས་ཡོང་ང་མེད།

b) *khong   da.lta   nang   - la   bzhugs   - yong.nga.med*
   s/he+H   now   home   - OBL   stay+H   - PERF+EPI 2+EGO+NEG

He probably isn't at home now. (He told the speaker he was going shopping today.)

(344)   ?   ཁྱེད་རང་མ་ཕེབས་ན་ཁོང་ཤི་ཡོང་ང་ཡོད།

a)   ?   *khyed.rang   ma   - phebs   - na   khong   shi   - yong.nga.yod*
       you+H   NEG   - come+H   - if   s/he+H   die   - PERF+EPI 2+EGO

If you hadn't come, he probably would have died. (He wanted to jump out of the window.)

    ?   ཁྱེད་རང་མ་ཕེབས་ན་ང་ཤི་ཡོང་ང་ཡོད།

b)   ?   *khyed.rang   ma   - phebs   - na   nga   shi   - yong.nga.yod*
       you+H   NEG   - come+H   - if   I   die   - PERF+EPI 2+EGO

If you hadn't come, I probably would have died. (The speaker was about to drown in a body of water.)

2. Verbal endings of the imperfective past, the present and the future

The endings *gi.yong.nga.yod* and *gi.yong.nga.med* are used in imperfective contexts regardless of the time-context of the statement (past, present, future). They can be combined with different verbal classes: with controllable verbs as in example (345), or with incontrollable verbs, as in example (346, not accepted by all consultants):

(345)   སྒྲོལ་མ་ད་ལྟ་ཡོང་གི་ཡོང་ང་ཡོད།

    sgrol.ma   da.lta   yong   - gi.yong.nga.yod
    Dolma   now   come   - IMPF+EPI 2+EGO

Dolma is most likely on her way here. (When the speaker met her, she said she would come to the same restaurant that the speaker was headed to: he is in the restaurant already, but Dolma hasn't arrived yet.)

(346)   ?   ཁོང་ཕལ་ཆེར་ན་གི་ཡོང་ང་ཡོད།

    ?   *khong   phal.cher   na   - gi.yong.nga.yod*
       s/he+H   perhaps   be ill   - IMPF+EPI 2+EGO

She is probably ill. (She didn't show up.)

Nonetheless, their use with some verbs is excluded, e.g. the affective verb *dga'* 'love'. The combination with this verb is considered ungrammatical, as in example (347a). Instead, the sentence with the adjective *dga'.po* and the copula *yong.nga.yod* meaning 'to probably like' is employed, as shown in example (347b):

170

(347)   * ཁོང་སྒྲོལ་དཀར་ལ་དགའ་གི་ཡོང་ང་ཡོད།

a)   * *khong   sgrol.dkar   - la   dga'   - gi.yong.nga.yod*
     s/he+H   Dolkar   - OBL   love   - IMPF+EPI 2+EGO

Intended statement: He probably is in love with Dolkar.

ཁོང་སྒྲོལ་དཀར་ལ་དགའ་པོ་ཡོང་ང་ཡོད།

b)   *khong   sgrol.dkar   - la   dga'.po   yong.nga.yod*
    s/he+H   Dolkar   - OBL   like   exist (EPI 2+EGO)

He probably likes Dolkar. (The speaker knows that the person in question helped Dolkar quite a bit.)

To sum up, the verbal endings and copulas of the type *yong.nga.yod* differ from other epistemic types by the absence of the perfective past ending and by the fact that this type has only one affirmative (and negative) copula that certain native speakers use as an existential copula and others as an essential copula. This type is less frequent than certain epistemic types discussed above (see Sections 2.1–2.7), and it is not widely accepted: some Tibetan speakers find most of the above examples in this section grammatical, whereas others reject the majority of them. This also holds true for conditional sentences.

2.10 EPISTEMIC VERBAL ENDINGS WITH THE MORPHEME *yong*

2.10.1 EPISTEMIC ENDING *mi.yong.ngas*

Formal, semantic and pragmatic characteristics

This epistemic ending is diachronically formed with the negative particle *mi*, the verb *yong* 'be possible' and the interrogative particle *ngas* corresponding literary to "Won't it be possible?" (as in example 348a). Originally interrogative, it now has an epistemic meaning. It has undergone a process of phonological change and reduction from [*mijoŋŋä*] to [*majõŋä*] or [*mõŋä*]). Other combinations containing *yong* and *ngas*, e.g. **yong.ngas, *gi.mi.yong.ngas,* do not exist in Tibetan, as shown in the following example (348b):

(348)   ན་ཚ་འདི་དྲག་མི་ཡོང་ངས།

    a) *na.tsha   'di   drag   - mi.yong.ngas*
        illness   this   recover   - FUT+EPI 1+FACT
    [She] will probably recover. (The speaker is a doctor, and is knowledgeable about this disease.)

    * ན་ཚ་འདི་དྲག་གི་མི་ཡོང་ངས།

    b) * *na.tsha   'di   drag   - gi.mi.yong.ngas*
          illness   this   recover   - IMPF+EPI 1+FACT
    Intended statement: [She] will probably recover.

In spite of its negative form, *mi.yong.ngas* conveys a positive meaning: the speaker considers something more probable than not. The degree of certainty is lower than that of some other epistemic types, for example *yod.kyi.red,* and thus corresponds to EPI 1. Regarding the evidential meaning of *mi.yong.ngas*, since it implies access to information acquired in an indirect or direct manner, it can generally be classified as factual. This epistemic ending is only used in future contexts. It is preceded by the past stem of the lexical verb. It is compatible with verbs of all verbal classes in third person sentences, as shown in example (349). In first person sentences, *mi.yong.ngas* is often used with verbs of physical sensation: see example (352) below. This epistemic ending is frequently employed in the spoken language.

(349)　　ཁོང་ལྷ་སར་ཕྱིན་མི་ཡོང་ངས།

a)　*khong*　　*lha.sa*　*- r*　　*phyin*　　*- mi.yong.ngas*
　　s/he+H　　Lhasa　- OBL　　go (PAS)　- FUT+EPI 1+FACT

She will probably go to Lhasa. (She often goes there.)

དེ་རིང་ངར་པ་ཕས་གཤེ་གཤེ་བཏང་མི་ཡོང་ངས།

b)　*de.ring*　*nga*　*- r*　　*pa.pha*　*- s*　　*gshe.gshe*　*btang*
　　today　　I　- OBL　father　- ERG　scold　　VBZ

　　- mi.yong.ngas
　　- FUT+EPI 1+FACT

Father will probably scold me today. (The speaker is late. Father usually
scolds him when he is late.)

ཨ་ཚི།　　ཁྱི་འདི་ཤི་མི་ཡོང་ངས།

c)　*a.tsi*　*khyi*　*'di*　*shi*　*- mi.yong.ngas*
　　oh no　dog　this　die　- FUT+EPI 1+FACT

Oh, my goodness! Will that dog not die? (Looking at a wounded dog,
the speaker feels pity for it, and wishes that it wouldn't die.)

The verbal ending *mi.yong.ngas* (350a) is employed in similar contexts as the construction
mdog.kha.po-red (350b). This is illustrated in the following example:

(350)　　ཁོང་ལ་གསུངས་དང་། ཁོང་གིས་ཁྱེད་རང་ལ་རོགས་པ་བྱས་མི་ཡོང་ངས།

a)　*khong*　*- la*　　*gsungs*　*- dang*　*khong*　*- gis*　　*khyed.rang*
　　s/he+H　- OBL　tell+H　　- IMP　　s/he+H　- ERG　　you+H

　　- la　　*rogs.pa*　　*byas*　　　　*- mi.yong.ngas*
　　- OBL　　help　　VBZ (PAS)　　- FUT+EPI 1+FACT

Tell her. Maybe she will help you. (Guessing from his personal or general
experience, the speaker thinks that if the addressee talks to her in a
pleasing way, she might help him.)

ཁོང་ལ་གསུངས་དང་། ཁོང་གིས་ཁྱེད་རང་ལ་རོགས་པ་བྱེད་མདོག་ཁ་པོ་རེད།

b)　*khong*　*- la*　　*gsungs*　*- dang*　*khong*　*- gis*　　*khyed.rang*
　　s/he+H　- OBL　tell+H　　- IMP　　s/he+H　- ERG　　you+H

　　- la　　*rogs.pa*　　*byed*　　　　*- mdog.kha.po*　*- red*
　　- OBL　　help　　VBZ (PRS)　- EPI 1　　　　　- AUX (FACT)

Tell her. Perhaps she will help you. (The speaker makes an inference
based on the fact that she can do what the addressee needs; therefore, he
thinks she might help him.)

173

This epistemic ending is also used in conditional sentences to express a present real condition:

(351) ངས་སྐད་ཆ་འདི་འདྲས་བཤད་ན་ཁོང་ཚིག་པ་ཟ་མི་ཡོང་ངས།

nga	- s	skad.cha	'di.'dras	bshad	- na	khong	tshig.pa
I	- ERG	speech	like this	say	- if	s/he+H	anger

za	- mi.yong.ngas
VBZ	- FUT+EPI 1+FACT

If I talk like this, he will perhaps get angry. (The speaker surmises based
on previous experience)

In first person sentences, the verbal ending *mi.yong.ngas* is rarely used with controllable verbs.
If it is, however, the use of this ending conveys that the action does not depend on the speaker's
will: see example (352). *Mi.yong.ngas* is often used with first person after endopathic verbs
(verbs of physical sensation) such as *grod.khog ltogs* 'be hungry', *khyag* 'be cold', *cham.pa
brgyab* 'catch a cold': see example (353).

(352) ང་ལས་ཀ་བྱས་མི་ཡོང་ངས།

nga	las.ka	byas	- mi.yong.ngas
I	work	VBZ (PAS)	- FUT+EPI 1+FACT

I wonder if I will work. (It doesn't depend on the speaker.)

(353) ང་འཁྱག་མི་ཡོང་ངས།

a)
nga	'khyag	- mi.yong.ngas
I	be cold	- FUT+EPI 1+FACT

I might get cold. (Lit. 'Won't I be cold? ' The speaker is going out early
in the morning.)

ང་ཆམ་པ་བརྒྱབ་མི་ཡོང་ངས།

b)
nga	cham.pa	brgyab	- mi.yong.ngas
I	a cold	VBZ	- FUT+EPI 1+FACT

It feels like I am catching a cold. Or: I might be catching a cold. (The
speaker is not feeling well.)

It is sometimes possible to use epistemic adverbs of the type *gcig.byas.na* 'perhaps', and
phal.cher 'probably' in sentences with *mi.yong.ngas*; see example (354). However, this verbal
ending is more often employed without an epistemic adverb. It is incompatible with adverbs
expressing near-absolute certainty, such as *gtan.gtan* 'certainly' (354c):

(354)   ཁོང་ཕལ་ཆེར་ང་ར་དགའ་པོ་བྱས་མི་ཡོང་ངས།

a) *khong*   *phal.cher*   *nga*   *- r*   *dga'.po*   *byas*   *- mi.yong.ngas*
   s/he+H   probably   I   - OBL   like   VBZ (PAS)   - FUT+EPI 1+FACT

   He will probably love me. (The speaker surmises, based on his behaviour.)

   ཁོང་གཅིག་བྱས་ན་ང་ར་དགའ་པོ་བྱས་མི་ཡོང་ངས།

b) *khong*   *gcig.byas.na*   *nga*   *- r*   *dga'.po*   *byas*   *- mi.yong.ngas*
   s/he+H   perhaps   I   - OBL   Glad   VBZ (PAS)   - FUT+EPI 1
                                                                          +FACT

   He might love me [one day]. (The speaker surmises, based on his behaviour.)

   * ཁོང་གཏན་གཏན་ང་ར་དགའ་པོ་བྱས་མི་ཡོང་ངས།

c) * *khong*   *gtan.gtan*   *nga*   *- r*   *dga'.po*   *byas*   *- mi.yong.ngas*
   s/he+H   certainly   I   - OBL   glad   VBZ (PAS)   - FUT+EPI 1
                                                                        +FACT

   Intended statement: He will certainly be in love with me.

2.10.2 EPISTEMIC ENDINGS AND COPULAS *yong* AND *mi.yong*

2.10.2.1 Semantic and pragmatic characteristics

The word *yong* is polysemic: it can function as a lexical verb, a secondary verb, an evidential ending or copula, or an epistemic ending or copula. As a lexical verb, *yong* can either function as a controllable verb conveying the meaning of 'come', or a non-controllable verb conveying a sense of 'happen', 'obtain', 'appear' or 'be possible'. *Yong* is also a directional and aspectual verb indicating a direction towards the speaker, or an inchoative, progressive, or iterative aspect (see Section 3.2.14, as well as Tournadre & Konchok Jiatso 2001: 89–96).

As a grammatical word, it is subject to a process of phonological reduction (pronounced [*jõ*]); the negative counterpart *mi.yong* is pronounced [*majõ*]) and used in a variety of meanings (of which see below); some of these convey as well the epistemic meaning of doubt or uncertainty.

Just as with the ending *mi.yong.ngas*, *yong* and *mi.yong* can generally be classified as factual markers as they imply information acquired through direct or indirect means. However, just as with the type *yod.kyi.red*, Tibetan consultants suggest that they tend to use *yong* when relying upon their own experience (*nyams.myong* 'experience'). As a result, *yong* should be viewed as more subjective compared to other types such as *yod. 'gro* or *mdog.kha.po-red*. The degree of certainty expressed by the epistemic endings and copulas *yong* and *mi.yong* is fairly high, corresponding to EPI 2. These two verbal endings may be used in both past and future contexts, as well as in the generic present. They are compatible with controllable as well as with non-controllable verbs of different verbal classes:

(355)   ཨ་ལའི་   མ་གཡུགས།   འདིར་བཞག   ཁོང་གིས་བཟས་ཡོང་།

a) *a.la'i   ma   - g.yugs   'dir   bzhag   khong   - gis   bzas*
    ah   NEG - throw   here   put   s/he+H - ERG   eat (PAS)

    - *yong*[82]
    - FUT+EPI 2+FACT

Wait, do not throw it away! Put it here! She will probably eat it. (She likes this food.)

ཁོང་སང་ཉིན་སླེབས་ཡོང་།

b) *khong   sang.nyin   slebs   - yong*
    s/he+H   tomorrow   arrive   - FUT+EPI 2+FACT

She will probably arrive tomorrow. (She said she would come on the 10th or the 11th. It is now the evening of the 10th, and she has not arrived yet.)

In the spoken language, *yong* and *mi.yong* used in an epistemic meaning are fairly infrequent compared to other epistemic types such as *yod.kyi.red, yod.'gro, yod.pa.'dra*. Tibetan speakers disagree on the acceptability of some sentences containing *yong*: some consider them grammatical, whereas others do not. As in other cases, these endings as well demonstrate generational differences in the use of epistemic verbal endings. As opposed to consultants of an older generation, consultants of a younger generation consider the majority of the examples employing *yong* and *mi.yong* to be ungrammatical. This disagreement is illustrated by the following examples:[83]

(356)   ?   འགྲེལ་བཤད་བྱེད་ཡག་གི་དེབ་འདི་ཕལ་ཆེར་ཁོང་གིས་བྲིས་ཡོང་།

    ? *'grel.bshad   byed   - yag   - gi   deb   'di   phal.cher*
       explain   VBZ (PRS) - NOM - GEN   book   this   perhaps

    khong   - gis   bris   - yong
    s/he+H   - ERG   write (PAS) - PFV+EPI 2+FACT

Probably he was the one who wrote the manual. (The speaker knows that there was a manuscript at the residence of the person in question.)

---

[82] This sentence is similar to the sentence with the epistemic suffix *mdog.kha.po*, i.e. *za - mdog.kha.po - red* (see Section 2.6), or to the sentence with the epistemic ending *'gro*, i.e. *bzas - 'gro* (see Section 2.4), which convey the meaning of "He will probably eat it."

[83] Similarly, the following examples are rejected by some consultants: (358b), (359b), (361), (362), (364), (365).

176

(357)　　?　ཁོང་ཕལ་ཆེར་ལས་ཀ་བྱས་མི་ཡོང་།

a) *?* *khong* *phal.cher* *las.ka* *byas* - *mi.yong*
   　s/he+H　probably　work　VBZ (PAS)　- FUT+EPI 2+FACT+NEG

   She won't probably work. (The speaker knows her and thinks that she won't want to work.)

　　?　ང་ན་མི་ཡོང་།

b) *?* *nga* *na* - *mi.yong*
   　I　be ill　- FUT+EPI 2+FACT+NEG

   I can't fall ill. (The speaker does not feel quite well but he thinks he won't fall ill.)

In the above examples, *yong* is used in a past context, as in example (356), and in a future context, as in example (357). The lexical verb, however, is always in the past stem: example (358a) illustrates the impossibility of using the present-future stem of the verb *za* 'eat':

(358)　　*　ཁོང་གིས་ཟ་ཡོང་།

a) * *khong* - *gis* *za* - *yong*
   　s/he+H　- ERG　eat (PRS)　- FUT+EPI 2+FACT

   Intended statement: He'll probably eat [this food].

　　ཁོང་གིས་བཟས་ཡོང་།

b) *khong* - *gis* *bzas* - *yong*
   　s/he+H　- ERG　eat (PAS)　- FUT+EPI 2+FACT

   He'll probably eat [this food]. (The speaker knows he likes this kind of food.)

The epistemic endings *yong* and *mi.yong* may sometimes be employed in conditional sentences, as in the following example:

(359)　　མོ་ཊ་མགྱོགས་པོ་བཏང་ན་བརྡུང་ཡོང་།

a) *mo.Ta* *mgyogs.po* *btang* - *na* *brdung* - *yong*
   　car　fast　drive　- if　smash　- FUT+FACT

   If [you] drive fast, there is a risk of a car crash. (The speaker bases his assertion on personal experience.)

　　ཆང་མང་པོ་བླུགས་ན་ང་ར་བཟི་ཡོང་།

b) *chang* *mang.po* *blugs* - *na* *nga* *ra.bzi* - *yong*
   　chang　a lot　pour　- if　I　be drunk　- FUT+EPI 2+FACT

   If [you] pour [me] a lot of *chang,* I will probably get drunk. (The action is not contingent on the speaker's will.)

177

2.10.2.2 Various functions and meanings of the verbal endings and copulas *yong* and *mi.yong* (epistemic and non-epistemic)

1. Imminent danger

The epistemic ending *yong* often conveys a sense of imminent danger or risk. It is used with third person and non-controllable verbs in near future contexts. It is only used for undesirable events (see Tournadre & Konchok Jiatso 2001: 95–96). As it conveys the meaning of 'There is a danger of …', it corresponds to sentences with the lexical expression of epistemic modality containing the noun *nyen.kha* 'danger' (see example 26 in Section 1.1.2).

(360)   འདི་མ་ཟ། ན་ཡོང་།

a) | *'di* | *ma* | *- za* | *na* | *- yong* |
|---|---|---|---|---|
| this | NEG | - eat (IMP) | be ill | - FUT+EPI 2+FACT |

Do not eat this! You will be sick. (The speaker's experience is such that if he ate the food in question, he would be sick. Thus, the other person should be wary of eating this food as well.)

འདིར་མ་བཞག ཁྱིས་བཟས་ཡོང་།

b) | *'dir* | *ma* | *- bzhag* | *khyi* | *- s* | *bzas* | *- yong* |
|---|---|---|---|---|---|---|
| here | NEG | - put | dog | - ERG | eat (PAS) | - FUT+EPI 2+FACT |

Don't put it here! The dog will (certainly) eat it. (Implication: There is a danger that the dog will eat it up.)

2. Threat, annoyance

The verbal ending or copula *yong* may convey other meanings beyond that of imminent danger. It often conveys negative connotations, and therefore is used in contexts implying threat, irritation or annoyance, as illustrated in the examples below:

(361)   རང་ཁ་བདེ་པོ་ཡོང་།

rang	*kha.bde.po*	*yong*
you	cheeky	be (FACT)

You are cheeky. (Threat: If you keep on doing [a given action], I'll teach you!)

(362)   ངས་ཇ་འདི་བཏུངས་མི་ཡོང་།

nga	*- s*	*ja*	*'di*	*btungs*	*- mi.yong*
I	- ERG	tea	this	drink (PAS)	- FUT (FACT)

Don't worry! I won't drink the tea. (Expression of annoyance: The speaker is annoyed as the other person thinks that he will drink up the tea.)

(363) ངས་ལབ་མི་ཡོང་།

> nga   - s   lab   - mi.yong
> I   - ERG eat (PAS)   - FUT(FACT+NEG)

Don't be afraid. I won't tell [anyone]. (Expression of irritation, or a promise)

3. Habitual events and the speaker's experience

The verbal ending and copula *yong* is employed to evoke habitual events or the speaker's past experience (actions or events that the speaker experienced during his lifetime). The copula *yong* combines with adjectives. See example (364) below, employing *yong* as a copula, as well as example (365), where it has the function of a verbal ending:

(364) བོད་ལ་གནམ་གཤིས་གྲང་མོ་ཡོང་།

> a) bod   - la   gnam.gshis   grang.mo   yong
>   Tibet - OBL   weather   cold   be (FACT)

The weather in Tibet is cold. (The implication is that this is the usual weather pattern in Tibet.)

བོད་ཟས་འདི་ཞིམ་པོ་མི་ཡོང་།

> b) bod.zas   'di   zhim.po   mi.yong
>   Tibetan meal   this   good   exist (FACT+NEG)

This Tibetan meal is not good. (The speaker has had this kind of meal before.)

(365) སྔོན་མ་ཡིན་ན་ཚོང་པ་མང་པོ་རྒྱ་གར་ལ་ཕྱིན་ཡོང་།

> a) sngon.ma   yin   - na   tshong.pa   mang.po   rgya.gar   - la
>   formerly   be   - if   merchant   many   India   - OBL
>
>   phyin   - yong
>   go (PAS)   - PFV+FACT

Formerly, many merchants travelled to India. (The speaker recalls that when he was young, many merchants travelled there.)

པེ་ཅིང་ལ་དགུན་ཁ་གངས་བབས་ཡོང་།

> b) pe.cing   - la   dgun.kha   gangs   babs   yong [84]
>   Beijing   - OBL   winter   snow   fall   be (FACT)

It snows in Beijing in the winter.

---

[84] Taken from Zhou, Xie, eds. (2003: 139).

4. Allocentric future

Yong is also used to mark allocentric future actions: the speaker guarantees that he will perform an action for the sake of another person (see Tournadre & Konchok Jiatso 2001: 95). It is often used in sentences with verbs of movement. The agent is always marked by the ergative; the verb is controllable and in the past stem:

(366)   ངས་བཏང་ཡོང་།

nga   - s   btang - yong
I   - ERG   VBZ   - FUT ALL

I'll go and send it for you.

To conclude, the epistemic verbal endings with the morpheme *yong*: *mi.yong.ngas* and *yong* (*mi.yong*) are not paradigm-like. *Mi.yong.ngas* is formally negative, but semantically positive. The epistemic endings and copulas *yong* and *mi.yong* are homonymous with the evidential ending and copula *yong* and *mi.yong*. While *mi.yong.ngas* is quite frequent in the spoken language, *yong* and *mi.yong* are not. Some native speakers reject many sentences with these endings.

2.11 EPISTEMIC VERBAL ENDINGS AND COPULAS WITH THE MORPHEME *bzo*

2.11.1 FORMAL, SEMANTIC AND PRAGMATIC CHARACTERISTICS

From a diachronic point of view, this type of epistemic ending and copula contains the morpheme *bzo* (the etymology of the word *bzo* refers back to 'shape'), combined with the final auxiliary *'dug* (or exceptionally *yod*),[85] e.g. *yod.bzo.'dug*. The use of other final auxiliaries is not possible (*yod.red, yin, red*).

Negative endings are formed by adding the negative particle *mi* before *'dug*, e.g. *gi.yod.bzo.mi.'dug*: see example (367a). The negative auxiliary *med*, **gi.med.bzo.'dug*, as an example (367b), is not used.

(367)   ཁོང་མི་འདིར་ཞེད་ཀྱི་ཡོད་བཟོ་མི་འདུག

    a) *khong   mi   'di - r   zhed   - kyi.yod.bzo.mi.'dug*
        s/he+H person this - OBL be afraid - IMPF+EPI 2+SENS+NEG

        It doesn't look like she is afraid of that person. (The speaker sees her arguing with the person in question.)

    * ཁོང་མི་འདིར་ཞེད་ཀྱི་མེད་བཟོ་འདུག

    b) * *khong   mi   'di - r   zhed   - kyi.med.bzo.'dug*
           s/he+H person this - OBL be afraid - IMPF+EPI 2+SENS+NEG

        Intended statement: It doesn't seem she is afraid of that person.

The epistemic copulas of this type are the essential copulas *yin.bzo.'dug* and *yin.bzo.mi.'dug*, as well as the existential copulas *yod.bzo.'dug* and *yod.bzo.mi.'dug*:

(368)   མི་འདི་བོད་པ་ཡིན་བཟོ་མི་འདུག

    a) *mi   'di   bod.pa   yin.bzo.mi.'dug*
        person this Tibetan be (EPI 2+SENS+NEG)

        It doesn't seem like this person is a Tibetan. Or: This person doesn't look like a Tibetan. (The speaker bases his statement on visual perception.)

---

[85] *Bzo*-endings with the auxiliary *yod* are very infrequent in standard spoken Tibetan and—as they are rejected by the younger generation of Tibetan consultants— appear to be falling out of use. They will not therefore be treated in detail in this work.

ཚོ་བཟང་ལ་ཚིག་མཛོད་ཆེན་མོ་ཡོད་བཟོ་འདུག

b) *blo.bzang* - *la* *tshig.mdzod chen.mo* *yod.bzo.'dug*
   Lobzang - OBL Great dictionary exist (EPI 2+SENS)

It seems Lobzang has [a copy of] the *Great Dictionary*. (The speaker makes an inference based on the fact that Lobzang is carrying around a very thick book; the *Great Dictionary* is also very thick.)

This epistemic type forms the following paradigm:

Affirmative endings:	Negative endings:
yod.bzo.'dug	*yod.bzo.mi.'dug*
pa.yin.bzo.'dug	*pa.yin.bzo.mi.'dug*
gi.yod.bzo.'dug	*gi.yod.bzo.mi.'dug*
bzo.'dug	*bzo.mi.'dug*

Other combinations are not grammatical, e.g. **gi.yin.bzo.'dug.*

Moreover, in SST, there are constructions with the morpheme *bzo* that are in the process of grammaticalization (suffixation):

V - *pa : 'i : bzo : 'dug*   V - *pa : 'i : bzo : mi : 'dug*

V - *yag : gi : bzo : 'dug*   V - *yag : gi : bzo : mi : 'dug*

Concerning evidentiality, as the epistemic endings and copulas with the morpheme *bzo* contain the final element *'dug*, they have sensory connotations. From a semantic viewpoint, the *bzo*-endings resemble constructions with *mdog.kha.po* (see Section 2.6), as in (369), as well as *'dra*-endings (see Section 2.2), as in (370). [86] From a pragmatic viewpoint, in contrast to the other two epistemic types, *bzo*-endings are infrequent in the spoken language and, as suggested by Tibetan consultants, this type is used in a more formal speech register. The degree of probability conveyed by this type of ending appears to be somewhat higher than the degree of probability expressed by the *mdog.kha.po*-construction, and similar to the *'dra*-type, corresponding to degree EPI 2. The use of the copula *yod.bzo.'dug* and the construction *mdog.kha.po-'dug* are shown in example (369a); the use of the copulas *yin.bzo.'dug* and *yin.pa.'dra* are shown in example (370a):

---

[86] There are nonetheless some minor differences among these three types (*yod.bzo.'dug, -mdog.kha.po-'dug,* and *yod.pa.'dra*) due to the original meaning of the elements *bzo, mdog* and *'dra*. The element *bzo*, i.e. *bzo.lta* conveys the meaning of 'manner, appearance, shape, form'; the suffix *mdog.kha.po* is derived from *mdog* i.e., *kha.mdog,* meaning 'colour'; and finally, *'dra* means 'be like, be similar, look as if, seem, appear'.

(369)   ཁ་ལག་འདི་ཞིམ་པོ་ཡོད་བཟོ་འདུག

a) *kha.lag   'di   zhim.po   yod.bzo.'dug*
   meal   this   tasty   exist (EPI 2+SENS)

It looks like the meal is tasty. (The people eating the meal seem to be enjoying their food.)

ཁ་ལག་འདི་ཞིམ་མདོག་ཁ་པོ་འདུག

b) *kha.lag   'di   zhim   - mdog.kha.po   - 'dug*
   meal   this   be tasty   - EPI 1   - AUX (SENS)

The meal looks tasty. (Looking at the meal, the speaker thinks it is tasty, even though he hasn't tried it himself yet.)

(370)   ཕྲུ་གུ་འདི་ཁོང་གི་ཡིན་བཟོ་འདུག

a) *phru.gu   'di   khong   - gi   yin.bzo.'dug*
   child   this   s/he+H   - GEN   be (EPI 2+SENS)

The child looks like it's his. (The speaker makes an inference based on the fact that the child has many similar physical characteristics to the person in question.)

ཕྲུ་གུ་འདི་ཁོང་གི་ཡིན་པ་འདྲ།

b) *phru.gu   'di   khong   - gi   yin.pa.'dra*
   child   this   s/he+H   - GEN   be (EPI 2+SENS)

It looks like this child is his. (The speaker makes an inference based on the fact that the person is holding the child's hand or making some other such similar parental gesture.)

The frequency of the *bzo*-type is fairly low in the spoken language: it is lower than that of most of the other epistemic verbal endings. The older generation of Tibetans consider the majority of the combinations in this section — see example (371a) — as grammatical, but at the same time they suggest that this type is less common in the spoken language than it used to be. In contrast, younger Tibetans find most of the examples in this section formal or odd, and suggest using other epistemic types, e.g. *yod.pa.'dra*, or other epistemic means such as the lexical construction consisting of the adjective *'dra.po* and an existential copula (see Section 1.1.2); consider as well example (371b) below:[87]

---

[87] Examples 367a, 369a, 373, 374, 376b, 378, 380a, 381, 382b, 383, 384a, 385, 387, 388 are rejected by some native speakers.

(371)   ཉི་མ་ལ་དགོངས་པ་རག་ཡོད་བཟོ་མི་འདུག

a)   *nyi.ma   - la   dgongs.pa   rag   - yod.bzo.mi.'dug*
    Nyima   - OBL   leave of absence   get   - PERF+EPI 2+SENS+NEG

Nyima probably didn't get time off. (The speaker saw Nyima looking angry as he left the boss's office.)

ཉི་མ་ལ་དགོངས་པ་རག་པ་འདྲ་པོ་མི་འདུག

b)   *nyi.ma   - la   dgongs.pa   rag - pa   'dra.po   mi.'dug*
    Nyima   - OBL   leave of absence   get - NOM   similar   exist (SENS+NEG)

It doesn't look like Nyima got time off. (The speaker saw Nyima looking angry as he left the boss's office.)

In first person sentences, *bzo*-endings often imply that the speaker cannot remember the action. The main verb is usually followed by the secondary verb *myong* 'have an experience', as in example (372). However, such sentences are even less frequent than third person sentences. Other epistemic endings such as *yod.pa. 'dra* or *yod.pa.yod* are used instead.

(372)   ང་ས་ཆ་འདིར་སླེབས་མྱོང་ཡོད་བཟོ་འདུག

    nga   sa.cha   'di - r   slebs   myong   - yod.bzo.'dug
    I   place   this - OBL   come   have an experience   - PERF+EPI 2+SENS

It looks like I've been here before. (The locale looks somewhat familiar to the speaker.)

Bzo-endings can combine with some epistemic adverbs, e.g. *phal.cher* 'probably', as in example (373a); some Tibetan consultants also accept *gtan.gtan* 'certainly', whereas others do not. Combinations with *gcig.byas.na* 'perhaps' are considered as odd and ungrammatical: see example (373b):

(373)   ཉི་མ་ལ་ཕལ་ཆེར་དགོངས་པ་རག་ཡོད་བཟོ་མི་འདུག

a)   *nyi.ma   - la   phal.cher   dgongs.pa   rag   - yod.bzo.mi.'dug*
    Nyima   - OBL   probably   leave of absence   get   - PERF+EPI 2+SENS+NEG

It doesn't look like Nyima got a leave of absence. Or: Nyima probably didn't get a leave of absence. (The speaker saw that Nyima looked angry as he left the boss's office.)

*   ཉི་མ་ལ་གཅིག་བྱས་ན་དགོངས་པ་རག་ཡོད་བཟོ་མི་འདུག

b) * *nyi.ma   - la   gcig.byas.na   dgongs.pa   rag   - yod.bzo.mi.'dug*
    Nyima   - OBL   perhaps   leave of absence   get   - PERF+EPI 2+SENS+NEG

Maybe Nyima didn't get time off.

2.11.2 DESCRIPTION OF THE VERBAL ENDINGS

2.11.2.1 Verbal endings with the final auxiliary *'dug*

1. Verbal endings of the perfective past

In the perfective past, the following verbal endings are employed: *yod.bzo.'dug* and *yod.bzo.mi.'dug, pa.yin.bzo.'dug* and *pa.yin.bzo.mi.'dug*.

The epistemic endings *yod.bzo.'dug* and *yod.bzo.mi.'dug* are used in perfective contexts. They are compatible with verbs of all classes: see example (374a) for use with a controllable verb, and (374b) for use with a non-controllable verb. Sentences with these endings are more common without an animate agent. Their use in first person sentences is considered exceptional and generally ungrammatical, as in example (375). Instead, other epistemic types, e.g. *yod.pa.yod* or *yod.pa.'dra*, are employed.

(374)   ཁོང་གིས་ཁ་ལག་བཟས་ཡོད་བཟོ་འདུག

     a)   *khong*   *- gis*   *kha.lag*   *bzas*   *- yod.bzo.'dug*
        s/he+H   - ERG   food   eat (PAS)   - PERF+EPI 2+SENS

        She seems to have eaten. (The speaker sees an empty plate on the table.)

        ཆུ་ཚོད་འདི་གཞུག་ལ་ལས་ཡོད་བཟོ་འདུག

     b)   *chu.tshod*   *'di*   *gzhug*   *- la*   *las*[88]   *- yod.bzo.'dug*
        watch   this   afterwards   - OBL   be left behind   - PERF+EPI 2+SENS

        This watch seems to be slow. (It was three o'clock when the speaker left school, and it takes him about twenty minutes to get home. As he arrives home, the watch shows only ten past three.)

(375)   * ངས་དེབ་འདི་ཉོས་ཡོད་བཟོ་འདུག

     *   *nga*   *- s*   *deb*   *'di*   *nyos*   *- yod.bzo.'dug*
        I   - ERG   book   this   buy (PAS)   - PERF+EPI 2+SENS

        Intended statement: It seems I bought the book.

The epistemic endings *pa.yin.bzo.'dug* and *pa.yin.bzo.mi.'dug* are used in the perfective past, and may combine with verbs of all verbal classes in third person sentences, as in example (376). They usually do not combine with the first person, as in example (377). Instead, other types (e.g. *yod.pa.'dra*) are employed, depending on the context.

---

[88] In literary Tibetan, it is spelt *lus* 'be left behind'.

(376)　ཁོང་གིས་བོད་སྐད་ཨ་མདོ་ནས་སྦྱངས་པ་ཡིན་བཟོ་འདུག

a)　*khong - gis*　*bod.skad*　*a.mdo - nas*　*sbyangs*
s/he+H - ERG　Tibetan language　Amdo - ABL　learn

- *pa.yin.bzo.'dug*
- PFV+EPI 2+SENS

She seems to have learnt Tibetan in Amdo. (The speaker makes an inference based on the fact that she speaks with an Amdo accent.)

མི་དེ་བསད་པ་ཡིན་བཟོ་མི་འདུག

b)　*mi*　*de*　*bsad*　- *pa.yin.bzo.mi.'dug*
man　that　kill　- PFV+EPI 2+SENS+NEG

That man was not murdered, it seems. (The speaker perceives certain indications of suicide.)

(377)　* གློག་བརྙན་འདི་ངས་ལྟས་པ་ཡིན་བཟོ་འདུག

*　*glog.brnyan*　*'di*　*nga - s*　*ltas*　- *pa.yin.bzo.'dug*
movie　this　I - ERG　watch (PAS)　- PFV+EPI 2+SENS

Intended statement: It seems I have seen this movie.

2. Verbal endings of the imperfective past, the present and the future

In imperfective contexts (past or present) and in the future, the following verbal endings are used: *gi.yod.bzo.'dug* and *gi.yod.bzo.mi.'dug, bzo.'dug* and *bzo.mi.'dug*.

The epistemic endings *gi.yod.bzo.'dug* and *gi.yod.bzo.mi.'dug* are compatible with all verbal classes in third person sentences, as shown in example (378). In first person sentences, these verbal endings do not combine with affective verbs: see example (379).

(378)　ཁོང་ཚོ་ཁང་པ་དེར་བསྡད་ཀྱི་ཡོད་བཟོ་འདུག

a)　*khong - tsho*　*khang.pa*　*de - r*　*bsdad*　- *kyi.yod.bzo.'dug*
s/he+H - pl　house　that - OBL　stay　- IMPF+EPI 2+SENS

They seem to be staying in that house. (The speaker saw them enter the house in the evening.)

སྒྲོལ་མ་སློབ་ཚན་འདིར་དགའ་གི་ཡོད་བཟོ་མི་འདུག

b)　*sgrol.ma*　*slob.tshan*　*'di - r*　*dga'*　- *gi.yod.bzo.mi.'dug*
Dolma　class　this - OBL　like　- IMPF+EPI 2+SENS+NEG

Dolma does not seem to like this class. (The speaker makes an inference based on the fact that Dolma does not attend class.)

186

ཁོང་མགྱོགས་པོ་རྒྱ་ནག་ལ་འགྲོ་གི་ཡོད་བཟོ་འདུག

c) *khong mgyogs.po rgya.nag - la 'gro - gi.yod.bzo.'dug*
   s/he+H soon China - OBL go (PRS) - IMPF+EPI 2+SENS

It seems she will be going to China soon. (The speaker makes an inference based on the fact that she has recently acquired guidebooks to China.)

(379) * ང་མི་དེར་ཡིད་ཆེས་ཀྱི་ཡོད་བཟོ་འདུག

a) * *nga mi de - r yid.ches - kyi.yod.bzo.'dug*
   I man that - OBL believe - IMPF+EPI 2+SENS

Intended statement: I seem to believe that man.

Instead the example above, Tibetan consultants suggest the following sentence:

འདུག་སེ་ལྟ་དུས་ང་མི་དེར་ཡིད་ཆེས་ཡོད།

b) *'dug.se lta - dus nga mi de - r yid.ches yod*
   like this look (PRS) - when I man that - OBL believe exist (EGO)

I seem to believe that man.

The endings *bzo.'dug* and *bzo.mi.'dug* express possible future actions, as shown in examples (380) and (381). The lexical verb is generally in the present-future stem, as shown in example (380a), and not in the past stem, as shown in example (380b):

(380) ཁོང་གཞིས་ཀ་རྩེར་འགྲོ་བཟོ་འདུག

a) *khong gzhis.ka.rtse - r 'gro - bzo.'dug*
   s/he+H Shigatse - OBL go (PRS) - FUT+EPI 2+SENS

It seems she will go. (The speaker heard her saying she was thinking of going there.)

? ཁོང་ཕྱིན་བཟོ་འདུག

b) ? *khong phyin - bzo.'dug* [89]
   s/he+H go (PAS) - FUT+EPI 2+SENS

It seems she will go.

(381) དེ་རིང་ཆར་པ་བཏང་བཟོ་མི་འདུག

de.ring char.pa btang - bzo.mi.'dug
today rain VBZ - FUT+EPI 2+SENS+NEG

It does not seem it is going to rain today. (The speaker infers from the fact that there are no clouds in the sky.)

---

[89] The present-future stem of the verb is preferred to the past stem. Sentences such as example (380b) are considered to be dialectal.

In first person sentences, *bzo.'dug* and *bzo.mi.'dug* are usually not compatible with controllable verbs, e.g. *'gro* 'go', *byed* 'do' (382a) but they may sometimes be used with non-controllable verbs (382b):

(382) * ང་འགྲོ་བཟོ་འདུག

    a) * *nga*   *'gro*   - *bzo.'dug*
        I   go (PRS)   - FUT+EPI 2+SENS

    Intended statement: It seems I will go [there].

    དེ་རིང་ང་ན་བཟོ་འདུག

    b) *de.ring*   *nga*   *na*   - *bzo.'dug*
        today   I   be ill   - FUT+EPI 2+SENS

    I seem to be getting ill today. (The speaker is not feeling well.)

2.11.2.2 Constructions with the morpheme *bzo*

1. Constructions of V (PAS) - *pa : 'i : bzo : 'dug* and V - *pa : 'i : bzo : mi : 'dug*

From a diachronic point of view, these constructions consist of a lexical verb in the past stem followed by the nominalizer *pa*, the genitive suffix *'i*, the morpheme *bzo*, (the negative particle *mi*), and the copula *'dug*. They express possible past actions having some relation to the present, and they convey sensory connotations as well. From a synchronic viewpoint, these constructions are in the process of grammaticalization, i.e., of developing into the suffixes *pa'i.bzo.'dug* or *pa'i.bzo.mi.'dug*. This process, however, has not yet been completed. They are written in the following way in this book: *pa : 'i : bzo : 'dug* and *pa : 'i : bzo : mi : 'dug*. These constructions may be used with verbs of all verbal classes with both the third person, as in examples (383) and (384a), as well as the first person, as seen in example (385). Sentences with the first person are, however, often found to be impossible: as in example (384b). The secondary verb *myong* 'have an experience' is generally employed in first person sentences; see example (385), implying recollection through visual perception:

(383) བསྟན་འཛིན་ཕ་ཡུལ་ལ་ཕེབས་པའི་བཟོ་འདུག

    bstan.'dzin   *pha.yul*   - *la*   *phebs*   - *pa : 'i : bzo : 'dug*
    Tenzin   native place   - OBL   go+H   - PERF+EPI 2+SENS

    It seems that Tenzin was [back] in his native land. (The speaker makes an inference based on the fact that Tenzin has acquired some items which are typical products of his native land.)

188

(384)   ཁོང་ལ་ཕྲུ་གུ་འཁོར་པའི་བཟོ་འདུག

a) *khong*   *- la*   *phru.gu*   *'khor*   *- pa : 'i : bzo : 'dug*
   s/he+H - OBL   child   be pregnant - PERF+EPI 2+SENS

It seems she is pregnant. (The speaker makes an inference based on the fact that she is vomiting a lot these days.)

    *   ངར་ཕྲུ་གུ་འཁོར་པའི་བཟོ་འདུག

b) * *nga*   *- r*   *phru.gu*   *'khor*   *- pa : 'i : bzo : 'dug*
   I   - OBL   child   be pregnant - PERF+EPI 2+SENS

Intended statement: I seem to be pregnant.

(385)   ང་དེབ་འདི་མཐོང་མྱོང་པའི་བཟོ་འདུག

   nga   *deb*   *'di*   *mthong*   *myong*   *- pa : 'i : bzo : 'dug*
   I   book   this   see   have an experience - PERF+EPI 2+SENS

I seem to have seen this book before. Or: I think I've seen this book before. (The book looks familiar to the speaker but he is not sure whether he has actually seen it before or not.)

In SST, there is as well an expression comprised of the elements *ra* and *cig* (derived from *'dra.po cig*, meaning 'a similar [one]') which are placed between *bzo* and *'dug*, i.e. diachronically V - *pa* - *'i* + *bzo* + *'dra.po* + *cig* + *'dug*, as seen in example (386a), or synchronically V - *pa : 'i : bzo : ra : cig : 'dug*, as seen in example (386b). This expression conveys sensory connotations and it has two meanings: the first conveys a sense of: 'appear, look like (but in reality not to be so)', whereas the second conveys a sense of: 'perhaps is', which is itself similar to *pa : 'i : bzo : 'dug*, as shown in example (386c):

(386)   * ཁོང་ཁ་ལག་བཟས་པའི་བཟོ་འདྲ་པོ་ཅིག་འདུག

a) * *khong*   *kha.lag*   *bzas*   *- pa*   *- 'i*   *bzo*   *'dra.po*   *cig*   *'dug*
   s/he+H   food   eat (PAS) - NOM - GEN   form   similar   one   exist (SENS)

   ཁོང་ཁ་ལག་བཟས་པའི་བཟོར་ཅིག་འདུག

b) *khong*   *kha.lag*   *bzas*   *- pa: 'i : bzo : ra : cig : 'dug*
   s/he+H   food   eat (PAS) - PERF+EPI 2+SENS

   1. She looks like she ate [something/a meal], [but she hasn't].
   2. She seems to have eaten. (There are traces of food around her mouth.).

ཁོང་ཁ་ལག་བཟས་པའི་བཟོ་འདུག

c) *khong*   *kha.lag*   *bzas*   - *pa : 'i : bzo : 'dug*
    s/he+H   food   eat (PAS) - PERF+EPI 2+SENS

    She seems to have eaten. (The speaker sees traces of food around her mouth.)

2. Constructions of V (PRS) - *yag : gi : bzo : 'dug* and V - *yag : gi : bzo : mi : 'dug*

From a diachronic viewpoint, this construction consists of a lexical verb in the present-future stem followed by the nominalizer *yag,* the genitive suffix *gi,* the morpheme *bzo,* (the negative particle *mi*), and the copula *'dug*. It conveys sensory connotations, and is usually used in present contexts (that may apply to future contexts as well). Just as in the preceding construction, from a synchronic viewpoint, this construction is undergoing a process of grammaticalization (*yag : gi : bzo : 'dug > yag.gi.bzo.'dug*). It can be used with different verbal classes in third person sentences, as shown in example (387). In first person sentences, it is usually employed with non-controllable verbs, as shown in example (388).

(387)   ཁོང་ཆང་ས་བརྒྱབ་ཡག་གི་བཟོ་འདུག

khong   *chang.sa*   *brgyab*   - *yag : gi : bzo : 'dug*
s/he+H   wedding   VBZ   - IMPF+EPI 2+SENS

It seems she is getting married. (The speaker saw her doing some preparations that are usually made before the wedding.)

(388)   ང་ཕལ་ཆེར་ཆམ་པ་བརྒྱབ་ཡག་གི་བཟོ་འདུག

a) *nga*   *phal.cher*   *cham.pa*   *brgyab*   - *yag : gi : bzo : 'dug*
    I   probably   cold   catch   - IMPF+EPI 2+SENS

    It seems I'm catching a cold. (The speaker can feel a cold coming on in his nose and throat.)

དེ་རིང་ང་ཡག་པོ་མ་ཡོང་ཡག་གི་བཟོ་འདུག

b) *de.ring*   *nga*   *yag.po*   *ma*   - *yong*   - *yag : gi : bzo : 'dug*
    today   I   good   NEG   - come   - IMPF+EPI 2+SENS

    I feel like something not good might happen to me today. (The speaker had a bad dream.)

To conclude, the position of this type of epistemic verbal ending and copula is fairly marginal in the system of SST epistemic types as its frequency in the spoken language is very low. To the best of my knowledge, however, this type has never been presented before, and so it merits discussion. Furthermore, it is noteworthy from the perspective of grammaticalization as it demonstrates the various degrees of grammaticalization of epistemic constructions into epistemic verbal endings.

190

III. SECONDARY VERBS AND EPISTEMIC VERBAL ENDINGS

3.1 SECONDARY VERBS

Between the lexical verb and the verbal ending, there is a syntactic position corresponding to that of a secondary verb.[90] The secondary verb specifies the meaning of the lexical verb. There are about twenty secondary verbs that are frequently used in standard spoken Tibetan. They include modal, aspectual and directional verbs. There are two types of secondary verbs.[91] The first type has a similar syntactic behaviour as lexical verbs, and is followed by TAM verbal endings: see example (389). The other one behaves like a nominalizer and as such can only be followed by auxiliaries that are identical to copulas: see example (390):

V	+	Sec 1	–	TAM verbal ending

1) Sec 1: *thub, dgos, chog*1 (modal), *shes, srid, nus, ran, tshar, bsdad, 'gro, yong, myong.*

(389)   མོ་རང་གིས་ལས་ཀ་འདི་བྱེད་ཐུབ་སོང་།

a) *mo.rang*   *- gis*   *las.ka*   *'di*   *byed*   *thub*   *- song*
   she   - ERG   work   this   VBZ (PRS)   be able   - PFV+SENS

   She was able to do this work.

ད་ལྟ་རང་འགྲོ་དགོས་ཀྱི་ཡོད་པ་འདྲ།

b) *da.lta*   *rang*   *'gro*   *dgos*   *- kyi.yod.pa.'dra*
   now   you   go (PRS)   must   - IMPF+EPI 2+SENS

   It looks like you have to go now. (Your parents are about to leave.)

---

[90] The term 'secondary verb' was introduced by Kesang Gyurme (*bya.tshig phal.ba*) and translated by Nicolas Tournadre (see Kesang Gyurme1992) and corresponds roughly to the English terms "modal verb" or "modal auxiliary" (for more details, see Coates 1997).

[91] The division of secondary verbs into two types was suggested in my D.E.A. dissertation, see Vokurková (2002).

2) Sec 2: *'dod, chog*2 (aspectual), *rtsis, long* and *grabs.*[92]

(390)   ཁོང་ལ་འགྲོ་ལོང་ཡོད་རེད།

   a)   *khong*   *- la*   *'gro*   *long*   *yod.red*
       s/he+H   - OBL   go (PRS)   have time   AUX (FACT)

    She has the time to go [there].

       བཀྲ་ཤིས་ཨམ་ཆི་བྱེད་རྩིས་ཡོད་པ་འདྲ།

   b)   *bkra.shis*   *am.chi*   *byed*   *rtsis*   *yod.pa.'dra*
       Tashi   doctor   VBZ (PRS)   intend   AUX (EPI 2+SENS)

    It looks like Tashi is intending to become a doctor. (The speaker makes
    an inference based on the fact that Tashi reads many books about
    medicine.)

From a semantic and syntactic viewpoint, many of the secondary verbs discussed above demonstrate a particular characteristic: some are employed only in one tense, some are used to convey more than one meaning, and some occupy the final position in the sentence and resemble thus verbal endings. Those verbs ccupying the final position are an example of the grammaticalization of a single lexical word into a verbal ending. This is the case of *dgos, chog, yong, tshar* and *myong*. They are preceded, with the exception of *myong*, by the past stem of the lexical verb (if this one is used in the spoken language). In this case, the agent is always in the first person. Moreover, the agent of sentences containing *dgos, chog* and *yong* is always in the ergative case, no matter the class of the lexical verb is, as in example (391). In sentences with transitive verbs containing *tshar*, the ergative is used, as in example (392). In sentences with a transitive verb followed by *myong*, the ergative is generally not used (see example 393) unless the agent is preceded by the object. *Dgos, chog* and *yong* express the egophoric allocentric future, whereas *tshar* and *myong* express the egophoric present perfect. From a phonetic viewpoint, they are all tonelesss. Compare the following examples:

(391)   ངས་བྱས་དགོས་ ⌠ ཆོག།

       nga   *- s*   *byas*   *- dgos / chog*
       I   - ERG   do (PAS)   - FUT+EGO ALL

       I'll do it (for you).

---

[92] The verbal status of *grabs* is problematic, see Section 3.2.15.

(392)   ངས་བྱས་ཚར།

nga	- s	byas	tshar	- Ø
I	- ERG	VBZ (PAS)	finish	- PERF+EGO

I have finished.

(393)   ང་བལ་ཡུལ་ལ་འགྲོ་མྱོང་།

a)

nga	bal.yul	- la	'gro	myong	- Ø
I	Nepal	- OBL	go (PRS)	have an experience	- PERF+EGO

I have gone to Nepal. (The speaker has had the experience of going to Nepal.)

ང་ཤིང་ཏོག་དེ་ཟ་མྱོང་།

b)

nga	shing.tog	de	za	myong	- Ø
I	fruit	that	eat (PRS)	have an experience	- PERF+EGO

I have eaten that fruit. (The speaker has had the experience of eating that kind of fruit.)

These secondary verbs differ in the degree of grammaticalization they have achieved by now. Since *myong* and *tshar* have still partially preserved their lexical meaning of 'have an experience of' and 'finish', respectively, in this work, they are both glossed as secondary verbs. The other three, *dgos, chog,* and *yong,* in their use as allocentric future endings, are glossed as verbal endings. It should, however, be emphasized that these charactersitics are restricted to utterances conveying certain information. In epistemic contexts, the allocentric endings *dgos, chog,* and *yong* are not used, and *tshar* and *myong* are followed by an epistemic verbal ending (see Sections 3.2.11 and 3.2.17).

In the article, "Final auxiliary verbs in Tibetan", Tournadre and Konchok Jiatso (2001: 88) describe the grammaticalization of four secondary verbs, among them *yong* and *tshar*, as follows:

"... [they] have kept their lexical meaning, although they also function as aspect and directional markers in the modern language. The study of these verbs is particularly interesting because they show synchronically various stages of polygrammaticalization."

3.2 USE OF SECONDARY VERBS WITH EPISTEMIC VERBAL ENDINGS

As stated above, in the Tibetan sentence, secondary verbs occupy a syntactic position between the lexical verb and the TAM verbal ending (whether evidential or epistemic). In this section, the use of secondary verbs with epistemic verbal endings, as well as restrictions on their use, will be analyzed and illustrated by examples.[93]

It should be emphasized that most of the examples contain an affirmative verbal ending. It is, however, generally possible to use the corresponding negative ending as well, unless the context of the sentence precludes this possibility. Affirmative and negative verbal endings differ only in polarity—negative endings imply a degree higher than 50% of the speaker's belief in the non-actuality of his utterance—but not in other parameters (see Section 1.2.1.2). See example (394a) below with the affirmative imperfective epistemic ending *gi.yod.pa.'dra,* and the negative imperfective epistemic ending *gi.med.pa.'dra*, as shown in example (394b):

(394)   ཁོང་པར་བརྒྱབ་ཆོག་གི་ཡོད་པ་འདྲ།

a)   *khong   par   brgyab   chog   - gi.yod.pa.'dra*
      s/he+H   photo   VBZ   be allowed   - IMPF+EPI 2+SENS

It seems he'll be allowed to take pictures. (The speaker sees other people taking pictures, and so assumes the subject of the sentence will be able to as well.)

ཁོང་འགྲུལ་པར་པར་བརྒྱབ་ཆོག་གི་མེད་པ་འདྲ།

b)   *khong   'grul.pa   - r   par   brgyab   chog   - gi.med.pa.'dra*
      s/he+H   tourist   - OBL   photo   VBZ   allow   - IMPF+EPI 2+SENS+NEG

It seems he doesn't allow the tourists to take pictures. (A monk in a monastery is waving at tourists while they are taking pictures. The speaker thinks this is probably because taking pictures is not allowed in the monastery.)

Just as with sentences with a lexical verb and an epistemic verbal ending, it is possible to use epistemic adverbs in sentences containing a secondary verb and an epistemic ending (or auxiliary). Their use is subject to certain restrictions depending on the epistemic ending and the context, among other factors. When these adverbs occur together with an epistemic ending (or auxiliary), they semantically impact the verbal ending and thus modify the epistemic significance

---

[93] Some examples are taken from Vokurková (2002).

of the whole sentence. It is often the case that the semantic connotations of the epistemic adverb are stronger than that of the verbal ending (see Section 1.1.1). The most frequently used epistemic adverbs implying probability are *gcig.byas.na* 'perhaps', *spyir.btang* 'generally, in principle' and *phal.cher* 'probably'. Below are examples of sentences employing a secondary verb that contain both an epistemic adverb and an epistemic verbal ending:

(395)   ཁོང་གཅིག་བྱས་ན་ལྷ་སར་འགྲོ་ཆོག་གི་ཡོད་པ་འདྲ།

a) *khong   gcig.byas.na   lha.sa   - r   'gro   chog   - gi.yod.pa. 'dra*
    s/he+H   perhaps   Lhasa   - OBL   go (PRS)   be allowed - IMPF+EPI 2+SENS

It seems he will be allowed to go to Lhasa. (The person who wants to go to Lhasa is leaving the office with a happy expression on his face.)

ང་སྤྱིར་བཏང་ནང་ལ་ཉལ་ཐུབ་པ་འདུག

b) *nga   spyir.btang   nang   - la   nyal   thub   - pa. 'dug*
    I   generally   inside - OBL   sleep   can   - FUT+EPI 3+SENS

I will probably be able to sleep at home. (The speaker is not at home but he thinks he will probably be able to reach home by night-time.)

3.2.1 MODAL VERB *thub* 'be able', 'can'

The secondary verb *thub* can combine with the majority of epistemic verbal endings: either perfect endings, e.g. *yod.pa.yod*, as shown in example (396a), or imperfective endings, e.g. *kyi.yod.kyi.ma.red*, as shown in example (396b). This secondary verb does not usually combine with perfective endings such as *pa.yin.pa. 'dra*, or *pa.yin.pa.yod* as in example (397a). The ending *bzo. 'dug*, shown in example (397b), as well as combinations with the other *bzo*-endings, are rare. The lexical verb preceding is in the present-future stem. Example (398) illustrates the use of *thub* with the first person.

(396)   ཁོང་ཕྱི་རྒྱལ་ལ་འགྲོ་ཐུབ་ཡོད་པ་ཡོད།

a) *khong   phyi.rgyal   - la   'gro   thub   - yod.pa.yod*
    s/he+H   abroad   - OBL   go (PRS)   be able   - PERF+EPI 2+EGO

She was probably able to go abroad. (The speaker doesn't remember if she was able to get a visa.)

ཁོང་རི་ལ་འགྲོ་ཐུབ་ཀྱི་ཡོད་ཀྱི་མ་རེད།

b) *khong   ri   - la   'gro   thub   - kyi.yod.kyi.ma.red*
    s/he+H   mountain - OBL   go (PRS)   be able   - IMPF+EPI 2+FACT+NEG

In all likelihood, she won't be able to go to the mountains. (The speaker bases his statement on the fact that she is elderly.)

(397)　　* ཁོང་ཕྱི་རྒྱལ་ལ་འགྲོ་ཐུབ་པ་ཡིན་པ་ཡོད།

    a)　* khong   phyi.rgyal   - la   'gro   thub   - pa.yin.pa.yod
          s/he+H   abroad   - OBL go (PRS) be able - PERF+EPI 2+EGO

    Intended statement: She was probably able to go abroad.

        * ཁོང་ལས་ཀ་བྱེད་ཐུབ་བཟོ་འདུག

    b)　* khong   las.ka   byed   thub   - bzo.'dug
          s/he+H   work   do (PRS) be able - FUT+EPI 1+SENS

    Intended statement: It looks like he will be able to work.

(398)　　ང་འགྲོ་ཐུབ་པ།

    nga   'gro   thub   - pa
    I   go (PRS) be able - FUT+EPI 3+SENS

    I must be able to walk. (An ailing woman comments on her attempts to get
    up from her seat.)

3.2.2 MODAL VERB *dgos* 'must', 'have to'

The verb *dgos* [94] (pronounced as *dgo* in the spoken language) is compatible with most perfect endings such as *yod.pa.'dra*, as shown in example (399a); imperfective endings such as *kyi.yod.pa.'dra*, as shown in example (399b); as well as with *mi.yong.ngas*. It is used with *pa.'dug* very infrequently. It would appear that the difference between the use of perfect and imperfective endings is rather aspectual than temporal. The lexical verb preceding *dgos* is in the present-future stem. This modal verb is not used with perfective endings such as *pa.yin.gyi.red*, as shown in example (400), or, for that matter, *pa.yod* or *pa.'dra*.

(399)　　ཁོང་ཚོགས་འདུ་ལ་འགྲོ་དགོས་ཡོད་པ་འདྲ།

    a)　khong   tshogs.'du - la   'gro   dgos   - yod.pa.'dra
         s/he+H meeting   - OBL go (PRS) have to - PERF+EPI 2+SENS

    It seems he has to go to that meeting. (The speaker saw him going into
    the office where the meeting will be taking place.)

        ཁོང་ཚོགས་འདུ་ལ་འགྲོ་དགོས་ཀྱི་ཡོད་པ་འདྲ།

    b)　khong   tshogs.'du - la   'gro   dgos   - kyi.yod.pa.'dra
         s/he+H meeting   - OBL go (PRS) have to - IMPF+EPI 2+SENS

    It seems he'll have to go to the meeting. (The speaker sees that no one
    else is available to go to the meeting.)

---

[94] The verb *dgos* also functions as a lexical verb meaning 'need' or 'want'. For more details, see Bartee, Nyima Droma (2000: 131–2), as well as Tournadre, Sangda Dorje (2003: 222–3).

(400)   * ཁོང་ཕྱག་ལས་གནང་དགོས་པ་ཡིན་གྱི་རེད།

       * *khong phyag.las gnang dgos   - pa.yin.gyi.red*
        s/he+H work+H   do+H   have to - PFV+EPI 2+FACT

Intended statement: He had to work, most likely.

3.2.3 MODAL VERB *'dod* 'want'

The verb *'dod* does not usually combine with epistemic endings: see example (401b).[95] It is compatible with epistemic auxiliaries, as shown in example (401a). It is often used in sentences expressing long-term, generic or repeated actions. To convey short-term volition in the spoken language, the verbs *snying.'dod* and *snying.bro* are employed. They are combined only with controllable verbs and are generally used with imperfective endings, as seen in example (402a). Their use with perfect endings is not excluded, however: see example (402b). As compared to *snying.'dod* and *snying.bro,* the secondary verb *'dod* can be characterized as more intense. It is preceded by the present-future stem of the lexical verb, and is compatible with the majority of epistemic auxiliaries.

(401)   མོ་རང་སློབ་གྲྭ་ཆེན་མོ་སློབ་སྦྱོང་བྱེད་འདོད་ཡོད་ཀྱི་རེད།

    a) *mo.rang   slob.grwa chen.mo   - r   slob.sbyong   byed*
       she   university   - OBL   study   VBZ (PRS)

       'dod   yod.kyi.red
       want   AUX (EPI 2+FACT)

       In all likelihood, she wants to study at university. (She has been preparing for the entrance exam.)

       * མོ་རང་རྒྱ་སྐད་སྦྱང་འདོད་ཀྱི་ཡོད་པ་ཡོད།

    b) * *mo.rang   rgya.skad   sbyang   'dod   - kyi.yod.pa.yod*
        she   Chinese   learn   want   - IMPF+EPI 2+EGO

       Intended statement: As far as I can remember, she wants to learn Chinese.

(402)   མོ་རང་སློབ་སྦྱོང་བྱེད་སྙིང་འདོད་ཀྱི་ཡོད་ཀྱི་རེད།

    a) *mo.rang   slob.sbyong   byed   snying.'dod   - kyi.yod.kyi.red*
       she   study   VBZ (PRS)   want   - IMPF+EPI 2+FACT

       In all likelihood, she wants to study [at the present time, general present]. (Instant volition, more frequent, She is a good student.)

---

[95] Tibetan consultants do not reject all the combinations of *'dod* with a verbal ending, however. See example (403a) below.

མོ་རང་སློབ་སྦྱོང་བྱེད་སྙིང་འདོད་ཡོད་ཀྱི་རེད།

b) *mo.rang*   *slob.sbyong*   *byed*   *snying.'dod*   *- yod.kyi.red*
   she   study   VBZ (PRS)   want   - PERF+EPI 2+FACT

In all likelihood, she wants to study [right now]. (Instant volition, less
frequent, She is a good student.)

Both of the sentences with the verb *snying.'dod* in example (402) convey a similar meaning as
the sentence with the verb *'dod* in example (401a). They differ in the duration of the agent's wish
to study (long-term vs. short-term), as well as in the intensity.

Although *'dod* combines, in principle, with verbal auxiliaries, some combinations with
imperfective epistemic endings are not rejected by native speakers; they are, however, considered
as dialectal for the most part: see the construction *kyi.yod-mdog.kha.po-red* in example (403a).
Other combinations, such as *kyi.yod.kyi.red* in example (403b), are considered to be
ungrammatical:

(403)   ཁོང་རྒྱ་གར་ལ་འགྲོ་འདོད་ཀྱི་ཡོད་མདོག་ཁ་པོ་རེད།

a) *khong*   *rgya.gar*   *- la*   *'gro*   *'dod*   *- kyi.yod*
   s/he+H   India   - OBL   go (PRS)   want   - IMPF

   - mdog.kha.po   *- red*
   - EPI 1   - AUX (FACT)

He probably wants to go to India. (Implication: he intends to be there for
a long time)

*   ཁོང་སློབ་སྦྱོང་བྱེད་འདོད་ཀྱི་ཡོད་ཀྱི་རེད།

b) *   *khong*   *slob.sbyong*   *byed*   *'dod*   *- kyi.yod.kyi.red*
     s/he+H   study   VBZ (PRS)   want   - IMPF+EPI 2+FACT

Intended statement: In all likelihood, he wants to study (e.g., at
university).

3.2.4 MODAL VERB *chog* 'be allowed', 'can' AND ASPECTUAL VERB *chog.chog* 'be ready'

In SST, the verb *chog* may have a modal (*chog1*) and an aspectual (*chog2*) meaning: as a modal
verb, it implies permission: see the use of *chog*1 in example (404); see as well the use of *chog*2 as
an aspectual verb of preparedness in example (405). The aspectual verb is reduplicated,
(*chog.chog*), behaving syntactically as a nominal phrase: it is thus followed by verbal auxiliaries.
On the contrary, the modal verb *chog* cannot be reduplicated, and can only be combined with
verbal endings.

198

(404) རང་འགྲོ་ཆོག་ག (རང་འགྲོ་ཆོག་པ་འདུག

rang   *'gro*   *chog*   *- ga* (i.e. *pa. 'dug*)[96]
you   go (PRS)   be allowed   - FUT+EPI 3+SENS

You will certainly be allowed to go. (The speaker thinks that the mother of
the person in question will give him permission to go to a certain
destination.)

(405) ཨ་མ་འགྲོ་ཆོག་ཆོག་ཡིན་མདོག་ཁ་པོ་རེད།

a.ma   *'gro*   *chog.chog*   *yin*   *- mdog.kha.po*   *- red*
mother   go (PRS)   be ready   AUX   - EPI 1   - AUX (FACT)

It looks mother is ready to go. (It is noon, so the speaker thinks that mother will
be ready to go.)

The modal verb *chog*

Since the modal verb *chog* implies a state of permission or 'being allowed [to do something]', it
is usually combined with imperfective endings. They are used either in a present-future context:
see the ending *gi.yod.'gro* in example (406a); or in an imperfective past context, as in example
(406b). Furthermore, *chog* is compatible with the future endings *a.yong, mi.yong.ngas, yong* and
pa.'dug, as in example (407).[97] It is not employed with perfect endings such as *yod.kyi.red,* as in
example (408a); with perfective endings such as *pa.yin.gyi.red,* as in example (408b), with
pa.'dra, as in example (408c), and with *bzo.'dug*. Finally, with *pa.yod* it is used in a different
meaning.[98] The lexical verb may be either in the present-future stem, as in example (406), or the
past stem, as in example (407). At times, *chog* expresses the same meaning as the modal verb
thub 'be able'.[99]

---

[96] In the spoken language. the epistemic ending *pa. 'dug >pa* is pronounced *ga* when preceded by *chog*.

[97] In SST, there is also an expression *chog.ga* conveying an optative meaning. See the following example:

ང་དབྱིན་ཇི་སྐད་ཡག་པོ་ཅིག་ཤེས་ཆོག་ག

nga   *dbyin.ji.skad*   *yag.po*   *cig*   *shes*   *chog.ga*
I   English   well   one   know   - FUT+OPTATIVE

If only I could speak English well.

[98] The secondary verb *chog* employed with the epistemic ending *pa.yod* (pronounced *ga.yod*) at times
conveys the meaning of 'deserve', and not 'be allowed' or 'be ready':

བྱ་དགའ་འདི་རང་ལ་སྤྲད་ཆོག་ག་ཡོད།

bya.dga'   *'di*   *rang*   *- la*   *sprad*   *chog*   *- ga.yod*
prize   this   you   - OBL   give   deserve   - FUT+EGO

You definitely deserve to get the prize. (The speaker thinks so as the other person
worked extremely hard on the project at hand. The speaker is expressing his own
personal judgement.)

[99] See Tournadre, Sangda Dorje (2003: 245).

(406) ཉི་མ་རྒྱ་གར་ལ་འགྲོ་ཆོག་གི་ཡོད་འགྲོ།

a) *nyi.ma   rgya.gar - la   'gro   chog   - gi.yod.'gro*
   Nyima   India   - OBL   go (PRS) be allowed - IMPF+EPI 1+FACT

Maybe Nyima will be allowed to go to India. (Many visas for India are being issued these days.)

ཟླ་ཉིན་ཉི་མ་རྒྱ་གར་ལ་འགྲོ་ཆོག་གི་ཡོད་འགྲོ།

b) *zla.nyin nyi.ma   rgya.gar   - la   'gro   chog*
   last year Nyima   India   - OBL   go (PRS) be allowed

   - gi.yod.'gro
   - IMPF+EPI 1+FACT

Maybe Nyima was allowed to go to India last year. (Since this year, Nyima did not obtain permission, the speaker tends to think that it is so because he was allowed to go last year.)

(407) ཉི་མ་རྒྱ་གར་ལ་ཕྱིན་ཆོག་ག / ཉི་མ་རྒྱ་གར་ལ་ཕྱིན་ཆོག་པ་འདུག

   nyi.ma   rgya.gar - la   phyin   chog   - ga (i.e. pa. 'dug)
   Nyima   India   - OBL   go (PAS) be allowed - FUT+EPI 3+SENS

Nyima will certainly be allowed to go to India. (The speaker saw that Nyima obtained a visa.)

(408) * ཉི་མ་རྒྱ་གར་ལ་ཕྱིན་ཆོག་ཡོད་ཀྱི་རེད།

a) * *nyi.ma   rgya.gar - la   phyin   chog   - yod.kyi.red*
     Nyima   India   - OBL   go (PAS) be allowed - PERF+EPI 2+FACT

Intended statement: It is very likely Nyima was allowed to go to India.

   * ཉི་མ་རྒྱ་གར་ལ་ཕྱིན་ཆོག་པ་ཡིན་གྱི་རེད།

b) * *nyi.ma   rgya.gar - la   phyin   chog   - pa.yin.gyi.red*
     Nyima   India   - OBL   go (PAS) be allowed - PFV+EPI 2+FACT

Intended statement: Most likely, Nyima was allowed to go to India.

   * ཁོང་གིས་བྱེད་ཆོག་པ་འདྲ།

c) * *khong   - gis   byed   chog   - pa.'dra*
     s/he+H - ERG   VBZ (PRS)   be allowed - PFV+EPI 2+SENS

Intended statement: It seems he was allowed to do [a certain action].

The aspectual verb *chog*

As stated above, in its aspectual function *chog* is reduplicated and is not used with verbal endings, as shown in example (410). It can be combined with both existential and essential auxiliaries, but with a difference in meaning. If used with an existential auxiliary, it conveys that 'something is ready', as shown in examples (409a) and (411a). When used with an essential

200

auxiliary, it conveys that 'someone is ready', as in examples (409b) and (411b). Compare the following examples with the evidential auxiliaries *yod* and *yin*:

(409)   རང་ ﹇ ལ་ ﹈ ཁ་ལག་ཟ་ཆོག་ཆོག་ཡོད་པས།

    a)   *rang*   *(- la)*   *kha.lag*   *za*   *chog.chog*   *yod*   *- pas*
          you   (- OBL)   meal   eat (PRS)   be ready   have (EGO)   - Q

          Do you have a ready meal (i.e. food that is already prepared and can be eaten right away)?

          རང་ཁ་ལག་ཟ་ཆོག་ཆོག་ཡིན་པས།

    b)   *rang*   *kha.lag*   *za*   *chog.chog*   *yin*   *- pas*
          you   meal   eat (PRS)   be ready   be (EGO)   - Q

          Are you ready to eat?

(410)   * ཉི་མ་རྒྱ་གར་ལ་འགྲོ་ཆོག་ཆོག་གི་ཡོད་འགྲོ།

    *   *nyi.ma*   *rgya.gar*   *- la*   *'gro*   *chog.chog*   *- gi.yod.'gro*
          Nyima   India   - OBL   go (PRS)   be ready   - IMPF+EPI 1+FACT

          Intended statement: Nyima is probably ready to go to India.

Similarly, this aspectual verb is compatible with such existential epistemic auxiliaries as *yod-mdog.kha.po-red* and *yod.pa.'dra,* as shown in example (411a); as well as with the corresponding essential auxiliaries *yin-mdog.kha.po-red, yin.pa.'dra*, and *yin.gyi.red*: see examples (411b) and (412). The lexical verb may be in either the present-future or the past stem, as shown in example (412):

(411)   དངུལ་སྤྲད་ཆོག་ཆོག་ཡོད་མདོག་ཁ་པོ་རེད།

    a)   *dngul*   *sprad*   *chog.chog*   *yod*   *- mdog.kha.po*   *- red*
          money   give   be ready   AUX   - EPI 1   - AUX (FACT)

          It looks like there is money ready to be given. (This refers to the object of the action, i.e. the money to be given.)

          དངུལ་སྤྲད་ཆོག་ཆོག་ཡིན་མདོག་ཁ་པོ་རེད།

    b)   *dngul*   *sprad*   *chog.chog*   *yin*   *- mdog.kha.po*   *- red*
          money   give   be ready   AUX   - EPI 1   - AUX (FACT)

          It looks like [you/one] is ready to give money. (This refers to the agent and the verbal action.)

(412)   ཉི་མ་འགྲོ་ཆོག་ཆོག་ཡིན་པ་འདྲ།

    a)   *nyi.ma*   *'gro*   *chog.chog*   *yin.pa.'dra*
          Nyima   go (PRS)   be ready   AUX (EPI 2+SENS)

          It seems Nyima is ready to go. (The speaker makes an inference based on the fact that Nyima is waiting with his bag.)

ཉི་མ་ཕྱིན་ཚོག་ཚོག་ཡིན་གྱི་རེད།

b) *nyi.ma   phyin   chog.chog   yin.gyi.red*
   Nyima   go (PAS)   be ready   AUX (EPI 2+FACT)

Nyima is most likely ready to go. (The speaker makes an inference based on the fact that Nyima finishes work at three pm. It is now six pm.)

3.2.5 MODAL VERB *shes* 'know'

The secondary verb *shes* can be combined with the vast majority of epistemic endings: imperfective endings, using *kyi.med.'gro'o*, as in example (413a); perfect endings, using *yod.kyi.red*, as in example (413b); and perfective endings, using *pa.yin.pa.'dra*, as in example (413c). It is also possible to combine *shes* with the following epistemic endings: *a.yong, pa.yod, pa.'dug, pa.'dra, mdog.kha.po-red, mi.yong.ngas* and *yong*. The preceding lexical verb is in the present-future stem: see example (414). The combination with the ending *bzo.'dug* is considered to be ungrammatical, as seen in example (415).

(413)   བུ་མོ་འདི་རི་མོ་འབྲི་ཤེས་ཀྱི་མེད་འགྲོ་འོ།

   a) *bu.mo   'di   ri.mo   'bri   shes   - kyi.med.'gro'o*
      girl   this   picture draw (PRS) know   - IMPF+EPI 1+FACT

   This girl maybe knows to draw (pictures). (She attends a drawing course.)

       ཁོང་གིས་དབྱིན་ཇི་སྐད་བརྒྱབ་ཤེས་ཡོད་ཀྱི་རེད།

   b) *khong   - gis   dbyin.ji.skad   brgyab   shes   - yod.kyi.red*
      s/he+H   - ERG   English language VBZ   know   - PERF+EPI 2+FACT

   Most likely, he learnt how to speak English. (He spent three years in England.)

       ཁོང་གིས་མོ་ཊ་བཏང་ཤེས་པ་ཡིན་པ་འདྲ།

   c) *khong   - gis   mo.Ta   btang   shes   - pa.yin.pa.'dra*
      s/he+H   - ERG   car   drive   know   - PFV+EPI 2+SENS

   It seems he learnt how to drive. (He is sitting behind the steering wheel.)

(414)   ཁོང་བོད་ཇ་བཟོ་ ⌠   *   བཟོས་ཤེས་ཀྱི་ཨ་ཡོད།

   khong   bod.ja   bzo   / bzos   shes   - kyi.a.yod*
   s/he+H   Tibetan tea   make (PRS) / make (PAS) know   - IMPF+EPI 3+EGO+NEG

   I doubt he can make Tibetan tea. (The speaker knows that the person in question is not familiar with Tibetan cuisine.)

202

(415)　　　* ཁོང་མོ་ཊ་བཏང་ཤེས་བཟོ་འདུག

　　　* *khong*　　*mo.Ta*　*btang*　*shes*　*- bzo.'dug*
　　　　　s/he+H　　car　　drive　　know　　- FUT+EPI 1+SENS

Intended statement: It looks like he'll know how to drive.

3.2.6 MODAL VERB *srid* 'be possible', 'can'

There is a considerable variation among native speakers concerning the acceptability of combinations of the verb *srid* with epistemic verbal endings. Some native speakers accept combinations of *srid* with various epistemic verbal endings, whereas others accept only cerain combinations, and some refuse all combinations, claiming that this secondary verb is semantically incompatible with epistemic verbal endings. The following imperfective or future verbal endings and constructions are accepted by some Tibetan speakers: *kyi.yod.'gro, kyi.a.yod, a.yong, pa.'dug, pa.yod, kyi.yod.pa.'dra, kyi.yod-mdog.kha.po-red, mdog.kha.po-red, kyi.yod.kyi.red, kyi.yod.sa.red, kyi.yod.bzo.'dug, mi.yong.ngas,* and *yong*: see example (416). Concerning perfect endings, the use of verbal endings with a sensory meaning is ungrammatical, as shown in example (417b) with *yod.pa.'dra, yod.bzo.'dug* and *pa.'dra*. Other perfect endings such as *yod.'gro, yod.kyi.red,* and *yod.pa.yod,* as shown in example (417a), are acceptable. Furthermore, *srid* is not compatible with non-controllable verbs: see example (418). The preceding lexical verb is in the present-future stem. The examples below marked with "?" are found grammatical by some native speakers and ungrammatical by others:

(416)　　? བོད་ལ་འགྲོ་སྲིད་ཀྱི་ཡོད་པ་འདྲ།

　　　? *bod*　　*- la*　　*'gro*　　*srid*　　*- kyi.yod.pa.'dra*
　　　　Tibet　　- OBL　　go (PRS)　be possible　- PRS+EPI 1+SENS

It seems it is possible to go to Tibet.

(417)　　? མི་དེ་སྐྱག་རྫུན་བཤད་སྲིད་ཡོད་ཀྱི་རེད་ ⌠ ཡོད་པ་ཡོད།

　　a)　? *mi*　　*de*　　*skyag.rdzun*　　*bshad*　　*srid*　　*- yod.kyi.red*
　　　　　man　　that　　lie　　　　　　say　　be possible　- PERF+EPI 2+FACT

　　/- yod.pa.yod
　　/- PERF+EPI 2+EGO

　　It is possible that this man was lying. (One of the workers went up to
　　speak with the boss. Later the boss changed his mind. The speaker thinks
　　that the man in question might have been lying about something.)

　　　* མི་དེ་སྐྱག་རྫུན་བཤད་སྲིད་ཡོད་པ་འདྲ་ ⌠ ཡོད་བཟོ་འདུག ⌠ པ་འདྲ།

　　b)　* *mi*　　*de*　　*skyag.rdzun*　　*bshad*　　*srid*　　　　*- yod.pa.'dra*

203

man	that	lie		say	be possible	- PERF+EPI 2+SENS

/yod.bzo. 'dug   */pa. 'dra*
/PERF+EPI 2+SENS   /PFV+EPI 2+SENS

Intended statement: It seems to be possible to tell lies.

(418)   * ཚར་པ་བཏང་སྲིད་ཀྱི་ཡོད་པ་ཡོད།

    * *char.pa*   *btang*   *srid*   *- kyi.yod.kyi.red*
      rain   VBZ   be possible   - IMPF+EPI 2+FACT

Intended statement: It is most likely possible that it will rain.

3.2.7 MODAL VERB *nus* 'dare'

The verb *nus* is, in general, compatible with imperfective verbal endings such as *kyi.yod.pa. 'dra* or *kyi.yod.kyi.red,* as in example (419a). Nonetheless, it is at times possible to employ the corresponding perfect and perfective verbal endings, as shown in examples (419b) and (419c). These are employed for single perfective actions, whereas imperfective endings are used for repeated and generic actions. Furthermore, *nus* can combine with other epistemic endings: *a.yong, pa.yod, pa. 'dug,* as shown in example (420), as well as with *pa. 'dra, bzo. 'dug, mi.yong.ngas, yong* and the *mdog.kha.po*-construction. The lexical verb is in the present-future stem, as shown in example (419).

(419)   ཁོང་འགྲོ་ནུས་ཀྱི་ཡོད་པ་འདྲ་ ⌐ ཀྱི་ཡོད་ཀྱི་རེད།

    a)   *khong*   *'gro*   *nus*   *- kyi.yod.pa. 'dra*   */ kyi.yod.kyi.red*
        s/he+H   go (PRS)   dare   - IMPF+EPI 1+SENS   / IMPF+EPI 2+FACT

      It seems she has the courage to go [there]. Or: She will most likely have the guts to go there.

    ཁོང་འགྲོ་ནུས་ཡོད་པ་འདྲ།

    b)   *khong*   *'gro*   *nus*   *- yod.pa. 'dra*
        s/he+H   go (PRS)   dare   - PERF+EPI 2+SENS

      It seems she dared to go [there]. (The speaker makes an inference based on the fact that yesterday she was saying she would not dare to go, but she is not at home now.)

    ཁོང་འགྲོ་ནུས་པ་ཡིན་པ་འདྲ།

    c)   *khong*   *'gro*   *nus*   *- pa.yin.pa. 'dra*
        s/he+H   go(PRS)   dare   - PFV+EPI 2+SENS

      It seems she dared to go. (The speaker observes some signs indicating that she has left.)

204

(420)   ང་དབྱིན་ཇི་སྐད་བརྒྱབ་ནུས་པ་མི་འདུག

nga	dbyin.ji.skad	brgyab	nus	- pa.mi.'dug
I	English language	VBZ	dare	- FUT+EPI 3+SENS+NEG

I certainly won't have the courage to speak English. (The speaker's knowledge of spoken English is slight.)

3.2.8 ASPECTO-TEMPORAL VERB *rtsis* 'intend [to do]', 'reckon or count [on doing]'

The verb *rtsis* can be combined only with existential verbal auxiliaries, as with *yod.pa.yod* in example (421) and the construction *yod-mdog.kha.po-red,* as in example (422); it cannot be combined with verbal endings. The lexical verb is in the present-future stem: see example (421):

(421)   ཁོང་མོག་མོག་བཟོ་ ∫ * བཟོས་རྩིས་ཡོད་པ་ཡོད།

khong	mog.mog	bzo	/ * bzos	rtsis	yod.pa.yod
s/he+H	momo	make (PRS)	/ make (PAS)	intend	AUX (EPI 2+EGO)

As far as I recall, she was probably intending to make *momos.* (The speaker seems to recollect that she told him she was going to make *momos,* but he isn't sure.)

(422)   ཁོང་དབྱིན་ཇི་སྐད་སྦྱང་རྩིས་ཡོད་མདོག་ཁ་པོ་རེད།

khong	dbyin.ji.skad	sbyang	rtsis	yod	- mdog.kha.po	- red
s/he+H	English language	learn	intend	AUX	- EPI 1	- AUX (FACT)

She is probably intending to learn English. (She has some English grammar books and dictionaries at her home.)

Furthermore, there is a construction in SST consisting of *rtsis* followed by the verb *byed* 'do', i.e. *rtsis byed,* which is compatible with imperfective verbal endings. Although in most sentences either the secondary verb *rtsis* (example 423a) or the expression *rtsis byed* can be used, the latter is the preferred, as shown in example (423b). From a semantic viewpoint, there is a difference between the use of the secondary verb *rtsis* and the expression *rtsis byed*: *rtsis* is used to talk about plans that are yet to be commenced, whereas *rtsis byed* implies that preparations have already started concerning the given action. Compare the following sentences with the epistemic auxiliary *yod.'gro* and the epistemic ending *kyi.yod.'gro.*

(423)   ཁོང་རྒྱ་གར་ལ་འགྲོ་རྩིས་ཡོད་འགྲོ།

a)
khong	rgya.gar	- la	'gro	rtsis	yod.'gro
s/he+H	India	- OBL	go (PRS)	intend	AUX (EPI 1+FACT)

Maybe he's intending to go to India. (He often talks about India, so the speaker infers that the person might have just such a plan.)

ཁོང་རྒྱ་གར་ལ་འགྲོ་རྩིས་བྱེད་ཀྱི་ཡོད་འགྲོ།

b) *khong*   *rgya.gar*   *- la*   *'gro*   *rtsis*   *byed*   *- kyi.yod.'gro*
    s/he+H   India   - OBL   go (PRS)   intend   VBZ (PRS)   - IMPF+EPI 1+FACT

Perhaps he is intending to go to India. (The person in question has been buying things he might need for the journey to India, so the speaker infers that perhaps he is planning to go there.)

3.2.9 ASPECTO-TEMPORAL VERB *ran* 'be time [to do]', 'have come [the time to do]'

The secondary verb *ran* is compatible with the majority of epistemic verbal endings. It is used with perfect endings such as *yod.'gro,* as seen in example (424a); imperfective endings such as *gyi.yod.'gro,* shown in example (424b); perfective endings such as *pa.yin.'gro,* shown in example (424c); with the verbal endings *pa.'dra* and *pa.yod,* shown here in a past-context in example (425a); and finally, with the construction *mdog.kha.po-red.* Taking into consideration the meaning of the verb *ran* ('be time [to do]', 'have come [the time to do]'), one can conclude that there is a semantic constraint on the use of this secondary verb in future contexts. Therefore, verbal endings employed only in the future, such as *a.yong, yong, mi.yong.ngas* and *pa.'dug*: see example (425b), are all incompatible with *ran.*

(424)   ནང་ལ་འགྲོ་རན་ཡོད་འགྲོ།

    a) *nang*   *- la*   *'gro*   *ran*   *- yod.'gro*
        home   - OBL   go (PRS)   be time   - PERF+EPI 1+FACT

    Maybe it's time to go now. (In reference to a single perfective action.)

    ཁང་གླ་སྤྲད་རན་གྱི་ཡོད་འགྲོ།

    b) *khang.gla*   *sprad*   *ran*   *- gyi.yod.'gro*
        rent   give   be time   - IMPF+EPI 1+FACT

    It is probably more than high time to pay the rent. (Concerning the temporal appropriateness of paying the rent, a repeated action)

    གླ་ལེན་རན་པ་ཡིན་འགྲོ།

    c) *gla*   *len*   *ran*   *- pa.yin.'gro* [100]
        salary   get   be time   - PFV+EPI 1+FACT

    It seems to be time to go and get my salary. (The speaker's name is on a list in the accounting department.)

---

[100] See note 49 and Section 1.2.2.1.2.

(425) ཁ་ལག་བཟོ་རན་པ་ཡོད།

a) *kha.lag   bzo   ran   - pa.yod*
    meal   make (PRS)   be time   - PFV+EPI 3+EGO

It must have been when it was time to cook. (The speaker usually prepares the meal at noon. It was about noon.)

    * ཁ་ལག་བཟོ་རན་པ་འདུག

b) * *kha.lag   bzo   ran   - pa.'dug*
      meal   make (PRS)   be time   - FUT+EPI 3+SENS

Intended statement: Surely, it is going to be time to prepare the meal.

3.2.10 ASPECTO-TEMPORAL VERB *long* 'have time [to do]'

Syntactically, the secondary verb *long* functions as a nominal phrase and thus is only compatible with existential verbal auxiliaries such as *yod.kyi.red,* as shown in example (426a), and not with verbal endings such as *gi.yod.kyi.red,* as shown in example (426b). The lexical verb is in the present-future stem. The first argument of the verb used with this secondary verb is obligatorily in the oblique case; see the examples below:

(426) རང་ལ་ཁ་ལག་ཟ་ལོང་ཡོད་ཀྱི་རེད།

a) *rang   - la   kha.lag   za   long   yod.kyi.red*
    you   - OBL   meal   eat (PRS)   have time   AUX (EPI 2+FACT)

You probably have time to eat. Or: I bet you have time to eat. (Someone complains that he has a lot of work and no time to eat. The speaker doesn't believe him.)

    * རང་ལ་ཁ་ལག་ཟ་ལོང་གི་ཡོད་ཀྱི་རེད།

b) * *rang   - la   kha.lag   za   long   - gi.yod.kyi.red*
      you   - OBL   meal   eat (PRS)   have time   - IMPF+EPI 2+FACT

Intended statement: Most likely, you do have time to eat.

(427) ཁོང་ལ་འགྲོ་ལོང་ཡོད་པ་འདྲ།

    khong   - la   'gro   long   yod.pa.'dra
    s/he+H   - OBL   go (PRS)   have time   AUX (EPI 1+SENS)

It seems she has the time to go [there]. (She is sitting and doing nothing, so the speaker infers that she has plenty of time to go to a certain destination.)

3.2.11 ASPECTO-TEMPORAL VERB *tshar* 'to finish', 'to end'

In addition to its lexical meaning 'to finish' or 'to end', the verb *tshar* may also convey the meaning of the adverbs 'already' and 'completely' (the terminative aspect): see example (428).[101] In accordance with its semantic scope, it generally is combined with perfect verbal endings such as *yod.pa.'dra*, as in example (429a). It is, though, sometimes possible to use *tshar* with perfective endings, as shown in example (429b), and exceptionally with imperfective endings, as shown in example (429c); the latter combinations are not, however, frequent. *Tshar* is also compatible with the endings *pa.'dra, pa.yod,* and *pa.'dug*: see example (430), but incompatible with the future endings *a.yong* and *bzo.'dug*. *Tshar* is preceded by the past stem of the lexical verb, as shown in example (429).

(428)   ཁོང་གི་ན་ཚ་དྲག་ཚར་པ་ཡོད།

     a)   *khong*   *- gi*   *na.tsha*   *drag*   *tshar*   *- pa.yod*
            s/he+H   - GEN   illness   recover   finish   - PFV+EPI 3+EGO

            She must have completely recovered. (She is attending classes again.)

       ཁོང་ཚོ་སླེབས་ཚར་པ་ཡིན་གྱི་རེད།

     b)   *khong*   *- tsho*   *slebs*   *tshar*   *- pa.yin.gyi.red*
            s/he+H   - pl   arrive   finish   - PFV+EPI 2+FACT

            They must have already arrived. (They left in the morning, and it is evening now.)

(429)   ཁོང་གིས་ཁ་ལག་བཟོས་ཚར་ཡོད་པ་འདྲ།

     a)   *khong*   *- gis*   *kha.lag*   *bzos*   *tshar*   *- yod.pa.'dra*
            s/he+H   - ERG   meal   make (PAS)   finish   - PERF+EPI 2+SENS

            It seems she finished the cooking. (The speaker makes an inference based on the fact that she is washing her hands.)

       ཁོང་གིས་ཁ་ལག་བཟོས་ཚར་པ་ཡིན་པ་འདྲ།

     b)   *khong*   *- gis*   *kha.lag*   *bzos*   *tshar*   *- pa.yin.pa.'dra*
            s/he+H   - ERG   meal   make (PAS)   finish   - PFV+EPI 2+SENS

            It seems she finished the cooking. (The speaker sees her carrying a tray with cooked food.)

---

[101] For more details, see Tournadre, Konchok Jiatso (2001: 96–8).

208

བོད་ནས་རྒྱུན་རྒྱུ་ཚོད་དང་པོར་ཉིན་གུང་ཁ་ལག་བཟས་ཚར་གྱི་ཡོད་པ་འདྲ།

c) khong   nam.rgyun   chu.tshod   dang.po   - r   nyin.gung   kha.lag
   s/he+H   usually   hour   first   - OBL noon   meal

   bzas   tshar   - gyi.yod.pa.'dra
   eat (PAS)   finish   - IMPF+EPI 2+SENS

It seems she usually finishes her lunch at 1 pm. (The speaker usually hears kitchen noises until that time.)

(430)   ཁོང་ཡི་གེ་མགྱོགས་པོ་བྲིས་ཚར་པ་འདུག

        khong   yi.ge   mgyogs.po   bris   tshar   - pa.'dug
        s/he+H   letter   soon   write (PAS) finish   - FUT+EPI 3+SENS

        Surely, she will soon finish (writing) the letter. (She is writing very quickly.)

The secondary verb *tshar* is often used in conditional sentences. It functions as an indicator of a perfective action, as shown in the example below:

(431)   ཁྱེད་རང་རོགས་པ་མ་བྱས་ན་ང་ཟག་ཚར་ཡོད་མདོག་ཁ་པོ་རེད།

        khyed.rang   rogs.pa   ma   - byas   - na   nga   zag   tshar
        you+H   help   NEG   - VBZ (PRS) - if   I   fall   finish
        - yod   - mdog.kha.po   - red
        - PERF   - EPI 1   - AUX (FACT)

        If you had not helped me, I would have fallen down [for good].

3.2.12 ASPECTO-TEMPORAL VERB *bsdad* 'stay'

The verb *bsdad* is often used to indicate a concomitant aspect leading to a resultant state with a progressive aspect (emphasizing the continuous character of the process).[102] It can be combined with the majority of epistemic verbal endings. It is compatible with imperfective endings such as *kyi.yod.pa.'dra* in example (432a); perfect endings such as *yod.pa.'dra* and *yod.kyi.red,* shown in examples (432b) and (433); perfective endings such as *pa.yin.pa.'dra* in example (432c); as well as other past or future endings such as *mdog.kha.po-red* or *'dug,* shown in example (434). Additionally, it is compatible with the endings *mi.yong.ngas* and *bzo.'dug.* It is usually preceded by the past stem of the lexical verb.

(432)   ཁོང་ནང་ལ་ལས་ཀ་བྱས་བསྡད་ཀྱི་ཡོད་པ་འདྲ།

        a) khong   nang   - la   las.ka   byas   bsdad   - kyi.yod.pa.'dra
           s/he+H   home   - OBL   work   VBZ (PAS)   stay   - IMPF+EPI 2+SENS

           It seems she (usually) works [while staying] at home. (She rarely leaves the house.)

---

[102] For more details, see Tournadre, Konchok Jiatso (2001: 98–101).

209

ཁོང་ནང་ལ་ལས་ཀ་བྱས་བསྡད་ཡོད་པ་འདྲ།

b) *khong*   *nang*   *- la*   *las.ka*   *byas*   *bsdad*   *- yod.pa. 'dra*
    s/he+H   home   - OBL   work   VBZ (PAS)   stay   - PERF+EPI 2+SENS

It seems she is staying at home to work [today].

ཁོང་ནང་ལ་ལས་ཀ་བྱས་བསྡད་པ་ཡིན་པ་འདྲ།

c) *khong*   *nang*   *- la*   *las.ka*   *byas*   *bsdad*   *- pa.yin.pa. 'dra*
    s/he+H   home   - OBL   work   VBZ (PAS)   stay   - PFV+EPI 2+SENS

It seems she stayed at home to work [in the past].

(433)   ཚེ་རིང་ན་བསྡད་ཡོད་ཀྱི་རེད།

      tshe.ring   *na*   *bsdad*   *- yod.kyi.red*
      Tshering   be ill   stay   - PERF+EPI 2+FACT

      Tsering is most likely still ill. (Tsering fell ill on Monday. It is only
      Wednesday today, so the speaker thinks that he is still ill.)

(434)   ཁོང་ལས་ཀ་བྱས་ནས་བསྡད་མདོག་ཁ་པོ་མི་འདུག

      khong   *las.ka*   *byas*   *- nas*   *bsdad*   *- mdog.kha.po*   *- mi.'dug* [103]
      s/he+H   work   VBZ (PAS)   - after   stay   - EPI 1   - AUX (SENS+NEG)

      He will probably not be able to work for a long time.

3.2.13 DIRECTIONAL AND ASPECTUAL VERB *'gro* 'go'

The secondary verb *'gro* has a variety of grammatical functions. It marks the inchoative and progressive aspects, direction from the speaker after verbs of movement, and cross-reference, as well as other meanings. For more details, refer to Tournadre, Konchok Jiatso (2001: 89–96).

Aspectual use of *'gro*

As an aspectual verb, *'gro* can only be combined with non-controllable verbs and imperfective verbal endings such as *gi.yod.pa. 'dra* , *gi.yod-mdog.kha.po-'dug,* and *gi.yod.kyi.red*: see examples (435) – (437). It functions as an indicator of the inchoative, progressive and iterative aspects. It conveys the disappearance of something or an entity, as well as a connection to other persons than the first person.[104] The aspectual function of *'gro* is illustrated in the examples below:

---

[103] Sometimes the particle of anteriority *nas*, pronounced *byas* in the spoken language, follows the lexical verb and precedes the secondary verb *bsdad*, as shown in example (434).
[104] For more details, see Tournadre, Konchok Jiatso (2001: 89–96).

210

(435) ཕྲུ་གུ་འདི་ཏེག་ཙ་འཁྱག་པ་ད་ཀ་ལམ་སང་ཆམ་པ་བརྒྱབ་འགྲོ་གི་ཡོད་པ་འདྲ།

phru.gu	*'di*	*teg.tsa*	*'khyag*	- *pa.da.ka*	*lam.sang*	*cham.pa*
child	this	a little bit	be cold	- IMM	immediately	a cold

brgyab	*'gro*	- *gi.yod.pa.'dra*
VBZ	go (PRS)	- IMPF+EPI 2+SENS

It seems whenever the child is a little bit chilly, it catches a cold.

(436) ཁོང་གཉིད་ཁུག་འགྲོ་གི་ཡོད་མདོག་ཁ་པོ་འདུག

khong	*gnyid.khug*	*'gro*	- *gi.yod*	- *mdog.kha.po*	- *'dug*
s/he+H	fall asleep	go (PRS)	- IMPF	- EPI 1	- AUX (SENS)

He is probably falling asleep. (The meeting is taking a long time and is very dull.)

(437) འདི་མགྱོགས་པོ་མ་བཟས་ན་སྐྱུར་འགྲོ་གི་ཡོད་ཀྱི་རེད།

'di	*mgyogs.po*	*ma*	- *bzas*	- *na*	*skyur*	*'gro*	- *gi.yod.kyi.red*
this	fast	NEG	- eat (PAS)	- if	sour	go (PRS)	- IMPF+EPI 2+FACT

We'd better eat this [food] soon or it will probably turn sour. (Usually, this kind of food goes sour quickly.)

As an ascpectual verb, *'gro* cannot be combined with perfect verbal endings such as *yod.kyi.red,* as shown in example (438a), or with future verbal endings such as *bzo.'dug,* as shown in example (439), as *'gro* is not used as an aspectual marker in past or future contexts. Thus only the present-future stem *'gro* and an imperfective ending are employed, as in example (438b); the past stem *phyin* with a perfect ending is not used, as in example (438a). Instead, in past contexts, the secondary verb *tshar* is used to denote the terminative aspect, as shown in example (438c):

(438) * འདི་སྐྱུར་ཕྱིན་ཡོད་ཀྱི་རེད།

a) *

'di	*skyur*	*phyin*	- *yod.kyi.red*
this	sour	go (PAS)	- PERF+EPI 2+FACT

Intended statement: It most likely turned sour.

འདི་སྐྱུར་འགྲོ་གི་ཡོད་ཀྱི་རེད།

b)

'di	*skyur*	*'gro*	- *gi.yod.kyi.red*
this	sour	go (PRS)	- IMPF+EPI 2+FACT

It will most likely turn sour.

འདི་སྐྱུར་ཚར་ཡོད་ཀྱི་རེད། ∫ ཡོད་མདོག་ཁ་པོ་རེད།

c)

'di	*skyur*	*tshar*	- *yod.kyi.red*	/- *yod*	- *mdog.kha.po*	- *red*
this	sour	finish	- PERF+EPI 2+FACT	/ - PERF	- EPI 1	- AUX (FACT)

It most likely turned sour. / It probably turned sour. (We have had [this food item] for almost a week now.)

(439)　　　* འདི་སྐྱུར་འགྲོ་བཟོ་འདུག

　　　* *'di*　*skyur*　*'gro*　　*- bzo. 'dug*
　　　　this　sour　　go (PRS)　- FUT+EPI 2+SENS

Intended statement: It will most likely turn sour.

Directional use of *'gro*

After verbs of movement, *'gro* implies direction away from the speaker or from another point in space. In past contexts, the past stem *phyin* is used instead of *'gro*. It is compatible with the majority of epistemic endings: see the use of the imperfective ending *gi.med.'gro'o* in example (440a); the use of the perfect ending *med.'gro'o* in example (440b); and finally, the use of the perfective ending *pa.yin.pa.'dra* in example (440c):

(440)　　　རྟ་རྒྱུག་འགྲོ་གི་མེད་འགྲོའོ།

　　a)　*rta*　*rgyug*　*'gro*　　*- gi.med.'gro'o*
　　　　horse　run　　go (PRS)　- IMPF+EPI 1+FACT

　　　The horse will probably run away. (If the horse is not tied up or hobbled.)

　　　རྟ་རྒྱུག་ཕྱིན་མེད་འགྲོའོ།

　　b)　*rta*　*rgyug*　*phyin*　*- med.'gro'o*
　　　　horse　run　　go (PAS)　- PERF+EPI 1+FACT

　　　Maybe the horse ran away. (No one had untied it.)

　　　ཁོང་རྒྱུག་ཤར་གློད་ཕྱིན་པ་ཡིན་པ་འདྲ།

　　c)　*khong*　*rgyug.shar*　*glod*　*phyin*　　*- pa.yin.pa.'dra*
　　　　s/he+H　run　　　VBZ　go (PAS)　- PFV+EPI 2+SENS

　　　It seems he ran as he went [there]. (The speaker makes an inference from the fact that the person was huffing and puffing.)

3.2.14 DIRECTIONAL AND ASPECTUAL VERB *yong* 'come'

Just as with *'gro,* the secondary verb *yong* has several grammatical functions. It marks the inchoative aspect, direction towards the speaker after verbs of movement, and cross-reference. For more details, refer to Tournadre, Konchok Jiatso (2001: 89–96).

Aspectual use of *yong*

As an aspectual verb, *yong* marks the inchoative, progressive and iterative aspects. It implies proximity on the part of the speaker, connection with the first person and a certain degree of being affected by the verbal action.[105] *Yong* can only be combined with non-controllable verbs. It is compatible with imperfective epistemic endings such as *gi.yod.pa.'dra, gi.a.yod,* as shown in examples (441) and (442). It is generally not used with other verbal endings.

(441)   ཚལ་འདི་སྐྱུར་ཡོང་གི་ཡོད་པ་འདྲ།

tshal	*'di*	*skyur*	*yong*	- *gi.yod.pa.'dra*
vegetables	this	sour	come	- IMPF+EPI 2+SENS

It seems these vegetables are going rotten [lit.: turning sour]. (The speaker can smell the rotting vegetables; *yong* implies direction towards the speaker.)

(442)   གྲང་མོར་ཆགས་ཡོང་གི་ཨ་ཡོད།

grang.mo	- *r*	*chags*	*yong*	- *gi.a.yod*
cold	- OBL	become	come	- IMPF+EPI 3+EGO+NEG

I don't think it's getting cold. (In this sentence, *yong* implies that the speaker has a direct personal interest in the current state of the weather, or that he will be directed affected by it.)

Compare the above example with the following sentence containing the secondary verb *'gro* 'go':

(443)   ཟླ་བ་བཅུ་པའི་ནང་ནས་གྲང་མོར་ཆགས་འགྲོ་གི་ཡོད་པ་འདྲ།

zla.ba	*bcu.pa*	- *'i*	*nang*	- *nas*	*grang.mo*	- *r*
month	tenth	- GEN	inside	- ABL	cold	- OBL

chags	*'gro*	- *gi.yod.pa.'dra*
become	go (PRS)	- IMPF+EPI 2+SENS

It seems like it starts to get cold in October. (In this sentence, *'gro* implies that the speaker is not too concerned about when it starts to get cold.)

Directional use of *yong*

After verbs of movement, *yong* implies direction towards the speaker. It is compatible with the majority of verbal endings: with imperfective endings, as shown in example (444); perfective endings, as shown in example (445), and perfect endings. The directional function of *yong* is illustrated below:

(444)   མོ་རང་རྒྱུག་ཡོང་གི་ཡོད་པ་འདྲ།

mo.rang	*rgyugs*	*yong*	- *gi.yod.pa.'dra*
she	run	come	- IMPF+EPI 2+SENS

She seems to be running towards us. (The speaker can see her in the distance as she approaches the speaker and the addressee.)

---

[105] For more details, see Tournadre, Konchok Jiatso (2001: 89–96).

213

(445)　　　 མོ་རང་རྒྱུག་ཡོང་པ་འདྲ།

      mo.rang   *rgyugs*   *yong*   *- pa.'dra*
      she   run   come   - PFV+EPI 2+SENS

It seems she came here running/ran here. (The speaker makes an inference from the fact that the person is out of breath.)

3.2.15 ASPECTO-TEMPORAL VERB *'gro'o* a) 'be ready/be about [to do]', b) 'have [just done/occured]'

The verbal status of *'gro'o,* which is derived from the word *grabs* used in literary Tibetan, is problematic. It is either considered as an adverb, as in *Bod-rgya tshig-mdzod chen-mo* [Great Tibetan-Chinese dictionary] (1985), or as a verb, as in Tournadre, Sangda Dorje (2003: 179).[106] Followed by a verbal auxiliary, *'gro'o* conveys either the meaning of 'be about [to (do)]' or 'have [just done]', depending on the auxiliary that follows it. From a syntactic viewpoint, *'gro'o* occupies the same position as secondary verbs that are followed by verbal auxiliaries (after the lexical verb and before the verbal auxiliary). It is impossible to use it with verbal endings. In this work, *'gro'o* is treated as an aspectual verb. When followed by existential auxiliaries such as *yod.pa.'dra* or *a.yod,* as in examples (446a) and (447a), with the lexical verb in the present-future stem, it expresses the extreme short-term future. When used with essential auxiliaries such as *yin.pa.'dra* or *a.yin,* as in examples (446b) and (447b), with the lexical verb in the past stem, it expresses the recent past.

(446)　　　ཁོང་ཁ་ལག་ཟ་འགྲོའི་ཡོད་པ་འདྲ།

  a) *khong*   *kha.lag*   *za*   *'gro'o*   *yod.pa.'dra*
      s/he+H   food   eat (PRS)   be about to   AUX (EPI 2+SENS)

It seems she is about to eat. (The speaker sees that she is setting the table.)

      ཁོང་ཁ་ལག་བཟས་འགྲོའི་ཡིན་པ་འདྲ།

  b) *khong*   *kha.lag*   *bzas*   *'gro'o*   *yin.pa.'dra*
      s/he+H   food   eat (PAS)   have just done   AUX (EPI 2+SENS)

It seems she has just eaten. (The speaker sees dirty dishes.)

(447)　　　ཁོང་སླེབས་འགྲོའི་ཨ་ཡོད།

  a) *khong*   *slebs*   *'gro'o*   *a.yod*
      s/he+H   come   be about to   AUX (EPI 1+SENS)

I doubt she is about to come. (Basing his assertation on personal experience, the speaker thinks it will take her a long time to arrive.)

---

[106] It is also used in a construction consisting of *'gro'o,* the verb *byed* 'do' and a verbal ending, corresponding to 'nearly/almost (do)'.

ཁོང་སྐྱེབས་འགྲོའོ་ལ་ཡིན།

b) *khong   slebs   'gro'o   a.yin*
   s/he+H   come   have just done   AUX (EPI 1+SENS)

I doubt she has just got here. (Basing his assertation on personal knowledge, the speaker thinks she has been here for a long time already.)

3.2.16 ASPECTO-TEMPORAL VERB *bzhag* 'put'

The aspectual verb *bzhag*[107] is employed to place stress to the final and post-process phase of the verbal event. It is compatible with volitional (controllable), bi- or trivalent verbs (See C. Simon, F. Robin, *Phasal-Aspect Marker Bzhag in Standard Tibetan*, paper presented in Yangon, 2014). Since it is used in perfective contexts, it generally combines with perfect epistemic endings, as shown in examples (448a) and (449a), and not with imperfective endings, as shown in examples (448b) and (449b):

(448) ཁོ་རང་གིས་པར་བརྒྱབ་བཞག་ཡོད་ཀྱི་རེད།

   a) *kho.rang   - gis   par   brgyab   bzhag   - yod.kyi.red*
       he   - ERG   photo   VBZ   put   - PERF+EPI 2+FACT

   In all likelihood he has taken [some] pictures.

     * ཁོ་རང་གིས་པར་བརྒྱབ་བཞག་གི་ཡོད་ཀྱི་རེད།

   b) * *kho.rang   - gis   par   brgyab   bzhag   - gi.yod.kyi.red*
        he   - ERG   photo   VBZ   put   - IMPF+EPI 2+FACT

   In all likelihood he will take pictures.

(449) ཁོ་རང་གིས་ཨ་མ་ལ་ལབ་བཞག་ཡོད་པ་འདྲ།

   a) *kho.rang   - gis   a.ma   - la   lab   bzhag   - yod.pa.'dra*
       he   - ERG   mother   - OBL   tell   put   - PERF+EPI 2+SENS

   It seems he has told mother.

     * ཁོ་རང་གིས་ཨ་མ་ལ་ལབ་བཞག་གི་ཡོད་པ་འདྲ།

   b) * *kho.rang   - gis   a.ma   - la   lab   bzhag   - gi.yod.pa.'dra*
        he   - ERG   mother   - OBL   tell   put   - IMPF+EPI 2+SENS

   It seems he will tell mother.

---

[107]Note that *bzhag* is used as well as a lexical verb meaning 'put', and as a verbal ending of the perfect tense, often spelt *shag* in this function (see Tournadre, Sangda Dorje (2003: 164).

3.2.17 EXPERIENTIAL SECONDARY VERB *myong* 'experience'

The verb *myong* implies that the agent of the sentence has already experienced the verbal action or state. It is only compatible with perfect epistemic verbal endings such as *yod.kyi.red,* as shown in example (450a). It cannot be combined with the corresponding imperfective endings such as *gi.yod.kyi.red,* as shown in example (450b); perfective endings such as *pa.yin.gyi.red,* as shown in example (450c); or with future endings such as *a.yong, pa. 'dug, mdog.kha.po-red, mi.yong.ngas, yong,* or *bzo. 'dug.* The lexical verb is in the present-future stem.

(450)   ཁོང་བོད་ཇ་འཐུང་མྱོང་ཡོད་ཀྱི་རེད།

    a)   *khong*   *bod.ja*   *'thung*   *myong*   *- yod.kyi.red*
         s/he+H   Tibetan tea   drink (PRS)   have an experience   - PERF+EPI 2+FACT
        She must have drunk Tibetan tea [at some point in the past]. (She is Tibetan.)

      * ཁོང་བོད་ཇ་འཐུང་མྱོང་གི་ཡོད་ཀྱི་རེད།

    b)   * *khong*   *bod.ja*   *'thung*   *myong*   *- gi.yod.kyi.red*
         s/he+H   Tibetan tea   drink (PRS)   experience   - IMPF+EPI 2+FACT
        Intended statement: She will surely have the experience of drinking Tibetan tea.

      * ཁོང་བོད་ཇ་འཐུང་མྱོང་པ་ཡིན་གྱི་རེད།

    c)   * *khong*   *bod.ja*   *'thung*   *myong*   *- pa.yin.kyi.red*
         s/he+H   Tibetan tea   drink (PRS)   experience   - PFV+EPI 2+FACT
        Intended statement: She must have drunk Tibetan tea [at some point in the past].

The secondary verb *myong* is often used in epistemic past contexts in first person sentences by the speaker to convey that he is unsure of his actions, often because he does not remember clearly what he has or hasn't done. *Myong* is especially employed with certain verbal categories, e.g. affective verbs, as shown in example (451) below. Without *myong* the sentence is usually considered as ungrammatical:

(451)   * ང་ཁོང་གི་རི་མོར་དགའ་ཡོད་ཀྱི་རེད།

    a)   * *nga*   *khong*   *- gi*   *ri.mo*   *- r*   *dga'*   *- yod.kyi.red*
         I   s/he+H   - GEN   painting   - OBL   like   - PERF+EPI 2+FACT
        Intended statement: Probably I liked his paintings.

216

ང་ཁོང་གི་རི་མོར་དགའ་མྱོང་ཡོད་ཀྱི་རེད།

b)
nga	khong	- gi	ri.mo	- r	dga'	myong	- yod.kyi.red
I	s/he+H	- GEN	painting	- OBL	like	experience	- PERF+EPI 2+FACT

I have probably liked his paintings [at one point]. (The speaker is trying to recall.)

3.3 SUMMARY OF THE COMPATIBILITY OF SECONDARY VERBS WITH EPISTEMIC VERBAL ENDINGS

Just as when lexical verbs are combined with epistemic verbal endings, there are several parameters that influence the use of modal, aspecto-temporal and directional secondary verbs with epistemic verbal endings. The most important parameters are the syntactic and semantic properties of the secondary verb; the tense-aspect; the verbal class of the lexical verb; the evidential meaning of the verbal ending; and person.

First, some secondary verbs behave syntactically as predicative adjectives, and thus they can only combine with verbal auxiliaries that are formally identical with copulas. Second, the use of secondary verbs with epistemic verbal endings is conditioned by the tense-aspect of the sentence (logical, epistemological, or pragmatic). Furthermore, from a semantic viewpoint, the majority of secondary verbs combine only with certain lexical verbs. As a result, some combinations are only applicable for certain verbal classes, and not for others. This also holds true for the parameter of person. The majority of combinations of secondary verbs with epistemic verbal endings (or auxiliaries) appear in third person sentences. Nevertheless, they can sometimes be employed in first person sentences as well, especially for memory-based statements. These combinations are generally subject to more restrictions than those with the third person. Finally, the context of each utterance is important in determining what type of epistemic verbal ending will be used.

Due to the interaction of these many and complex parameters, some secondary verbs are compatible with the majority of verbal endings, while others are subject to more constraints. Consequently, one can distinguish two groups of secondary verbs (see below). The third group consists of those secondary verbs that are compatible only with epistemic auxiliaries, and not with epistemic verbal endings:

1. Secondary verbs compatible with the majority of epistemic verbal endings are: *thub* 'can', *dgos* 'must', *shes* 'know', *ran* 'be time [to do]', *bsdad* 'stay', *'gro* (Dir) 'go', *yong* (Dir) 'come'.

2. Secondary verbs compatible only with certain epistemic verbal endings are: *chog1* 'may', *nus* 'dare', *srid* 'be possible', *tshar* 'finish', *myong* 'experience', *'gro* (Asp) 'go', *yong* (Asp) 'come'. The most problematic secondary verb is *srid* 'be possible'.

3. Secondary verbs compatible with epistemic verbal auxiliaries are: *'dod* 'want', *chog2* 'be ready', *rtsis* 'intend', *long* 'have time', *'gro'o* 'be about [to do]', 'have [just done/occured]'. Four of these five verbs are aspecto-temporal; only *'dod* 'want' is modal.

In addition, the following conclusions can be drawn: unlike evidential verbal endings, the majority of secondary verbs do not combine with perfective epistemic endings (e.g.

pa.yin.pa.yod). The aspectual verbs combining with verbal endings are, in general, compatible with perfect epistemic endings (e.g. *yod.pa.yod*). On the contrary, some modal verbs are only compatible with imperfective epistemic endings (e.g. *chog*1 and *nus*) as these verbs convey an imperfective meaning.

Finally, I would like to draw attention to other important parameters – the various idiolects of the speakers, as well as to their age: these are important factors which lead to differences among native speakers concerning the acceptability of certain combinations, their use and frequency. Similarly, there are also regional differences in the use between the variants spoken in the TAR (Lhasa) and in the diaspora.

CONCLUSION

The aim of this book has been to study and document a part of the grammar of standard spoken Tibetan which is certainly well known, yet hardly adequately documented. My extensive fieldwork has led me to conclude that in order to convey epistemic meanings, standard spoken Tibetan makes use of both lexical and grammatical means. As for the grammatical expression of epistemic meanings, it has developed into a complex system of epistemic verbal endings. The main goal of this book has been to identify and classify those epistemic endings that are employed in standard spoken Tibetan.

Since the present work is concerned with the spoken language, fieldwork was an important part of my research. Conducted between the years 2002 and 2016 mostly in central Tibet, but also in the diaspora, my fieldwork confirmed the division of Tibetan verbal endings into two sub-systems: evidential and epistemic. Although they share some functions, in the main the expression of tense-aspect and the evidential mode, they differ in the degree of certainty that the speaker attributes to his own utterance.

In addition, my research has confirmed that there are approximately a dozen various types of epistemic verbal endings commonly used in standard spoken Tibetan, all differing in their degrees of certainty, geographic use, and frequency. Most of these verbal endings form part of a tense-aspect paradigm. The paradigm consists of three forms: the perfective past, the perfect, and the imperfective. Several, but not all, epistemic types have a future form as well.

Regarding the criterion of the degree of certainty, I have classified these epistemic types according to three degrees of probability: EPI 1: epistemic verbal endings conveying a weaker degree of certainty of over 50%; EPI 2: epistemic verbal endings conveying a stronger degree of certainty corresponding to approximately 75%; and EPI 3: epistemic verbal endings conveying the strongest degree of certainty, close to 100%.

Another criterion distinguishing the various types of epistemic endings is geographic variation. Although some types are common in central Tibet and in the diaspora, there are other types that are frequently employed in Lhasa, but are less common or not used at all in the diaspora. In contrast, the most common epistemic type used in the diaspora, *yod.sa.red,* is not in frequent use by the natives of Lhasa.

And finally, these epistemic endings can be classified according to the parameter of frequency. The majority of the epistemic types that have been analyzed in this book are very frequent or quite frequent in standard spoken Tibetan. It should be, however, emphasized that epistemic verbal endings are much less common in the spoken language than evidential verbal endings. My fieldwork has demonstrated a considerable divergence in the use of epistemic verbal endings among native speakers due to various factors, including both dialectal (the influence of other dialects on standard Tibetan), and idiolectal (the preference of the speaker for a certain type of epistemic ending; absence of the use of epistemic endings).

The following conclusions can be drawn:

First, from a synchronic viewpoint, epistemic verbal endings are fused, non-analyzable units. Their diachronic development is not reflected in the mind of the native speakers when they use these endings. Nonetheless, apart from fully grammaticalized verbal endings, in SST there are expressions and constructions used to convey epistemic modality showing various degrees of grammaticalization of different lexical items.

Second, epistemic verbal endings are only used in affirmative and negative sentences. They do not normally appear in interrogative sentences. Similarly, they are not employed in the protasis of complex sentences (e.g. temporal or conditional). However, they may be used in the apodosis of conditional sentences (see below).

Third, epistemic verbal endings, just like evidential verbal endings, also convey secondary evidential meanings: sensory, factual and egophoric. This had been suggested for some epistemic types (see Tournadre, Sangda Dorje 2003) but until now had never been the subject of systematic study. Moreover, it has been demonstrated that epistemic verbal endings may be employed to convey other secondary meanings, such as the speaker's sense of obligation, hope, surprise and regret, depending on the actual context of the statement.

Fourth, perfective past endings and perfect endings generally differ in their scope of epistemic modality. Perfect endings (e.g. *yod.kyi.red*) have a sentence scope, relating to the whole sentence. On the contrary, perfective endings (e.g. *pa.yin.gyi.red*) have a restricted scope emphasizing one part of the sentence (e.g. the agent, the adverbial, or the predicate). Unlike sentences with past evidential verbal endings, in which perfective past endings are much more common than perfect endings and are generally subject to fewer constraints, in sentences with past epistemic verbal endings, the use of perfective endings is more restricted as regards, for example, verbal class and person.

Fifth, when the first person and an epistemic verbal ending occur together, they do not, in general, express the degree of the speaker's certainty of the actuality of his utterance, but instead convey either that the speaker does not recall clearly the action of the sentence, or that the action is not contingent on his will. In first person sentences, the secondary verb *myong* 'have an experience' is often employed.

Sixth, a number of epistemic verbal endings are used in the apodosis of conditional sentences. In general, perfect epistemic endings appear in past unreal conditionals (past counterfactuals), whereas imperfective or future epistemic endings appear in present conditionals. It is impossible to use perfective past endings in conditional sentences.

In conclusion: a fruitful direction of further study could be for researchers of Tibetan dialectology and Tibeto-Burman linguistics to compare the results of this study of epistemic modality in the language spoken in central Tibet with similar analyses of the epistemic systems of other Tibetan dialects and related languages. Likewise, this study of a language with a grammaticalized expression of epistemic modality will hopefully be of use to linguists engaged in a more general typological studies of epistemicity.

REFERENCES

AGHA, A. 1993. *Structural Form and Utterance Context in Lhasa Tibetan*. New York: Peter Lang.

AIKHENVALD, A. Y. 2004. *Evidentiality*. Oxford: Oxford University Press.

———. 2011. "Evidentials". *Oxford Bibliograpies Online*. http://oxfordbibliographiesonline.com/view/document/obo-9780199772810/obo-9780199772810–0014.xml.

AIKHENVALD, A. Y., DIXON, R. M. W. (eds.) 2003. *Studies in Evidentiality*. Amsterdam: John Benjamins Publishing Comp.

AUWERA, J. van der. 1998a. "Modality: The three-layered Scalar square", *Journal of Semantics* 13. Oxford: Oxford University Press. Pp. 181–195.

———. 1998b. "On combining negation and modality", in Caron Bernard (ed.) *Proceedings of the 16th International Congress of Linguists* (20–25 July 1997). New York: Elsevier.

———. 2001. "On the typology of negative modals", in Jack Hoeksema (ed.) *Perspectives on Negation and Polarity Items*. Amsterdam: Benjamins. Pp. 23–48.

AUWERA, J. van der, PLUNGIAN, V. 1998. "Modality's semantic map", *Linguistic Typology* 2. Pp. 79–124.

DRIEM, G. van. 1998. *Dzongkha. Languages of the Greater Himalayan Region*. Leyde. Vol. 1.

BACHE, C. 1985. *Verbal Aspect*. Odense: Odense University.

———. 1995. *The Study of Aspect, Tense and Action: Towards a Theory of the Semantics of Grammatical Categories*. Frankfurt am Main: Deter Lang.

BAILEY, G., WALKER, Ch. E. 2004. *Lhasa Verbs. A practical Introduction*. Tibetan Academy of Social Science.

BARNES, J. 1984. "Evidentials in the Tuyuca verb", *International Journal of American Linguistics* 50. Pp. 255–71.

BARTEE, E., NYIMA DROMA. 2000. *A Beginning Textbook of Lhasa Tibetan*. National Presss for Tibetan Studies.

BERNINI, G., RAMAT, P. 1996. *Negative Sentences in the Languages of Europe. A Typological Approach*. Berlin and NY: Mouton de Gruyter.

BEYER, S. V. 1992. *The Classical Tibetan Language*. New York: State University of New York.

BHAT, D. N. S. 1999. *The Prominence of Tense, Aspect and Mood*. Amsterdam – Philadelphia: John Benjamins Publishing Company.

BIELMEIER, R. 2000. "Syntactic, semantic, and pragmatic-epistemic functions of auxiliaries in Western Tibetan", in Balthasar Bickel (ed.) *Person and Evidence in Himalayan Languages. Special Issue of Linguistics of the Tibeto-Burman Area*. Vol. I, 23.2, pp. 79–125.

BOYE, C. 2006. *Epistemic meaning: A Cross-linguistic Study*. University of Copenhagen. PhD. Dissertation.

BROWN, K. (ed.) 2006. *Encyclopedia of Language and Linguistics*. Elsevier.

BYBEE, J. L. 1985. *Morphology: A Study of the Relation between Meaning and Form*. Amsterdam: John Benjamins Publishing Comp.

BYBEE, J. L., DALH, Ö. 1989. "The creation of tense and aspect systems in the languages of the world", *Studies in Language* 13. Pp. 51–103.

BYBEE, J. L., PERKINS, R. and PAGLIUCA, W. 1994. *The Evolution of Grammar: Tense, Aspect and Modality in the Languages of the World*. Chicago: University of Chicago.

BYBEE, J. L., FLEISCHMAN, S. (eds.) 1995. *Modality in Grammar and Discourse*. Amsterdam – Philadelphia: John Benjamins Publishing Comp.

CHAFE, W. L., NICHOLS, J. (eds.) 1986. *Evidentiality: The Linguistic Coding of Epistemology*. Norwood, NY: Ablex.

CHANG, B. S., CHANG, K. 1980. *Ergativity in Spoken Tibetan*. Vol. 51 Part 1. Bulletin of the Institute of History and Philology, Taipei: Academia Sinica.

CHOI, S. 1995. "The development of Epistemic Sentence-ending Modal Forms and Functions in Korean Children", in J. Bybee and S. Fleischman (eds.) *Modality in Grammar and Discourse*. Amsterdam – Philadelphia: John Benjamins Publishing Comp.

CHUNG, S., TIMBERLAKE, A. 1985. "Tense, aspect and mood", in T. Shopen (ed.) *Language Typology and Syntactic Descriptions*. Vol. 3, Cambridge: CUP. Pp. 202–258.

COATES, J. 1983. *The Semantics of Modal Auxiliaries*. London: Croom Helm.

COHEN, D. 1989. *L'aspect verbal*. Paris: Presses Universitaires de France.

COMRIE, B. 1976. *Aspect*. Cambridge: Cambridge University.

———. 1985. *Tense*. Cambridge: Cambridge University.

CONFAIS, J.-P. 1995. *Temps, Mode, Aspect. Les approches des morphèmes verbaux et leurs problèmes à l'exemple du français et de l'allemand*. Presses universitaires du Mirail.

CROFT, W. 1990. *Typology and Universals*. Cambridge University Press.

DAHL, Ö. 1985. *Tense and Aspect Systems*. Oxford, NY: Basil Blackwell.

———. (ed.) 2000. *Tense and Aspect in the Languages of Europe. Empirical Approaches to Language Typology*. Berlin: Mouton de Gruyter.

De HAAN, F. 1997. *The Interaction of Modality and Negation. A Typological Study*. New York & London: Garland Publishing, Inc.

———. 2005. "Typological approaches to modality", in W. Frawley (ed.) *The Expression of Modality*. Berlin: Mouton de Gruyter.

DeLANCEY, S. 1986. "Evidentiality and volitionality in Tibetan", in Chafe and Nichols (eds.) *Evidentiality: The Linguistic Coding of Epistemology*. Norwood, NY: Ablex. Pp. 203–13.

———. 1992. "The historical status of the conjunct/disjunct pattern in Tibeto-Burman", *Acta Linguistica Hafniensia* 25. Pp. 39–62.

———. 1997. " Mirativity: The grammatical marking of unexpected information", in F. Plank (ed.) *Linguistic typology*. Berlin – New York: Mouton de Gruyter. Pp. 33–52.

———. 2001. "The mirative and evidentiality", *Journal of Pragmatics* 33, no. 3. Pp. 369–382.

———. 2012. "Still mirative after all these years", *Linguistic Typology* 16, no. 3. Pp. 529–564.

DENDALE, P., TASMOWSKI, L. (eds.) 2001. "On Evidentiality", *Journal of Pragmatics* 33, no. 3, Amsterdam: Elsevier.

DENWOOD, P. 1999. *Tibetan*. Amsterdam: John Benjamins.

DIXON, R. M. W. 1994. *Ergativity*. Cambridge : Cambridge University Press.

DUCHET, J.-L. 1990. *L'auxiliaire en question*. Rennes: PUR 2 – CERLICO.

DRYER, M. S. 1988. "Universals of negative position", in Hammond, M., Moravcsik, E. & Wirth, J. (eds.) *Studies in Syntactic Typology*. Amsterdam: John Benjamins. Pp. 93–124.

FRANÇOIS, J. 2003. *La prédication verbale et les cadres prédicatifs*. Louvain – Paris – Dudley, MA: Editions Peeters.

FRAWLEY, W. (ed.) 2005. *The Expression of Modality*. Berlin: Mouton de Gruyter.

GARRETT, E. J. 2001. *Evidentiality and Assertion in Tibetan*. Ph.D. Dissertation. Los Angeles: University of California.

GESANG, J., GESANG, Y. 2002. *Bod kyi yul-skad rnam-bshad, Zangyu fangyan gailun* [An Introduction to Tibetan Dialects]. Beijing: Minorities Publishing House.

GOLDSTEIN, M. C. et al. 1991. *Essentials of Modern Literary Tibetan: A Reading Course and Reference Grammar*. New Delhi: Munshiram Manoharlal Publishers Pvt Ltd.

GOSSELIN, L. 2005. *Temporalité et modalité*. Duculot.

GUENTCHEVA, Z. (ed.) 1996. *L'Enonciation médiatisée*. Louvain – Paris: Editions Peeters.

GUENTCHEVA, Z. 2004. "La notion de médiation dans la diversité des langues", in R. Delamotte-Legrand (ed.) *Les médiations langagières: Des faits de langue aux discours*. Vol. 1. Rouen: PUR. Pp.11–33.

GUENTCHEVA, Z., LANDABURU, J. (eds.) 2007. *L'Enonciation médiatisée II: Le traitement épistémologique de l'information: illustration amérindiennes et caucasiennes.* Louvain – Paris: Editions Peeters.

HAEGEMAN, L. 1995. *The Syntax of Negation.* Cambridge: Cambridge University Press.

HALLIDAY, M. A. K. 1970. "Functional diversity in language as seen from a consideration of mood and modality in English", *Foundations of Language* 4. Pp. 225–42.

HASPELMATH, M. (ed.) 2005. *The World Atlas of Language Structures.* Martin Oxford: Oxford University Press.

HEINE, B. 1993. *Auxiliaries. Cognitive Forces and Grammaticalization.* Oxford University Press.

HERGE. 1991. *Tin-tin bod-la phyin-pa* [Tintin in Tibet], Tibetan translation. Casterman.

HILL, N. 2012. "'Mirativity' does not exist: hdug in 'Lhasa' Tibetan and other suspect", *Linguistic Typology* 16. Pp. 389–433.

HOPPER, P. J. (ed.) 1982. *Tense-Aspect: Between Semantics and Pragmatics.* Amsterdam: John Benjamins.

———. 1991. "On some principles of Grammaticalization", in Traugott, Heine (eds.) *Approaches to Grammaticalization: Focus on Theoretical and Methodological Issues.* Vol. 1. Amsterdam: John Benjamins. Pp. 17–35.

HU, Tan et al. 1989. *Lasa kouyu duben.* [A Textbook of Lhasa Dialect]. Beijing: Minzu chubanshe.

JOHANSON, L., UTAS, B. 2000. *Evidentials: Turkic, Iranian and Neighbouring Languages.* Berlin: Mouton de Gruyter.

sKAL-bZANG bSTAN-PA et al. 2002. *A-khu ston-pa.* Lhasa: Bod.ljongs mi.dmangs dpe.skrun.khang.

KESANG GYURME. 1992. *Le Clair Miroir.* Translated by H. Stoddard and N. Tournadre. Paris: Prajna.

KOZLOWSKA, M. 1998. "Bornage, télicité et ordre temporel", in *Le temps des événements. Pragmatique de la référence temporelle.* J. Moeschler (ed.) Editions Kimé. Pp. 221–244.

KRATZER, A. 1977. "What 'must' and 'can' must and can mean", *Linguistics and Philosophy* 1. Pp. 337–355.

———. 1981. "Partition and revision: The semantics of counterfactuals", *Journal of Philosophical Logic* 10. Pp. 201– 216.

KUNERT, H. P. 1984. *Aspekt, Aktionsart, Tempus.* Tübingen: Gunter Narr Verlag.

LaPOLLA, R. J. (ed.) 2000. *Linguistics of the Tibeto-Burman Area.* Vol. 23.2. University of California.

———. (ed.) 2001. *Linguistics of the Tibeto-Burman Area.* University of California. Vol. 24.1.

———. 2003. "Evidentiality in Qiang", in Aikhenvald, Dixon (eds.) *Studies in Evidentiality.* Amsterdam: John Benjamins. Pp. 63–78.

LE QUERLER, N. 1996. *Typologie des modalités.* Presses Universitaires de Caen.

LICHTENBERK, F. 1995. "Apprehensional Epistemics", in J. Bybee and S. Fleischman (eds.) *Modality in Grammar and Discourse.* Amsterdam/Philadelphia: John Benjamins Publishing Comp.

LHAKPA TSETEN. 1999. *Basic spoken Tibetan grammar patterns.* Lhasa: Tibet University.

MALONE, T. 1988. "The origin and development of Tuyuca evidentials", *International Journal of American Linguistics* 54, no. 2. Pp. 119–140.

MÉLAC, É. 2014. *L'évidentialité en anglais. Approche contrastive à partir d'un corpus anglais-tibétain.* Ph.D. Dissertation. Université de la Sorbonne nouvelle-Paris 3.

MIESTAMO, M. 2005. "Standard negation: The negation of declarative verbal main clauses in a typological perspective." *Empirical Approaches to Language Typology* 31. Berlin – New York: Mouton de Gruyter.

MIN, S. 2003. *A-mdo'i kha-skad slob-deb* [A Manual of Amdo Dialect]. Xining.

MOESCHLER, J. 1998. *Le temps des événements. Pragmatique de la référence temporelle.* Editions Kimé.

Nyi.chos bzang.po'i sgrung [Stories of Nyicho Sangpo]. 2000. Lhasa: Bod.ljongs mi.dmangs dpe.skrun.khang.

NØLKE, H. 1994a. "La dilution linguistique des responsabilités, Essai de description polyphonique des marqueurs évidentiels: il semble que et il paraît que", in Dendale P. et Tasmowski L. (eds.) *On Evidentiality (Journal of Pragmatics).* Pp. 84–94.

———. 1994b. *Linguistique modulaire: de la forme au sens.* Louvain – Paris: Peeters.

NUYTS, J. 2001a. *Epistemic Modality, Language, and Conceptualization: A Cognitive Pragmatic Perspective.* Amsterdam: John Benjamins Publishing Comp.

———. 2001b. "Subjectivity as an evidential dimension in epistemic modal expressions", in *Journal of Pragmatics* 33, no. 3. Pp. 383–400.

NYUTS, J., DENDALE, P. 1994. "Bibliographie sélective de l'évidentialité", *Langue Française* 102. Paris: Larousse. Pp. 121–125.

OISEL, G. 2006. *Emplois particuliers des suffixes médiatifs non-egophoriques dans le tibétain parlé de Lhassa.* Master 2 Thesis. Université Paris 8 – Saint-Denis.

———. 2013. *Morphosyntaxe et sémantique des auxiliaires et des connecteurs du tibétain littéraire: étude diachronique et synchronique.* Ph.D. Dissertation. Université de la Sorbonne nouvelle-Paris 3.

PALMER, F. 1986. *Mood and Modality.* Cambridge: Cambridge University Press.

———. 1990. *Modality and the English Modals.* London: Longman Linguistics Library.

PAPAFRAGOU, A. 1998. "The acquisition of modality: Implications for theories on semantic representation", *Mind & Language* 13, no. 3. Pp. 370–399.

———. 2000. *Modality: Issues in the Semantics-pragmatics Interface.* Oxford: Elsevier Science Ltd.

PARFIONOVICH, Y. M. 1982. *The Written Tibetan Language.* Moscow: Nauka.

PLANK, F. 1979. *Ergativity:Towards a Theory of Grammatical Relations.* London: Academic Press.

PLUNGIAN, V. A. 2001. "The place of evidentiality within the universal grammatical space", *Journal of Pragmatics* 33, no. 3. Pp. 349–357.

SAUSSURE, L. de. 1998. "L'approche référentielle : de Bauzée à Reichenbach", in Moeschler (ed.) *Le temps des événements, pragmatique de la référence temporelle.* Paris: Kimé.

SEARLE, J. R. 1977. *Speech Acts. An Essay in the Philosophy of Language.* Cambridge University Press.

SEARLE, J., VANDERVEKEN, D. 1985. *Foundations of Illocutionary Logic.* Cambridge: Cambridge University.

SHAFER, R. 1951. 'Studies in the morphology of the Bodic Verb', *Bulletin of the School of Oriental and African Studies* 13, Pp. 702–24, 1017–31.

SIMON, C., ROBIN, F. "Phasal-Aspect Marker Bzhag in Standard Tibetan". Paper presented at 24th Annual Meeting of the Southeast Asian Linguistics Society. Yangon, 27 May 2014.

SMITH, C. S. 1986. "A speaker-based approach to aspect", *Linguistics and Philosophy* 9. Pp. 97–115.

———. 1991. "The parameter of aspect." *Studies in Linguistics and Philosophy* 43. Dordrecht: Kluver

STEELE, S. et al. 1981. *An Encyclopedia of AUX: a Study in Cross-linguistic Equivalence.* Cambridge, Mass. and London: MIT Press.

SUN, J. T.-S. 1993. "Evidentials in Amdo-Tibetan" *Bulletin of the Institute of History and Philology, Academia Sinica* 63–4, Pp. 945–1001.

———. 1995. *The Typology of Tone in Tibetan.* Taiwan: Institute of History and Philology, Academia Sinica.

TAKEUCHI, T. 1990. "Chibettogo no jatsubu ni okeru jodōshi no kinō to sono hatten katei. The semantic functions of auxiliary verbs in Tibetan and their historical development", in Sakiyama and Satoh (eds.) *Ajia no shogengo to ippan gengogaku* [Asian Languages and General Linguistics]. Tokyo: Sanshodo. Pp. 6–16.

TEDESCHI, P. J., ZAENEN, A. (eds.) 1981. "Syntax and Semantics: Tense and Aspect." *Academic Press* 14.

THUB-bSTAN dBANG-PO et al. 2002. *Lha-sa'i kha-skad sbyong-deb* [A Textbook of Lhasa Dialect]. Lhasa: Bod.ljongs mi.dmangs dpe.skrun.khang.

TOURNADRE, N. 1994. "Personne et médiatifs en tibétain", *La Personne. Faits de langues* 3. Paris: PUF. Pp. 149–158.

———. 1995. "Tibetan ergativity and the trajectory model", *New Horizons in Tibeto-Burman Morphosyntax. Senri Ethnological Studies* 41. Osaka: National Museum of Ethnology.

———. 1996a. *L'Ergativité en tibétain, approche morphosyntaxique de la langue parlée.* Louvain: Peeters.

———. 1996b. "Comparaison des systèmes médiatifs de quatre dialectes tibétains (tibétain central, ladakhi, dzongkha et amdo)", in Guentchéva (ed.) *L'Enonciation médiatisée.* Pp. 195–213.

———. 2004. "Typologie des aspects verbaux et intégration à une théorie du TAM", *Bulletin de la Société de linguistique de Paris.* Vol. XCIX. fasc.1. Pp. 7–68.

———. 2005. "L'aire linguistique tibétaine et ses divers dialectes", *LALIES* 25.

———. 2008. "Arguments against the concept of 'conjunct'/'disjunct' in Tibetan", in B. Huber. *Chomolangma, Demawend und Kasbek. Festschrift für Roland Bielmeier.* Pp. 281–308.

TOURNADRE, N., KONCHOK JIATSO. 2001. "Final auxiliary verbs in literary Tibetan and in the Dialects", *Linguistics of the Tibeto-Burman Area* 24.1. University of California. Pp. 49–111.

TOURNADRE, N., LAPOLLA, R. 2014. "Towards a new approach to evidentiality. Issues and directions for research", *Linguistics of the Tibeto-Burman Area* 37, no. 2. John Benjamins Publishing Company. Pp. 240–262.

TOURNADRE, N., SANGDA, D. 2003. *Manual of Standard Tibetan. Language and Civilization.* Ithaca, New York: Snow Lions Publications.

TOURNADRE, N., SHAO, M. "Intentionality, Evidentiality and Epistemicity in Amdo Tibetan". In print.

TRAUGOTT, E. C., HEINE, B. (eds.) 1991. *Approaches to grammaticalization: Focus on Theoretical and Methodological Issues.* Amsterdam: John Benjamins.

YULE, G. 1998. *Pragmatics*. Oxford University Press.

VION, R. 2003. "Le concept de modalisation: vers une théorie linguistique des modalisateurs et des modalités", *Cercle linguistique d'Aix-en-Provence. La Grammaticalisation. La Terminologie. Travaux* 18. Aix en Provence: Publications de l'Université de Provence.

VITTRANT, A. 2004. *Les modalités et ses corrélats en birman*. Ph.D. Dissertation, ms. Université Paris 8 – Saint-Denis.

VITTRANT, A., ROBIN, F. 2007. "Réduplication dans les langues tibéto-birmanes: l'exemple du birman et du tibétain", *Faits de langue* 29. Pp. 77–98.

VOKURKOVÁ, Z. 2002. *La modalité en tibétain standard: Compatibilité des verbes secondaires avec les auxiliaires finaux*. Université Paris 8 – Saint-Denis. D.E.A. Dissertation.

———. 2007. "The process of grammaticalization of nominalizing morphemes and auxiliaries in spoken Standard Tibetan", in J. Vacek and A. Oberfalzerová (eds.) *Folia linguarum Orientis selecta* (FLOS): *Ethnolinguistics, Sociolinguistics and Culture*. Vol. 1. Prague: Charles University Press. Pp. 115–130.

———. 2008. *Epistemic modalities in spoken Standard Tibetan*. Prague: Charles university. Ph.D. Dissertation, ms.

———. 2009. "The lexical and grammatical expression of epistemic meanings in spoken Tibetan", in J. Vacek and A. Oberfalzerová (eds.) *Mongolo-Tibetica Pragensia '09. Ethnolinguistics, Sociolinguistics, Religion and Culture* 2, no. 2. Prague: Charles University and Triton. Pp. 59–76.

———. 2010. "Epistemic modality in Tibetan: The use of secondary verbs with epistemic verbal endings", *Mongolo-Tibetica Pragensia '10. Ethnolinguistics, Sociolinguistics, Religion and Culture* 2, no. 2. Prague: Charles University and Triton. Pp. 35–58.

———. 2011a. "Evidential and epistemic modality in standard spoken Tibetan", in T. Mortelmans, J. Mortelmans and W. De Mulder (eds.) *In the Mood for Mood*. Cahiers Chronos 23. Editions Rodopi B. V., Amsterdam – New York, Pp. 117–139.

———. 2011b. "The use of epistemic verbal endings in different syntactic structures in spoken Tibetan", in J. Vacek and A. Oberfalzerová (eds.) *Mongolo-Tibetica Pragensia '11. Ethnolinguistics, Sociolinguistics, Religion and Culture* 4, no. 2. Prague: Charles University and Triton. Pp. 57–68.

———. 2012. "The various lexical and grammatical functions of the verb *dgos* in spoken Tibetan", in J. Vacek and A. Oberfalzerová (eds.) *Mongolo-Tibetica Pragensia '12. Ethnolinguistics, Sociolinguistics, Religion and Culture* 5, no. 1. Prague: Charles University and Triton. Pp. 109–126.

————. 2014. "Expressing permission, possibility, ability and preparedness in spoken Tibetan with special attention to the secondary verb *chog*", in J. Vacek and A. Oberfalzerová (eds.) *Mongolo-Tibetica Pragensia '14. Ethnolinguistics, Sociolinguistics, Religion and Culture* 7, no. 1. Prague: Charles University and Triton.

WILLETT, T. 1988. "A cross-linguistic survey of the grammaticalization of evidentiality", *Studies in Language* 12, no. 1. Pp. 51–97.

WYLIE, T. 1959. "A Standard system of Tibetan transcription", *Harvard Journal of Asiatic Studies (HJAS)* 22. Pp. 261–67.

WANG, Zhijing 1994. *Zangyu lasa kouyu yufa.* [A Grammar of Spoken Lhasa Tibetan]. Beijing: Zhongyang minzu daxue chubanshe.

ZEISLER, B. 2004. *Relative Tense and Aspectual Values in Tibetan Languages.* A comparative study. Berlin: Mouton de Gruyter.

ZHOU Jiwen, XIE Houfang (eds.) 2003. *Zangyu lasahua yufa* (*bod kyi lha.sa'i skad kyi brda.sprod*) [A Grammar of Lhasa Tibetan]. Beijing: Minzu chubanshe.

DICTIONARIES and NEWSPAPERS

Bod-kyi-dus-bab [Tibet Times], Newspaper published in Dharamsala.

Bod-rgya tshig-mdzod chen-mo [Great Tibetan-Chinese Dictionary]. Reprinted in two volumes. Beijing: Minzu chubanshe. 1993.

Bod-rgya shan-sbyar gyi lha-sa-'i kha-skad tshig-mdzod [Tibetan-Chinese Dictionary of the Lhasa Dialect]. Beijing: Minzu chubanshe. 1983.

DAS, C. S. 1979. *Tibetan-English Dictionary*. Kyoto: Rinsen Book Company.

GOLDSTEIN, M. C. (ed.) 2001. *The New Tibetan-English Dictionary of Modern Tibetan.* Berkley, Los Angeles, London: University of California Press.

bKRASHIS TSERING, LIU, Dejun. *English-Tibetan-Chinese Dictionary*. Beijing: Minzu chubanshe. 1991.

ROERICH, G. N. 1983. *Tibetsko-russko-anglijskij slovar' s sanskritskimi paralleljami* (11 volumes). Moskva: Izdatel'stvo nauka.

GLOSSARY

allocentric: Allocentric endings are used to indicate that the speaker is performing the action on behalf of the interlocutor.

autolalic: The term 'autolalic' is used in contexts when one is talking to oneself about what one has done or wishes to do. It is employed only with the first person singular.

controllable (also volitional): In SST, there are verbs that indicate controllable actions, i.e. actions that depend, in principle, on the agent's will or control. They can be used with all types of verbal endings. On the contrary, non-controllable verbs imply actions that do not depend on the agent's will or control. The verbal endings of non-controllable verbs are more restricted than those of controllable verbs. Useful as well is the differentiation between the *controllability of a verb* (i.e. the semantic meaning of some verbs is controllable, implying the agent's control, for example the verb 'to eat' as opposed to non-controllable verbs e.g. 'be ill'), and the *volitionality of an action* (i.e., whether an action is carried out intentionally or not: although some verbs are controllable, an action can be carried out unwillinglingly, for example the sentence: 'I have unwillingly eaten a worm') (Camille Simon, personal communication).

directional: The term 'directional' refers to those secondary verbs (see below) that are used with verbs of motion to indicate whether the action is carried out towards or away from the speaker, or a specific reference point in space.

egophoric: The egophoric evidential implies personal knowledge or experience, or intention of the speaker. He is the source of information of the action, in which he is often directly engaged or implicated. There are several kinds of egophoric endings: intentional, receptive, habitual, allocentric.

endopathic: The term 'endopathic' refers to certain feelings or sensation accessible only to the speaker.

ergative: The ergative case marks the agent of transitive verbs. With the instrumental, it forms the two functions of the agentive case.

essential: Essential (also stative) verbs or copulas imply an essential quality inherent in the person or the thing.

evidential: Evidentials are used to specify the speaker's access to the information underlying his statement. In SST, there are two major ways of classifying these: 1) into one indirect, and four direct types (the factual, the sensory, the inferential and the egophoric); or 2) into a three-fold system: direct, indirect, and reported. Evidentials are conveyed by a system of verbal endings.

factual: The factual evidential is employed when the speaker judges his utterance to be comprised of definite and objective information. How the information was gained is not specified: the access can be indirect (general knowledge, a historic fact), or direct (a specific fact). Consequently, the factual can be considered as a 'default' evidential or as Mélac (2014) puts it, as not a genuine evidential.

first person sentence: The term 'first person' corresponds to the term "first person subject" in other languages. In such sentences, the first person is the first argument of a verb and is used in a variety of functions, such as to express the agent of an action, the patient, the goal, and so on.

honorific: In SST, there are several registers of politeness, two of which are essential: ordinary and polite. The polite register is marked by honorific and humilific terms. Honorific terms are used with the second and third persons; humilific terms are employed with the first person. These terms are mainly comprised of nouns, personal pronouns and verbs. They differ from their "ordinary" counterparts.

humilific: see honorific

inferential: This evidential conveys the information that the speaker bases his utterance on an inference or a deduction. The speaker has observed some kind of evidence, or present result, of a past action.

receptive: The receptive egophoric ending conveys the sense of direction towards the speaker. He is the patient of the action, or its addressee.

secondary: The term 'secondary' is used for a group of verbs placed between the lexical verb and the verbal ending (or the auxiliary). This group consists of modal, aspectual and directional verbs.

sensory: The sensory evidential conveys that the access to information the speaker has obtained is sensory in nature. It is often visual, but it may be any other sense: auditive, tactile, olfactory, or gustatory.

thrid person sentence: The term "third person" corresponds to the term "third person subject" in other languages. In such sentences, the third person is the first argument of a verb and is used in a variety of functions, such as the agent of an action, the patient, the goal, and so on.

verbalizer: Verbalizers are verbs with the empty or generalized sense such as 'do' or 'send'. They are preceded by a noun that specifies the action. In SST, constructions consisting of a noun and a verbalizer are very frequent.

Appendix: List of TAM verbal endings in standard Spoken Tibetan

PERFECTIVE ENDINGS

Positive (meaning)	Negative (meaning)	Evidential	Epistemic	Usage
pa.yin	*med*	egophoric	Ø	Lhasa, Diaspora
pa.red	*yod.ma.red*	factual	Ø	Lhasa, Diaspora
song	*ma.song*	sensory	Ø	Lhasa, Diaspora
byung	*ma.byung*	egophoric	Ø	Lhasa, Diaspora
pa.yod	*pa.med*	egophoric	EPI 3	Lhasa, Diaspora
pa.yin.pa.yod	*pa.yin.pa.med*	egophoric mnemic	EPI 2	Lhasa
–	*pa.a.yin*	egophoric	EPI 3	mainly Lhasa
pa.yin.'gro	*pa.min.'gro*	factual	EPI 1	mainly Lhasa
pa.min.'gro'o	*pa.yin.'gro'o*	factual	EPI 1	mainly Lhasa
pa.yin.gyi.red	*pa.yin.gyi.ma.red*	factual	EPI 2	Lhasa, Diaspora
pa.yin.pa.'dra	*pa.min.pa.'dra*	sensory	EPI 2	mainly Lhasa
pa.'dra	*ma +V - pa.'dra, V+ med.pa.'dra*	sensory	EPI 2	mainly Lhasa
pa.yin.sa.red	*pa.yin.sa.ma.red*	sensory	EPI 2	mainly Diaspora
pa.yin.bzo.'dug	*pa.yin.bzo.mi.'dug*	sensory	EPI 2	rare in spoken Tibetan
yong	*mi.yong*	factual	Ø, EPI 2	Lhasa
pa.yin-mdog.kha.po-red/'dug	*pa.yin-mdog.kha.po-ma.red/mi.'dug*	factual/ sensory	EPI 1	Lhasa

PERFECT ENDINGS

Positive (meaning)	Negative (meaning)	Evidential	Epistemic	Usage
yod	*med*	egophoric	Ø	Lhasa, Diaspora
yod.red	*yod.ma.red*	factual	Ø	Lhasa, Diaspora
'dug	*mi.'dug*	sensory	Ø	Lhasa, Diaspora
		inferential	Ø	Diaspora
bzhag (also spelt *shag*)	*mi.'dug*	inferential	Ø	mainly Lhasa
yod.pa.yod	*yod.pa.med*	egophoric mnemic	EPI 2	Lhasa
–	*a.yod*	egophoric	EPI 3	mainly Lhasa
yod.'gro	*med.'gro*	factual	EPI 1	mainly Lhasa
med.'gro'o	*yod.'gro'o*	factual	EPI 1	mainly Lhasa
yod.kyi.red	*yod.kyi.ma.red*	factual	EPI 2	Lhasa, Diaspora
yod.pa.'dra	*med.pa.'dra*	sensory	EPI 2	mainly Lhasa
yod.sa.red	*yod.sa.ma.red*	sensory	EPI 2	mainly Diaspora
yod.bzo.'dug	*yod.bzo.mi.'dug*	sensory	EPI 2	rare in spoken Tibetan
yong.nga.yod	*yong.nga.med*	egophoric	EPI 2	Lhasa
yod-mdog.kha.po-red/'dug	*yod-mdog.kha.po-ma.red/mi.'dug*	factual/sensory	EPI 1	Lhasa

IMPERFECTIVE (PRESENT and PAST) ENDINGS

Positive (meaning)	Negative (meaning)	Evidential	Epistemic	Usage
gi.yod	gi.med	egophoric	Ø	Lhasa, Diaspora
gi.'dug (gis)	gi.mi.'dug	sensory	Ø	Lhasa, Diaspora
gi.yod.red	gi.yod.ma.red	factual	Ø	Lhasa, Diaspora
gi.yod.pa.yod	gi.yod.pa.med	egophoric mnemic	EPI 2	Lhasa
—	gi.a.yod	egophoric	EPI 3	mainly Lhasa
gi.yod.'gro	gi.med.'gro	factual	EPI 1	mainly Lhasa
gi.med.'gro'o	gi.yod.'gro'o	factual	EPI 1	mainly Lhasa
gi.yod.kyi.red	gi.yod.kyi.ma.red	factual	EPI 2	Lhasa, Diaspora
gi.yod.pa.'dra	gi.med.pa.'dra	sensory	EPI 2	mainly Lhasa
gi.yod.sa.red	gi.yod.sa.ma.red	sensory	EPI 2	mainly Diaspora
gi.yod.bzo.'dug	gi.yod.bzo.mi.'dug	sensory	EPI 2	rare in spoken Tibetan
gi.yong.nga.yod	gi.yong.nga.med	egophoric	EPI 2	Lhasa
gi.yod-mdog.kha.po-red/'dug	gi.yod-mdog.kha.po-ma.red/mi.'dug	factual/ sensory	EPI 1	Lhasa

FUTURE ENDINGS

Positive (meaning)	Negative (meaning)	Evidential	Epistemic	Usage
gi.yin	gi.min	egophoric	Ø	Lhasa, Diaspora
gi.red	gi.ma.red	factual	Ø	Lhasa, Diaspora
rgyu.yin	—	egophoric (deontic)	Ø	Lhasa, Diaspora
rgyu.red	—	factual (deontic)	Ø	Lhasa, Diaspora
chog	—	egophoric allocentric	Ø	mainly Lhasa
dgos	—	egophoric allocentric	Ø	mainly Lhasa
yong	—	egophoric allocentric; factual	Ø; EPI 2	mainly Lhasa
rgyu.yin.pa.yod	—	sensory	EPI 2	Lhasa
rgyu.yin.'gro	—	factual	EPI 1	mainly Lhasa
rgyu.min.'gro'o	—	factual	EPI 1	mainly Lhasa
rgyu.yin.gyi.red	—	factual	EPI 2	Lhasa, Diaspora
rgyu.yin.pa.'dra	—	sensory	EPI 1	mainly Lhasa
rgyu.yin.sa.red	—	sensory	EPI 2	mainly Diaspora
rgyu.yin.bzo.'dug	—	sensory	EPI 1	rare in spoken Tibetan
rgyu.yong.nga.yod	—	egophoric	EPI 2	Lhasa
rgyu.yin-mdog.kha.po-red/'dug	—	factual/sensory	EPI 1	Lhasa
pa.'dug	pa.mi.'dug	sensory	EPI 3	Lhasa
pa.yod	pa.med	egophoric	EPI 3	Lhasa
—	a.yong	egophoric	EPI 3	mainly Lhasa
'gro	—	factual	EPI 1	Lhasa
sa.red	sa.ma.red	sensory	EPI 2	mainly Diaspora
bzo.'dug	bzo.mi.'dug	sensory	EPI 2	rare in spoken Tibetan
mi.yong.ngas	—	factual	EPI 1	Lhasa
mdog.kha.po-red/'dug	mdog.kha.po-ma.red/mi.'dug	factual/sensory	EPI 1	Lhasa